WORKSHOPS IN COMPUTING
Series edited by C. J. van Rijsbergen

Also in this series

continued on back page...

V.S. Alagar, Laks V.S. Lakshmanan and F. Sadri (Eds.)

Formal Methods in Databases and Software Engineering

Proceedings of the Workshop on Formal Methods in Databases and Software Engineering, Montreal, Canada, 15–16 May 1992

Published in collaboration with the British Computer Society

BCS

Springer-Verlag
London Berlin Heidelberg New York
Paris Tokyo Hong Kong
Barcelona Budapest

V.S. Alagar, PhD

Laks V.S. Lakshmanan, PhD

F. Sadri, PhD

Department of Computer Science
Concordia University
1455 de Maisonneuve Blvd. West
Montreal, Quebec, H3G 1M8, Canada

ISBN 3-540-19812-1 Springer-Verlag Berlin Heidelberg New York
ISBN 0-387-19812-1 Springer-Verlag New York Berlin Heidelberg

British Library Cataloguing in Publication Data
A catalogue record for this book is available from the British Library

Library of Congress Cataloging-in-Publication Data
A catalog record for this book is available from the Library of Congress

Typesetting: Camera ready by contributors
34/3830-543210 Printed on acid-free paper

Preface

Logic and object-orientation have come to be recognized as being among the most powerful paradigms for modeling information systems. The term "information systems" is used here in a very general context to denote database systems, software development systems, knowledge-base systems, proof support systems, distributed systems and reactive systems. One of the most vigorously researched topics common to all information systems is "formal modeling". An elegant high-level abstraction applicable to both application domain and system domain concepts will always lead to a system design from "outside in"; that is, the aggregation of ideas is around real-life objects about which the system is to be designed. Formal methods when applied with this view in mind, especially during early stages of system development, can lead to a formal reasoning on the intended properties, thus revealing system flaws that might otherwise be discovered much later. Logic in different styles and semantics is being used to model databases and their transactions; it is also used to specify concurrent, distributed, real-time, and reactive systems. The notion of "object" is central to the modeling of object-oriented databases, as well as object-oriented design and programs in software engineering. Both database and software engineering communities have undoubtedly made important contributions to formalisms based on logic and objects. It is worthwhile bringing together the ideas developed by the two communities in isolation, and focusing on integrating their common strengths.

The Montreal Workshop on Formal Methods in Databases and Software Engineering was held at Concordia University, Montreal on 15-16 May 1992. It was organized by the Formal Methods and Knowledge-Base Systems Research Group of the Department of Computer Science and aimed to foster closer collaboration between database and software engineering researchers. A fundamental goal of this workshop was to encourage active discussion between the research groups in an informal setting so that their discussions would lead to the identification of common research problems, promote a better awareness of the techniques and technologies developed within the areas of databases and software engineering, contribute to an understanding of significant differences and commonalities, and open up new research directions. Although this was the first workshop of its kind and was put together in a short time, the response to the workshop announcement was excellent: we were able to put together an exciting two-day session with four invited speakers and eight other speakers. The invited speakers were:

Michael Kifer (SUNY, Stony Brook, New York)
Deepak Kapur (SUNY, Albany, New York)
Lynn Marshall (BNR, Ottawa)
Jiawei Han (Simon Fraser, Vancouver)

There were close to forty participants from all the Montreal based Universities and industries. A copy of the proceedings was made available to many of the participants in advance and was distributed to other participants at the workshop site. After each talk sufficient time was given for discussion and dialogue. These arrangements proved to be very effective and the participants appreciated the opportunity for active interaction and numerous lively discussions. These proceedings contain eleven of the twelve papers presented at the workshop.

Several people and bodies have contributed in various ways to the success of this workshop and we are deeply indebted to all of them. We thank all the speakers/authors and the participants for contributing to a truly intellectually stimulating event. We acknowledge the financial support provided by the Faculty of Engineering and Computer Science. We gratefully acknowledge the organizational support enthusiastically volunteered by Ramesh Achuthan, Ramesh Ahooja, Alanoly Andrews, Karima Ashraf, Piero Colagrosso, Fangqing Dong, Hasan Jamil, Iyer Subramanian, Heather Johnstone, Dimitri Kourkopoulos, Daniel Nonen and Shiri Nematollaah. Without their assistance the workshop could not have taken place.

Our thanks are due to Halina Monkiewicz for local arrangements and our special thanks to Terry Czernienko for her superb professional assistance through all the stages of the workshop–mailing, announcements, the preparation of participants' proceedings, and the preparation of the papers for this volume. Last but not least, we would like to thank Fonds Pour La Formation De Chercheurs Et L'Aide à La Recherche (FCAR) for supporting our project on Critical Feasibility Issues in the Design of Integrated Knowledge-Base Systems, which enabled the efforts and strengths of our Formal Methods and Knowledge-Base Systems group to mature to a state where this workshop was possible.

November 1992   V.S. Alagar
                                                Laks V.S. Lakshmanan
                                                            F. Sadri

Contents

Transaction Logic:
An (Early) Exposé*

Anthony J. Bonner[†]   and   Michael Kifer[‡]

University of Toronto

Department of Computer Science

Toronto, Ontario, Canada

Abstract

This paper is an informal account of *Transaction Logic*—a new logic recently introduced in [4]. Transaction Logic was devised to deal with the phenomena of state changes in logic programming, databases, and AI. Transaction Logic has a natural model theory and a sound and complete proof theory. Unlike many other logics, however, it is suitable for *programming* transactions, transactions that accomplish state transitions in a logically correct manner. Transaction logic amalgamates such features as hypothetical *and* committed updates, dynamic constraints on transaction execution, nondeterminism, and bulk updates. Transaction Logic also appears to be suitable as a logical model of hitherto non-logical phenomena, including so-called *procedural knowledge* in AI, and the *behavior* of object-oriented databases, especially methods with side effects.

1   Introduction

We offer an informal introduction to a novel logic, called Transaction Logic (abbreviated $\mathcal{TR}$), that is specifically designed to deal with the updating of arbitrary logical theories, especially databases and logic programs. Unlike most logics of action, $\mathcal{TR}$ is a declarative formalism for specifying and executing procedures that update and permanently change a database, a logic program or an arbitrary logical theory. Like classical logic, $\mathcal{TR}$ has a "Horn" version that has *both* a procedural and a declarative semantics, as well as an efficient SLD-style proof procedure. The Horn version is of particular interest since it allows transactions to be defined as logic-programs. This paper presents the model theory and proof theory of $\mathcal{TR}$, and develops many of its applications.

$\mathcal{TR}$ was designed with several application in mind, especially in databases, logic programming, and AI. It was therefore developed as a general logic, so that it could solve a wide range of update-related problems. The full paper, [4],

---

*This work was supported in part by NSF grant CCR-9102159 and a grant from New York Science and Technology Foundation. Work done while on sabbatical leave from Stony Brook University. This author wishes to thank Computer Systems Research Institute of University of Toronto for their support. Present address: Department of Computer Science, SUNY at Stony Brook, Stony Brook, NY 11794, U.S.A.

[†]email: bonner@db.toronto.edu

[‡]email: kifer@cs.sunysb.edu

has an extensive discussion of a number of applications of $\mathcal{TR}$, both practical and theoretical. We outline several of these applications here.

1. $\mathcal{TR}$ provides a logical account for many update-related phenomena. For instance, in logic programming, $\mathcal{TR}$ provides a logical treatment of the assert and retract operators in Prolog. This effectively extends the theory of logic programming to include updates as well as queries. In object-oriented databases, $\mathcal{TR}$ can be combined with object-oriented logics, such as F-logic [10], to provide a logical account of *methods*, that is, of programs that reside "inside" objects and update their internal states. Thus, while F-logic covers the structural aspect of object-oriented databases, its combination with $\mathcal{TR}$ would account for the behavioral aspect as well. In AI, $\mathcal{TR}$ suggests a logical account of planning and design. STRIPS-like actions[1] and many aspects of hierarchical and non-linear planning are easily expressed in $\mathcal{TR}$. Although there have been previous attempts to give these phenomena declarative semantics, until now there has been no unifying *logical* framework that accounts for them all. $\mathcal{TR}$ provides just such a framework.

2. $\mathcal{TR}$ is a full-fledged logic. As such, it is more flexible and expressive than procedural systems in specifying transactions. Like procedural languages, $\mathcal{TR}$ is a language where simple actions can be combined into complex ones; but in $\mathcal{TR}$, actions can be combined in a greater variety of ways. In procedural languages, sequential composition is the only combinator, whereas in $\mathcal{TR}$, each logical operator combines actions in its own way. The result is that $\mathcal{TR}$ can specify transactions at many levels of detail, from the procedural to the declarative. At one extreme, the user may spell out an exact sequence of operations in excruciating detail. At the other extreme, he may specify loose constraints that the transaction must satisfy. In general, sequences and constraints can be arbitrarily mixed, and in this way, procedural and declarative knowledge are seamlessly integrated.

3. Because of its generality, $\mathcal{TR}$ supports a wide range of functionality in several areas. This functionality includes database queries and views; unification and rule-base inference; transaction and subroutine definition; deterministic and non-deterministic actions; static and dynamic constraints; hypothetical and retrospective transactions; and a wide class of tests and conditions on actions, including pre-conditions, post-conditions, and intermediate conditions. Furthermore, many problems related to the updating of incomplete information can be dealt with efficiently. Perhaps most important, these diverse capabilities are *not* built into $\mathcal{TR}$ separately. Rather, they all derive from a small number of basic ideas embodied in a single logic.

4. Commercial database systems are poor at specifying transactions. For example, in standard SQL, one can only define relatively simple updates, and even then, one must often abandon the relational algebra and resort to relatively awkward subqueries. More seriously, one cannot define

---

[1] STRIPS was an early AI planning system that simulated the actions of a robot arm [6].

transaction procedures in SQL. The main reason for this is that there is no way to combine simple transactions into more complex ones. This limitation should be contrasted with SQL's elegant view mechanism, in which views can easily be combined to produce other views. The result is that to define transactions, a user must go outside of SQL and embed it within a procedural language, such as C. A problem with this approach is that embedded SQL is an order of magnitude more difficult to use than pure SQL. In addition, embedded SQL is much less amenable to type checking and query optimization than SQL. Actually, it should not be surprising that difficult problems arise in trying to define updating transactions, since relational databases are founded on relational algebra (or, equivalently, first-order logic), which is a language for expressing *queries*, not updates. A solution, then, is to develop a logic that can serve as a foundation for queries *and* transactions. $\mathcal{TR}$ is just such a logic.

5. For a wide class of problems, $\mathcal{TR}$ avoids what is known in AI as the *frame problem*. The frame problem arises because, to reason about updates, one must specify what does *not* change, as well as what does. Many ingenious solutions have been proposed to deal with the frame problem, but most of them have aimed at the very general case of *arbitrary* reasoning about updates to arbitrary logical theories. As such, the proposed solutions have been conceptually complex and computationally intractable, even for simple updates. Fortunately, many interesting and important problems do not require a completely general solution to the frame problem. $\mathcal{TR}$, for example, was designed so that the frame problem does not arise when actions are *executed* or *planned*. This is possible for two reasons. First, transactions in $\mathcal{TR}$ are specified in terms of a small set of basic updates. Once the frame problem is solved for these updates, the solution propagates automatically to complex actions. Thus, $\mathcal{TR}$ programmers do not experience the frame problem, just as conventional programmers do not. In addition, the proof theory for $\mathcal{TR}$ actually updates the database during inference, just as procedural systems update the database during execution. This contrasts sharply with other logical formalisms, like the situation calculus, which reason about updates, but never actually change the database. In this way, $\mathcal{TR}$ provides simple, efficient handling of the frame problem, for both the specification and execution of transactions.

On the surface, there would appear to be many other candidates for a logic of transactions, since many logics reason about updates or about the related phenomena of time and action. However, despite a plethora of action-logics, database researchers continue to complain that there is no clear declarative semantics for database updates [2, 1]. In fact, no action logic has ever been adopted by a database or logic programming system, and none has become a core of database or logic-programming theory. This is in stark contrast to classical logic, which is the foundation of database queries and logic programming, both in theory and in practice.

There appear to be a few simple reasons for this unsuitability of existing action logics.

One major problem is that most logics of time or action are *hypothetical*, that is, they do not permanently change the database. Instead, these logics reason about what *would* happen *if* certain sequences of actions took place.

For instance, they might infer that *if* the pawn took the knight, then the rook *would* be threatened. Such systems are useful for reasoning about alternatives, but they do not actually *accomplish* state transitions. Hence, these logics do not provide executable specifications. Contrast this with $\mathcal{TR}$, a logic where *both* real and hypothetical updates are possible. Procedures in $\mathcal{TR}$ may commit their updates (and thus permanently change the database), reason about these updates without committing them, or they may do any combination thereof.

Another major problem is that most logics of time or action were not designed for programming. Instead, they were intended for specifying *properties* of programs and for reasoning about them. In such systems, one might say that action A precedes action B, and that B precedes C, from which the system would infer that A precedes C. Thus, these formalisms are useful for *reasoning about* actions, but are not that useful for *specifying* what the actions A, B and C actually do, and even less so for executing them.

A related problem is that many logics of action cannot assign names to composite transactions. In their intended context (of reasoning about sequences of actions), this is not a shortcoming. However, this renders such logics inappropriate for programming transactions, since specifying transactions without a naming facility is like programming without subroutines. From a programmer's standpoint, the lack of a straightforward naming facility defeats the purpose of using logic in the first place, which is to free the user from the drudgery of low-level details.

Another problem is that many logics (and all relational databases) make a clear distinction between non-updating queries and actions with side effects. However, this distinction is blurred in object-oriented systems, where both queries and updates are special cases of a single idea: method invocation (or message passing). In such systems, an update can be thought of as a query with side effects. In fact, every method is simply a *program* that operates on the data. $\mathcal{TR}$ models this uniformity naturally, treating all methods equally, thereby providing a logical foundation for object-oriented databases.

The important point here is that, unlike most formalisms of action, $\mathcal{TR}$ is not *forced* to distinguish between updates and queries; but the distinction always exists as an *option*. This is possible because an application can introduce logical sorts, one for queries, and one for updates. This is comparable to the distinction in deductive databases between base predicates and derived predicates. Even when an application makes such distinctions, $\mathcal{TR}$ treats all predicates uniformly, just as classical logic does. Most other logics are not capable of this uniform treatment, since they see queries as propositions, but updates (or actions) are seen as entities of a different, incompatible nature. For instance, in situation calculus [12], actions are function terms, while in Dynamic and Process Logics [7, 8], actions are modal operators.

Although $\mathcal{TR}$ is different from logics of action, it is comparable to declarative query languages, like Prolog and SQL. In Prolog, for instance, one does not reason about logic programs. Instead, one specifies and executes them. Thus, given a logic program and a database of atomic facts, one can ask, "Is $p(a)$ true?", but one cannot ask not, "Will $p(a)$ *always* be true, i.e., for *every* database?" Logics of action are aimed at the latter kind of question (applied to actions); $\mathcal{TR}$ is aimed at the former, but without sacrificing the ability to handle the latter.

The system that comes closest in spirit to $\mathcal{TR}$ is Prolog. Although Prolog is not a logic of action *per se*, transactions can be defined in Prolog via the operators *assert* and *retract*. Prolog transactions have some of the properties that we want to model: (i) updates are real, not hypothetical; (ii) named procedures can be composed from simpler procedures; (iii) all predicates can have both a truth value and a side effect on the database; and (iv) the frame problem does not arise. Unfortunately, updates in Prolog are non-logical operations. Thus, each time a programmer uses "assert" or "retract" operators, he moves further away from declarative programming. In addition, Prolog has the opposite problem *vis a vis* most action logics: updates are always committed and cannot be rolled back. It is therefore not possible for a Prolog update to have post-conditions. For instance, one cannot perform an update tentatively, test its outcome, and then commit the update only if some condition is met. Due to these drawbacks, transactions are often the most awkward of Prolog programs, and the most difficult to understand, debug, and maintain.

In addition, updates in Prolog are not integrated into a complete logical system. It is therefore not clear how *assert* and *retract* should interact with other logical operators such as disjunction and negation. For instance, what does $assert(X) \lor assert(Y)$ mean? or $\neg assert(X)$? or $assert(X) \leftarrow retract(Y)$? Also, how does one logically account for the fact that the order of updates is important? Finally, what does it mean to update a database that contains arbitrary logical formulas? None of these questions is addressed by Prolog's classical semantics or its update operators.

$\mathcal{TR}$ provides a general solution to the aforementioned limitations, both of Prolog and of action logics, by providing a syntax and a semantics in which updates can be combined with logical operators to build a large number of interesting and useful formulas.

Syntactically, $\mathcal{TR}$ extends first-order logic with a single binary operator, $\otimes$, which we call *serial conjunction*. Intuitively, the formula $\psi \otimes \phi$ means, "First execute transaction ψ, and then execute transaction ϕ." Serial conjunction may be combined arbitrarily with the standard logical operators, such as $\land$, $\lor$ and $\neg$, to build a wide variety of formulas, such as $\neg[b(X) \otimes c(X)]$ and $\forall X[a(X) \leftarrow b(X) \otimes c(X)]$.

Semantically, $\mathcal{TR}$ is related to Process Logic [8], but is different from it in several important respects. As in Process Logic, a model in $\mathcal{TR}$ consists of a set of states, and actions cause transitions from one state to another. In fact, an action may cause a sequence of transitions, passing from an initial state, through intermediate states, to a final state. Like Process Logic, formulas in $\mathcal{TR}$ are *not* evaluated at states. Instead, they are evaluated on *paths*, which are sequences of states. This property enables $\mathcal{TR}$ to express a wide range of constraints on transaction execution. Unlike Process Logic, however, $\mathcal{TR}$ does not distinguish between programs and propositions: In $\mathcal{TR}$, every formula is both a proposition and a program. This is a natural way to model database transactions, since a transaction can both change the database and— as a query—return an answer. Thus, pure queries and pure updates are merely two extremes on a spectrum of possible transactions. In fact, in $\mathcal{TR}$, a single notion of truth subsumes two ideas: (i) the classical concept of a truth value, and (ii) the hitherto non-logical concept of a "side effect" on the database. This uniformity renders $\mathcal{TR}$ suitable for a number of diverse applications in areas such as relational databases, object-oriented databases, logic programming, and Artificial Intelligence. More discussion of the relationship between $\mathcal{TR}$ and process logics appears in [4].

Like classical logic, $\mathcal{TR}$ has a "Horn" version that is of particular interest for logic programming. In Horn $\mathcal{TR}$, a transaction is defined by Prolog-style rules in which the premise specifies a *sequence* of queries and updates. Furthermore, just as $\mathcal{TR}$ is an extension of classical first-order logic, Horn $\mathcal{TR}$ is an extension of classical Horn-clause logic.

Horn $\mathcal{TR}$ has a clean and simple proof theory that is sound and complete with respect to its model theory. This proof theory is described in detail in [4]. Two versions are presented, a bottom-up version based on natural deduction, and a top-down version based on resolution. As in classical Horn logic, the resolution-based proof theory is probably the one that would be used in practice. The proof theory for Horn $\mathcal{TR}$ is much simpler than the proof theory for full $\mathcal{TR}$, which involves encoding $\mathcal{TR}$ in a more general logic of state transitions. The latter will be discussed in a forthcoming report [3].

2   Overview and Introductory Examples

From the user's point of view, using $\mathcal{TR}$ is similar to using Prolog or using a relational database system. That is, the user may specify rules and he may pose queries and request updates. In $\mathcal{TR}$, the user sees no obvious or immediate difference between queries and updates. An update is just a query with side effects (which can be detected only by issuing subsequent queries). In general, the user issues transactions, and the system responds by displaying answers and updating the database. This section provides simple examples of how this behavior appears to the user and how it is described formally. The examples also illustrate several dimensions of $\mathcal{TR}$'s capabilities.

One of these capabilities, *non-deterministic transactions,* should be mentioned at the outset. Non-determinism has applications in many areas, but it is especially well-suited for advanced applications, such as those found in Artificial Intelligence. For instance, the user of a robot simulator might instruct the robot to build a stack of three blocks, but he may not say (or care) which three blocks to use. Likewise, the user of a CAD system might request the system to run an electrical line from one point to another, but without fixing the exact route, except in the form of loose constraints (*e.g.*, do not run the line too close to wet or exposed areas). These are the kinds of non-deterministic transactions that $\mathcal{TR}$ can specify. In such transactions, the final state of the database is non-deterministic, as it depends on choices made by the system at run time. $\mathcal{TR}$ enables users to specify what choices are allowed. When a user issues a non-deterministic transaction, the system makes particular choices (which may be implementation-dependent), putting the database into one of the allowed new states.

For all but the most elementary applications, a transaction execution will be characterized not just by an initial and a final state, but rather by a sequence of *intermediate* states that it passes through. For example, as a robot simulator piles block upon block upon block, the transaction execution will pass from state to state to state. Like the final state, intermediate states may not be uniquely determined at the start of the execution. For example, the robot may have some (non-deterministic) choice as to which block to grasp next. We call such a sequence of database states the *execution path* of the transaction. $\mathcal{TR}$ represents execution paths explicitly. By doing so, it can express a wide range of constraints on transaction execution. For example, a user may require every intermediate state to satisfy some condition, or he may forbid certain sequences of states.

To describe the execution of transactions formally, we use statements of the following form, which express a form of logical entailment in $\mathcal{TR}$, called *executional entailment*:

$$\mathbf{P}, \mathbf{D}_0, \ldots, \mathbf{D}_n \models \psi \tag{1}$$

Here, $\mathbf{P}$ and each $\mathbf{D}_i$ is a logical formula, as is ψ. Intuitively, $\mathbf{P}$ is a set of transaction definitions, ψ is a transaction invocation, and $\mathbf{D}_0, \ldots, \mathbf{D}_n$ is a sequence of databases, representing all the states of transaction execution. Statement (1) means that $\mathbf{D}_0, \ldots, \mathbf{D}_n$ is an execution path of transaction ψ. That is, if the current database state is $\mathbf{D}_0$, and if the user issues the transaction ψ (by typing $? - \psi$, as in Prolog), then the database *may* go from state $\mathbf{D}_0$ to state $\mathbf{D}_1$, to state $\mathbf{D}_2$, etc., until it finally reaches state $\mathbf{D}_n$, after which the transaction terminates. We emphasize the word "may" because ψ may be a non-deterministic transaction. As such, it may have many execution paths beginning at $\mathbf{D}_0$, possibly of different length. The proof theory for $\mathcal{TR}$ can derive each of these paths, but only one of them will be (non-deterministically) selected as the actual execution path; the final state, $\mathbf{D}_n$, of that path then becomes the new database.

Unlike other formalisms, $\mathcal{TR}$ does not draw a thick line between transactions and queries. In fact, any transaction, ϕ, that does not cause a state change can be viewed as a query. This state of affairs is formally expressed by the statement $\mathbf{P}, \mathbf{D}_0 \models \phi$, a special case of statement (1) in which $n = 0$. In this case, $\mathbf{D}_0$ is a sequence of databases of length 1. This uniform treatment of transactions and queries is crucial for successful adaptation of $\mathcal{TR}$ to the object-oriented domain,[2] because many object-oriented systems do not syntactically distinguish between state-changing methods and information-retrieving methods.

Several other aspects of statement (1) should be mentioned at this point. First, the transaction base $\mathbf{P}$ can be *any* formula in $\mathcal{TR}$. In practice, though, it will often be a conjunction of Prolog-like rules, which we will represent as a finite set of formulas. In any case, regardless of its form, we call $\mathbf{P}$ a *transaction base*. As the name suggests, transaction bases define transactions and, as a special case, queries. The databases, $\mathbf{D}_1, \ldots, \mathbf{D}_n$, are also finite sets of formulas; however, they are classical first-order formulas. These formulas are *not* restricted to be ground atomic facts, and it is entirely possible for each $\mathbf{D}_i$ to contain Prolog-like rules. The difference between a database and a transaction base is that formulas in a transaction base may use full syntax of $\mathcal{TR}$, while formulas in a database are limited to the syntax of first-order logic, a subset of $\mathcal{TR}$.

Statements of the form (1) provide a formal view of all that is possible in the transaction system. However, this formal view is somewhat different from the user's view of the system. From his perspective, a $\mathcal{TR}$ logic program

---

[2]by combining $\mathcal{TR}$ with F-logic [10], for example.

has two parts: a transaction base, **P**, which the programmer provides,[3] and a *single* current database, **D**, which he wishes to access and possibly modify. The transaction base is immutable; that is, it cannot be changed by other transactions. In contrast, the database constantly changes—it is updated when the user executes transactions defined in **P**. In particular, if **D** contains Prolog-style rules, they, too, can be modified.

The rest of this section illustrates our notation and the capabilities of $\mathcal{TR}$ through a number of simple examples. The examples illustrate how $\mathcal{TR}$ uses logical operators to combine simple actions into complex ones. These operators include the standard ones, such as $\wedge$, $\vee$ and $\neg$, and a new operator of sequential composition, $\otimes$. For the purpose of illustration, our example databases are sets of ground atomic formulas, and insertion and deletion of atomic formulas are elementary update operators. However, $\mathcal{TR}$ is not restricted to this type of database nor to these particular elementary updates.

2.1 Simple Transactions

This subsection introduces some of the basic ideas of $\mathcal{TR}$. Starting with purely declarative queries, we show how $\mathcal{TR}$ extends classical logic to represent procedural phenomena, such as updates and action-sequences. We then show how these ideas can be combined to form more complex transactions. The examples of this subsection focus on simple, deterministic transactions, ones that a user might issue directly to a $\mathcal{TR}$ interpreter. Subsequent subsections illustrate more sophisticated transactions.

Since $\mathcal{TR}$ queries are a special kind of transaction, they are defined in the transaction base, **P**, just as other transactions are. These definitions are similar to Horn rules in logic programming, and we refer to them as *serial-Horn* formulas. These formulas draw inferences from base facts just as logic programs and deductive databases do. In fact, if the transaction base consists entirely of first-order formulas, then entailment in $\mathcal{TR}$ reduces to first-order entailment. That is, if **P** and ϕ are both first-order formulas, then

$$\mathbf{P}, \mathbf{D} \models \phi \qquad \textit{iff} \qquad \mathbf{P} \wedge \mathbf{D} \models^c \phi$$

where $\models^c$ denotes classical entailment. In this way, classical logic—the medium in which queries are traditionally expressed—is the starting point for $\mathcal{TR}$. Logic programs, deductive databases, and first-order knowledge-bases can thus be adopted for use in $\mathcal{TR}$ with minimal (if any) change. That is, they are upward compatible with $\mathcal{TR}$.

Example 2.1 (Classical Inference) Suppose that the database, **D**, contains the atom q, and that the transaction base, **P**, contains the rule $p \leftarrow q$. By typing $?- p$, the user is posing a query, asking the $\mathcal{TR}$ interpreter if p is true. In this case, p can be inferred from the contents of the database and the transition base, so the interpreter returns "true." Likewise, the interpreter returns "true" if the user types $?- q$, or if he types $?- p \wedge q$. Note that in each case,

---

[3]The term "programmer" should be taken here in a broad sense. For instance, parts of the transaction base may be provided by the knowledge-base engineer, by the database administrator, or by any number of system or application programmers.

the database remains unchanged. We represent this behavior formally by the following three statements:

$$\mathbf{P}, \mathbf{D} \models p \qquad \mathbf{P}, \mathbf{D} \models q \qquad \mathbf{P}, \mathbf{D} \models p \wedge q$$

☐

In $\mathcal{TR}$, all transactions are a combination of queries and updates. Queries do not change the database, and can be expressed in classical logic, as Example 2.1 shows. In contrast, updates do change the database, and are expressed in an extension of classical logic. We refer to the simplest kind of updates as *elementary*. In principle, there is no restriction on the changes that an elementary update can make to a database, though in practice, we expect them to be simple and cheap. In this overview, we use the insertion and deletion of atomic formulas as canonical examples of elementary updates. Other kinds of elementary updates, such as SQL-style *bulk* updates, can be found in [4].

Elementary updates are atomic in that they cannot be decomposed into simpler updates. We therefore represent them by atomic formulas. Like all atomic formulas, elementary updates have a truth value; but in addition, they have a side effect on the database. We represent this idea formally by statements of the following form:

$$\mathbf{P}, \mathbf{D}_1, \mathbf{D}_2 \models u$$

This statement says that the atomic formula u is (the name of) an update that changes the database from state $\mathbf{D}_1$ to state $\mathbf{D}_2$. Although any atomic formula can be an update, it is a good programming practice to reserve a special set of predicate symbols for this purpose. For example, for each predicate symbol p, we shall use another predicate symbol $ins{:}p$ to represent insertions into p. Likewise, we use the predicate symbol $del{:}p$ to represent deletions from p.

Example 2.2 (Elementary Updates) If p is a binary predicate symbol, then the atoms $ins{:}p(a, b)$ and $del{:}p(a, b)$ are elementary updates. Intuitively, the atom $ins{:}p(a, b)$ means, "insert the atom $p(a, b)$ into the database," while $del{:}p(a, b)$ means, "delete $p(a, b)$ from the database." From the user's perspective, typing ?− $ins{:}p(a, b)$ to the interpreter changes the database from $\mathbf{D}$ to $\mathbf{D} + \{p(a, b)\}$. Likewise, typing ?− $del{:}p(a, b)$ changes the database from $\mathbf{D}$ to $\mathbf{D} - \{p(a, b)\}$. We express this behaviour formally by the following two statements, which are true for any transaction base $\mathbf{P}$:

$$\mathbf{P}, \mathbf{D}, \mathbf{D} + \{p(a, b)\} \models ins{:}p(a, b)$$
$$\mathbf{P}, \mathbf{D}, \mathbf{D} - \{p(a, b)\} \models del{:}p(a, b)$$

☐

Here we use the operator "+" to denote set union when it is applied to databases. This is possible because all examples in this paper will deal with databases that are sets (or conjunctions) of ground atomic formulas. Thus, the expression $\{p, q\} + \{r, s\}$ denotes the set $\{p, q, r, s\}$, which in turn stands for the formula $p \wedge q \wedge r \wedge s$. Likewise, we use the operator "−" for set difference. For instance,

$\{p, q, r, s\} - \{q, s\}$ denotes $\{p, r\}$, which stands for $p \wedge r$. It is hoped that this notation will not mislead the reader into thinking that, say, $\mathbf{D} + \{p(a, b)\}$ above represents a model—it does not. In general, $\mathbf{D}$ can be a set of arbitrary first-order formulas.

We emphasize here that insertions and deletions are *not* built into the semantics of $\mathcal{TR}$. Thus, there is no *intrinsic* connection between the names p, *ins:p* and *del:p*. Our use of these names is merely a convention for purposes of illustration. In fact, p, *ins:p* and *del:p* are ordinary predicates of $\mathcal{TR}$, where the connection between them is established via axioms of the so called *transition base*, as explained later.

$\mathcal{TR}$ is not committed to any particular set of elementary updates. Indeed, we expect that each database system will want its own repertoire of elementary updates, tuned to the applications at hand. Within each database system, though, we expect this repertoire of updates to be relatively stable. Thus, for most users of a given system, it will *appear* as though there is a fixed set of elementary updates. The user's job is to combine elementary updates into complex transactions using the facilities provided by $\mathcal{TR}$.

A basic way of combining transactions is to sequence them, *i.e.*, to execute them one after another. For example, one might take money out of one account and then, if the withdrawal succeeds, deposit the money into another account. To combine transactions sequentially, we extend classical logic with a new binary connective, $\otimes$, which we call *serial conjunction*. The formula $\psi \otimes \phi$ denotes the composite transaction consisting of transaction ψ followed by transaction ϕ.[4] Unlike elementary updates, sequential transactions often have intermediate states, as well as initial and final states. We express this behavior formally by statements like the following:

$$\mathbf{P}, \mathbf{D}_0, \mathbf{D}_1, \mathbf{D}_2 \models \psi \otimes \phi$$

This statement says that the transaction $\psi \otimes \phi$ changes the database from $\mathbf{D}_0$ to $\mathbf{D}_1$ to $\mathbf{D}_2$. Here, $\mathbf{D}_1$ is an intermediate state.

Example 2.3 (Serial Conjunction) The expression *ins:a* $\otimes$ *ins:b*, where a and b are ground atomic formulas, denotes a sequence of two insertions. This transaction means, "First insert a into the database, and then insert b." Thus, if the initial database is $\mathbf{D}$, and if the user issues a transaction by typing $? - $ *ins:a* $\otimes$ *ins:b*, then during execution, the database will change from $\mathbf{D}$ to $\mathbf{D} + \{a\}$ to $\mathbf{D} + \{a, b\}$. We express this behaviour formally by the following statement, which is true for any transaction base $\mathbf{P}$:

$$\mathbf{P}, \mathbf{D}, \mathbf{D} + \{a\}, \mathbf{D} + \{a, b\} \models \text{ } ins\text{:}a \otimes ins\text{:}b$$

□

---

[4]Logics of action sometimes use a semicolon to denote serial conjunction. We have avoided this notation for two reasons: (*i*) in Prolog, a semicolon means disjunction, and (*ii*) there is no natural symbol to stand for the dual of the semicolon (as we shall see, this dual is a useful operator in its own right). In contrast, $\oplus$ naturally stands for the dual of $\otimes$. We can therefore rewrite $\neg(\psi \otimes \phi)$ as $\neg\psi \oplus \neg\phi$.

2.2 Tests and Conditions

Serial conjunction applies not only to updates, but to any transaction, including queries. We can therefore place queries that act as tests anywhere in a sequence of updates. This allows us to monitor the progress of a transaction, and force it to abort if certain conditions are not met.

In the simplest case, we can define pre-conditions by placing a query at the beginning of a transaction. For instance, before withdrawing money from an account, we should check that enough money is available. If there is, then the transaction can continue, and the database can be updated; if not, then the transaction should abort, and the database should remain in its original state.

Example 2.4 (Pre-Conditions) If the atom b is a query (*i.e.*, has no side effects), then the expression $b \otimes ins{:}c$ denotes a test followed by an update. Intuitively, it means, "check that b is true, and if so, insert c into the database." In other words, if b is true in the initial database state, then the transaction succeeds and the database is changed from $\mathbf{D}$ to $\mathbf{D} + \{c\}$; otherwise, the transaction fails and the database remains in the initial state, $\mathbf{D}$. Formally,

$$\begin{aligned} &\textit{if} &&\mathbf{P}, \mathbf{D} \models b \\ &\textit{then} &&\mathbf{P}, \mathbf{D}, \mathbf{D} + \{c\} \models b \otimes ins{:}c \end{aligned}$$

□

By placing tests at other points in a transaction, sophisticated behavior can be specified in a simple and natural way. For instance, tests at the end of a transaction act as post-conditions, which query the *final* state of the database. If these tests succeed, then the transaction commits and the database is permanently changed. Otherwise, if the tests fail, then the transaction aborts and the database is rolled back to its original state. Post-conditions are particularly useful for aborting transactions that have forbidden side effects. For instance, a move in chess is forbidden if it puts you into check. Likewise, changes to a circuit design may be forbidden if the new design violates certain conditions (*e.g.*, limits on cost, size, or power consumption). It is worth noting that post-conditions can be awkward, if not impossible to express in other formalism of action, such as the situation calculus [12, 15].

Example 2.5 (Post-Conditions) If the atom b is a query (*i.e.*, has no side effects), then the expression $ins{:}c \otimes b$ denotes an update followed by a test. Intuitively, it means, "insert c into the database, and then check that b is true." In other words, the database state is first changed from $\mathbf{D}$ to $\mathbf{D} + \{c\}$. If b is true in the final state, then the transaction succeeds and the change is committed; otherwise, the transaction fails and the database is rolled back to the initial state, $\mathbf{D}$. Formally,

$$\begin{aligned} &\textit{if} &&\mathbf{P}, \mathbf{D} + \{c\} \models b \\ &\textit{then} &&\mathbf{P}, \mathbf{D}, \mathbf{D} + \{c\} \models ins{:}c \otimes b \end{aligned}$$

□

2.3 Non-Deterministic Transactions

In addition to being sequenced, transactions in $\mathcal{TR}$ can be combined using any of the classical connectives. Two of these connectives, disjunction and existential quantification, can be used to build non-deterministic transactions. For instance, the formula $\psi \vee \phi$ means, "do transaction ψ or do transaction ϕ." Likewise, the formula $\exists X \, \phi(X)$ means, "do transaction $\phi(c)$ for some value c."

Example 2.6 (Classical Disjunction) If the user issues a transaction by typing $?- ins{:}a \vee ins{:}b$, then after execution, the final database will be either $\mathbf{D} + \{a\}$ or $\mathbf{D} + \{b\}$. In effect, the user has stated that he doesn't care which update is made, so the system chooses one of them and executes it. Formally, *both* of the following statements are true, for any transaction base $\mathbf{P}$:

$$\mathbf{P}, \mathbf{D}, \mathbf{D} + \{a\} \; \models \; ins{:}a \vee ins{:}b$$
$$\mathbf{P}, \mathbf{D}, \mathbf{D} + \{b\} \; \models \; ins{:}a \vee ins{:}b$$

□

In addition to defining non-deterministic transactions, classical disjunction is also needed (in combination with negation) to define implication, exactly as in classical logic. Implication is illustrated later in this section.

When non-determinism results from classical disjunction, alternatives are fixed and independent of the database. However, when existential quantification is used, the number of alternatives can be infinite and data-dependent.

Example 2.7 (Existential Quantification) Suppose the user issues the transaction $?- ins{:}q(X)$ (or, equivalently, $?- \exists X \, ins{:}q(X)$). The database system will then insert a tuple, $\langle c \rangle$, into relation q non-deterministically. That is, after execution, the database state will be $\mathbf{D} + \{q(c)\}$, for some (unspecified) value c. Formally, the following statement is true for every value c in the Herbrand universe:

$$\mathbf{P}, \mathbf{D}, \mathbf{D} + \{q(c)\} \; \models \; \exists X \, ins{:}q(X)$$

□

Example 2.8 (Copying Tuples Non-Deterministically) Consider the transaction $?- \exists X \, [p(X) \otimes ins{:}q(X)]$, which requests the system to copy a tuple from p to q non-deterministically. The system will first non-deterministically choose a tuple, $\langle c \rangle$, from relation p, and then insert the tuple into relation q. Formally, for every value c,

$$if \quad \mathbf{P}, \mathbf{D} \models p(c)$$
$$then \quad \mathbf{P}, \mathbf{D}, \mathbf{D} + \{q(c)\} \; \models \; \exists X \, [p(X) \otimes ins{:}q(X)]$$

For instance, suppose the database $\mathbf{D}$ contains the atoms $p(b)$, $p(c)$ and $p(d)$. Then there are three choices for X: b, c, and d. Each choice results in a different update, since either $q(b)$, $q(c)$, or $q(d)$ will be inserted into $\mathbf{D}$. Formally, the following three statements are all true:

$$\mathbf{P, D, D} + \{q(b)\} \ \models \ \exists X \, [p(X) \otimes ins:q(X)]$$
$$\mathbf{P, D, D} + \{q(c)\} \ \models \ \exists X \, [p(X) \otimes ins:q(X)]$$
$$\mathbf{P, D, D} + \{q(d)\} \ \models \ \exists X \, [p(X) \otimes ins:q(X)]$$

□

2.4 Rules

Rules are formulas of the form $p \leftarrow \phi$, where p is an atomic formula and ϕ is any $\mathcal{TR}$ formula. As in classical logic, this formula is just a convenient abbreviation for the formula $p \vee \neg\phi$. This is the formal, declarative interpretation of rules. In addition, rules in $\mathcal{TR}$ have a procedural interpretation. Intuitively, the formula $p \leftarrow \phi$ means, "to execute p, it is sufficient to execute ϕ." This procedural interpretation is important because it provides $\mathcal{TR}$ with a subroutine facility and makes logic programming possible. For instance, in the rule $p(X) \leftarrow \phi$, the predicate symbol p acts as the name of a procedure, the variable X acts as an input parameter, and the formula ϕ acts as the procedure body, or definition (exactly as in Horn-clause logic programming). Although the rule-body may be any $\mathcal{TR}$ formula, it will frequently be a serial conjunction. In this case, the rule has the form $a_0 \leftarrow a_1 \otimes a_2 \otimes \dots \otimes a_n$, where each a_i is an atomic formula. With such rules, users can define transaction subroutines and write transaction logic programs. Note that this facility is possible because transactions are represented by predicates. This property distinguishes $\mathcal{TR}$ from other logics of action, especially those in which actions are modal operators. In such logics, subroutines are awkward, if not impossible, to express. Finally, for notational convenience, we assume that all free variables in a rule are universally quantified outside the rule. Thus, the rule $p(X) \leftarrow \phi$ is simply an abbreviation for $\forall X \, [p(X) \leftarrow \phi]$.

Example 2.9 (A Simple Rule) The rule $c \leftarrow ins:a \otimes ins:b$ defines a transaction called c. Intuitively, this rule says, "to do c, first insert a into the database, and then insert b." Thus, if the user invokes transaction $?-c$, then the database changes from $\mathbf{D}$ to $\mathbf{D} + \{a\}$ to $\mathbf{D} + \{a, b\}$. Formally, if transaction base $\mathbf{P}$ contains this rule, then the following statement is true:

$$\mathbf{P, D, D} + \{a\}, \mathbf{D} + \{a, b\} \ \models \ c$$

The simplicity of our examples may have blurred an important point made earlier, namely, that the database itself may be a full-fledged deductive database. For instance, $\mathbf{D}$ may contain the rule $d \leftarrow a \wedge b$. In this case, the query $?-d$ would be answered affirmatively if asked *after* the transaction c has been executed. That is, the following statement would be true:

$$\mathbf{P, D, D} + \{a\}, \mathbf{D} + \{a, b\} \ \models \ c \otimes d$$

In addition, transactions can modify the rules found in the database. For instance, a transaction may be programmed to delete the formula $d \leftarrow a \wedge b$ from the database.

□

The rule in Example 2.9 defines a deterministic transaction c. However, rules can also define non-deterministic transactions. To take a simple example, the rule $c \leftarrow \phi \vee \psi$ defines c to be the non-deterministic transaction $\phi \vee \psi$. More generally, rules can define non-deterministic transactions even without mentioning disjunctions explicitly. This is possible because, as in classical logic, a rule like $c \leftarrow (\phi \vee \psi)$ is equivalent to a conjunction of two rules, $(c \leftarrow \phi) \wedge (c \leftarrow \psi)$.

Even a single rule can give rise to non-determinism. This is possible because, as in classical logic, a rule like $\forall X\, [p \leftarrow \phi(X)]$ is equivalent to the rule $p \leftarrow \exists X\, \phi(X)$, and the body of the latter rule is a non-deterministic transaction. Another way to see this is to think of the former rule as a conjunction of its instances, $p \leftarrow \phi(a)$, for all a. Each of these instances provides an alternate way of executing p, thereby introducing non-determinism.

Example 2.10 (Copying Tuples Non-Deterministically) Example 2.8 shows how one can copy a tuple from one relation to another non-deterministically. We can give this transaction a name by adding the following rule to the transaction base:

$$copy \leftarrow p(X) \otimes ins\text{:}q(X)$$

Formally, this rule is equivalent to $copy \leftarrow \exists X\, [p(X) \otimes ins\text{:}q(X)]$. Note that the body of this rule is exactly the formula used in Example 2.8. Intuitively, this rule says, "to execute $copy$, first choose a tuple from relation p non-deterministically; then insert this tuple into relation q." Observe that the set of non-deterministic alternatives is data-dependent. Formally, for every value c,

$$
\begin{aligned}
\text{if} \quad & \mathbf{P}, \mathbf{D} \models p(c) \\
\text{then} \quad & \mathbf{P}, \mathbf{D}, \mathbf{D} + \{q(c)\} \models copy
\end{aligned}
$$

This means that we cannot know in advance what the exact outcome of copying will be. However, if the rule above is the only rule defining $copy$, then we can make the following statement, which is true for any pair of databases, $\mathbf{D}_1$ and $\mathbf{D}_2$:

$$
\begin{aligned}
\text{if} \quad & \mathbf{P}, \mathbf{D}_1, \mathbf{D}_2 \models copy \\
\text{then} \quad & \mathbf{P}, \mathbf{D}_1 \models p(c) \\
\text{and} \quad & \mathbf{P}, \mathbf{D}_2 \models q(c)
\end{aligned}
$$

for some value c. $\qquad\qquad\qquad\qquad\qquad\qquad\qquad\qquad\qquad\qquad\qquad\quad\square$

2.5   Transaction Bases

This section gives simple but realistic examples of transaction bases comprised of finite sets of rules. The examples show how updates can be combined with queries to define complex transactions. In each example, the body of each rule is a sequence of atomic formulas, some of which are queries and some of which are updates.

Example 2.11 (Financial Transactions) Suppose the balance of a bank account is given by the relation *balance(Acct, Amt)*. To modify this relation, we are provided with a pair of elementary update operations: *del:balance(Acct, Amt)* to delete a tuple from the relation; and *ins:balance(Acct, Amt)*, which inserts a tuple into the relation. Using these two updates, we define four transactions: *change:balance(Acct, Amt1, Amt2)* to change the balance of an account from one amount to another; *withdraw(Amt, Acct)* to withdraw an amount from an account; *deposit(Amt, Acct)* to deposit an amount into an account; and *transfer(Amt, Acct1, Acct2)* to transfer an amount from one account to another. These transactions are defined by the following four rules:

$$transfer(Amt, Acct1, Acct2) \leftarrow$$
$$withdraw(Amt, Acct1) \otimes deposit(Amt, Acct2)$$

$$withdraw(Amt, Acct) \leftarrow$$
$$balance(Acct, Bal) \otimes change:balance(Acct, Bal, Bal - Amt)$$

$$deposit(Amt, Acct) \leftarrow$$
$$balance(Acct, Bal) \otimes change:balance(Acct, Bal, Bal + Amt)$$

$$change:balance(Acct, Bal1, Bal2) \leftarrow$$
$$del:balance(Acct, Bal1) \otimes ins:balance(Acct, Bal2)$$

In the second and third rules, the atom *balance(Act, Bal)* is a query that retrieves the balance of the specified account. All other atoms are updates. □

Example 2.12 (Non-Deterministic Robot Actions) The rules below define actions that simulate the movements of a robot arm in the blocks world [14]. States of this world are defined in terms of three database predicates: $on(x, y)$, which says that block x is on top of block y; $clear(x)$, which says that nothing is on top of block x; and $color(x, c)$, which says that c is the color of block x. The rules below define six actions that change the state of the world. Each action evaluates its premises in the order given, and the action fails if any of its premises fail (in which case the database is left in its original state).

$$stackSameColor(Z) \leftarrow$$
$$color(Z, C) \otimes stackTwoColors(C, C, Z)$$

$$stackTwoColors(C_1, C_2, Z) \leftarrow$$
$$color(X, C_1) \otimes color(Y, C_2) \otimes stackTwoBlocks(X, Y, Z)$$

$$stackTwoBlocks(X, Y, Z) \leftarrow$$
$$move(Y, Z) \otimes move(X, Y)$$

$$move(X, Y) \leftarrow$$
$$pickup(X) \otimes putdown(X, Y)$$

$$pickup(X) \leftarrow$$
$$clear(X) \otimes on(X, Y) \otimes del:on(X, Y) \otimes ins:clear(Y)$$

$$putdown(X, Y) \leftarrow$$
$$X \neq Y \otimes clear(Y) \otimes ins:on(X, Y) \otimes del:clear(Y)$$

The basic actions are $pickup(X)$ and $putdown(X, Y)$, meaning, "pick up block X," and "put down block X on top of block Y," respectively. Both are defined in terms of elementary inserts and deletes to database relations. The remaining rules combine simple actions into more complex ones. For instance, $move(X, Y)$ means, "move block X to the top of block Y," and $stackTwoBlocks(X, Y, Z)$ means, "stack blocks X and Y on top of block Z." These actions are deterministic: Each set of argument bindings specifies only one robot action.

In contrast, the two actions $stackTwoColors$ and $stackSameColor$ are *non-deterministic*. For instance, $stackTwoColors(C1, C2, Z)$ means, "stack two blocks, of colors C_1 and C_2, on top of block Z." The action does not say which two blocks to use, only their colors. To perform the action, the inference system searches the database for blocks of the appropriate color that can be stacked. If several such blocks are available, the system chooses any two non-deterministically. The action $stackSameColor(Z)$ means, "stack two blocks on top of Z that are the same color as Z." Again, the inference system searches the database for appropriate blocks. In this way, by defining non-deterministic actions, a user can specify what to do (declarative knowledge) as well as how to do it (procedural knowledge). □

It is worth noting that the rules in Example 2.12 involve queries as well as updates. In the last rule, for instance, the atom $clear(Y)$ (which itself may be defined by other deductive rules) is a Boolean test that must return *true* in order for the transaction to continue. In the first rule, the atom $color(Z, C)$ is a query that retrieves the color C of the block Z. The second rule is, perhaps, the most interesting. Here, the atoms $color(X, C_1)$ and $color(Y, C_2)$ are non-deterministic queries. They retrieve two blocks, X and Y, of colors C_1 and C_2, respectively. The particular blocks retrieved by these queries then determine the course of action taken in the rest of the transaction.

Example 2.13 (Recursive, Non-Deterministic Actions) Suppose the transaction base of Example 2.12 is augmented by the two rules below. Then the transaction $stack(N, X)$ tries to stacks N blocks on top of X. If it succeeds, the database is updated and the transaction returns *true*; if it fails (perhaps because N blocks are not available), then the database remains in its original state, and the transaction returns *false*.

$$stack(N, X) \leftarrow N > 0 \otimes move(Y, X) \otimes stack(N - 1, Y)$$
$$stack(0, X) \leftarrow$$

In order to stack N blocks on X, the first rule moves a single block, Y, onto X, and then recursively tries to stack $N - 1$ blocks on Y. Since the second rule has an empty premise, it terminates the recursion by doing nothing, thereby stacking no blocks on top of X. □

2.6 Constraints

Section 2.3 showed how classical disjunction creates non-determinism. Now we show how classical conjunction constrains it.

In general, the transaction $\psi \wedge \phi$ is more deterministic than either ϕ or ψ by themselves. This is because any execution of $\psi \wedge \phi$ must be an allowed execution of ψ and an allowed execution of ϕ. We illustrate this idea in two ways: first, through an informal example of robot navigation (i.e., a routing problem), and then through two formal and abstract examples. More elaborate and formal examples appear in [4].

Consider the following conjunction of two robot actions:

"Go to the kitchen" ∧ "Don't pass through the bedroom"

Note that each conjunct is a non-deterministic action, since there are many ways in which it can be carried out. In $\mathcal{TR}$, this conjunction would be equivalent to the following:

"Go to the kitchen without passing through the bedroom."

This action is more constrained than either of the two original conjuncts by themselves. In this way, conjunction reduces non-determinism and can specify what is *not* to be done.

Two points about classical conjunction are worth noting. First, it does not cause the conjuncts to be executed as two separate transactions. Instead, it combines them into a single, more tightly constrained transaction. Second, classical conjunction constrains the *entire execution* of a transaction (*i.e.*, the way in which it is carried out), not just the final state of the transaction. It can therefore express *dynamic* integrity constraints.

In general, classical conjunction constrains transactions in two ways: (i) by forcing non-deterministic transactions to execute in certain ways, and (ii) by causing transactions to fail. The following examples illustrate these points.

Example 2.14 (Transaction Failure: I)   If a user issued the transaction $?-\ ins{:}b \wedge del{:}b$, then the transaction would fail,[5] leaving the database unchanged. The transaction fails because it is not possible to simultaneously insert and delete one and the same atom into a database. Formally, the following statements are both true:

$$\mathbf{P}, \mathbf{D}, \mathbf{D} + \{b\} \;\models\; ins{:}b \qquad \mathbf{P}, \mathbf{D}, \mathbf{D} - \{b\} \;\models\; del{:}b$$

but the following statement is false, for every database $\mathbf{D}'$:

$$\mathbf{P}, \mathbf{D}, \mathbf{D}' \;\models\; ins{:}b \wedge del{:}b$$

□

The transaction in Example 2.14 fails because its conjuncts, $ins{:}b$ and $del{:}b$, terminate at different database states. However, a conjunction $\psi \wedge \phi$ may fail even though the component-transactions, ψ and ϕ, terminate at the *same* state. This is possible because the execution paths of ψ and ϕ may pass through *different* intermediate states, and there may be no execution path that is common to ϕ and ψ.

Example 2.15 (Transaction Failure: II) Each of the transactions, $ins{:}b \otimes ins{:}c$ and $ins{:}c \otimes ins{:}b$, transforms a database, $\mathbf{D}$, into the database $\mathbf{D} + \{b, c\}$. However, they pass through different intermediate states. The former passes through state $\mathbf{D} + \{b\}$, while the latter passes through state $\mathbf{D} + \{c\}$. The conjunction $ins{:}b \otimes ins{:}c \wedge ins{:}c \otimes ins{:}b$ therefore fails, since there is no single sequence of states that is a valid execution path of both conjuncts. Formally, the following two statements are both true:

---

[5] We use the term "failure" in the same sense as it is used in Prolog, which is not quite the same as in transaction management theory.

$$\mathbf{P}, \mathbf{D}, \mathbf{D} + \{b\}, \mathbf{D} + \{b, c\} \ \models \ ins{:}b \otimes ins{:}c$$

$$\mathbf{P}, \mathbf{D}, \mathbf{D} + \{c\}, \mathbf{D} + \{b, c\} \ \models \ ins{:}c \otimes ins{:}b$$

Nevertheless, the following statement is false for any database sequence:[6]

$$\mathbf{P}, \mathbf{D}, \mathbf{D}_1, \ldots, \mathbf{D}_n \ \models \ ins{:}b \otimes ins{:}c \wedge ins{:}c \otimes ins{:}b$$

□

Example 2.16 (Reducing Non-Determinism) The transactions $ins{:}a \vee ins{:}c$ and $ins{:}a \vee ins{:}b$ are both non-deterministic. However, starting from database $\mathbf{D}$, both transactions can follow the same path and terminate at $\mathbf{D} + \{a\}$. In fact, this is the only database that can be reached by both transactions.[6] Hence, if the user issued the transaction $(ins{:}a \vee ins{:}b) \wedge (ins{:}a \vee ins{:}c)$, then after execution, the final database would be $\mathbf{D} + \{a\}$. Formally, the following statement is true:[6]

$$\mathbf{P}, \mathbf{D}, \mathbf{D}' \ \models \ (ins{:}a \vee ins{:}b) \wedge (ins{:}a \vee ins{:}c) \quad \textit{iff} \quad \mathbf{D}' = \mathbf{D} + \{a\}$$

In this way, classical conjunction reduces non-determinism and, in this particular example, yields a completely deterministic transaction. □

In [4], we show that $\mathcal{TR}$ is a rich language for expressing constraints. Much of this richness comes from serial conjunction, especially when combined with negation. For example, each of the following formulas has a natural meaning as a constraint:

- $\neg(a \otimes b \otimes c)$ means that the sequence $a \otimes b \otimes c$ is not allowed.

- $\phi \otimes \neg\psi$ means that transaction ψ must *not* follow transaction ϕ.

- $\neg(\phi \otimes \neg\psi)$ means that transaction ψ *must* follow transaction ϕ.

These formulas can often be simplified by using the dual operator $\oplus$, which we call *serial disjunction*. For example, the last formula can be rewritten as $\neg\phi \oplus \psi$ [4].

3   Syntax

The syntax of $\mathcal{TR}$ distinguishes two kinds of formulas: *transaction formulas* and *elementary transitions*. The former define composite transactions, and the latter define elementary updates.

Transaction formulas are the formulas that most users will work with, using them to define transactions and formulate queries. Transaction formulas extend first-order formulas with two new connectives, $\otimes$ and $\oplus$, called *serial conjunction* and *serial disjunction*, respectively.

Formally, transaction formulas are defined recursively as follows. An *atomic transaction formula* is an expression of the form $p(t_1, \ldots, t_n)$, where $p \in \mathcal{P}$ is a

---

[6] Assuming b and c are not implied by $\mathbf{D}$.

predicate symbol, and $t_1, \ldots, t_n$ are terms. If ϕ and ψ are transaction formulas, then so are $\phi \vee \psi$, $\phi \wedge \psi$, $\phi \oplus \psi$, $\phi \otimes \psi$, $\neg \phi$, $(\forall X)\phi$, and $(\exists X)\phi$, where X is a variable.

The following are examples of transaction formulas:

- $b(X) \otimes c(X, Y)$

- $a(X) \vee \neg[b(X) \otimes c(X, Y)]$

- $\forall X[a(X) \vee \neg b(X) \oplus \neg c(X, Y)]$

Intuitively, the formula $\psi \otimes \phi$ means, "Do ψ and then do ϕ," and the formula $\psi \oplus \phi$ means, "Do ψ now or do ϕ later." Formally, $\oplus$ and $\otimes$ are dual, so that $\neg(\psi \oplus \phi)$ is equivalent to $\neg\phi \otimes \neg\psi$. Note that classical first-order formulas are transaction formulas that do not use $\otimes$ and $\oplus$.

Transaction formulas combine simple transactions into complex ones. However, we also need a way to specify *elementary* changes to a database. One way to define such transitions is to build them into the semantics as in [11, 13, 5]. The problem with this approach is that adding new kinds of elementary transitions leads to a redefinition of the very notion of a model and thus to a revamping of the entire theory, including the need to reprove soundness and completeness results. In other words, such theories are not extensible. This is a serious problem, since the ability to add new transitions is by no means an esoteric whim. For instance, a transition called *relational assignment* [4] is especially important to SQL-style bulk updates. Furthermore, Katsuno and Mendelzon [9] pointed out that, generally, state transitions belong to two major categories—*updates* and *revisions*—and even within each category several different flavours of such transitions are worth looking at. Thus, there appears to be no small, single set of elementary transitions that is best for all purposes.

For this reason, rather than commit $\mathcal{TR}$ to a fixed set of elementary transitions, we have chosen to treat the elementary transitions as a *parameter* of $\mathcal{TR}$. Each set of elementary transitions thus gives rise to a different version of the logic. To achieve this, elementary transitions are defined by logical axioms. Unlike the axioms in most logics, however, elementary transitions have a special status and are expressed in a special language.

Elementary transitions are specified by formulas of the form $\langle \phi, \psi \rangle u$, where ϕ, ψ are closed first-order formulas and u is a ground (*i.e.*, variable-free) atomic formula, called the *name* of the transition.[7] Intuitively, this formula says that u is an update that transforms database ϕ into database ψ. For instance, in Section 2, the predicates *ins:b* and *del:b* would be defined by an enumerable set of elementary transitions consisting of the formulas $\langle \mathbf{D}, \mathbf{D} + \{b\} \rangle$ *ins:b* and $\langle \mathbf{D}, \mathbf{D} - \{b\} \rangle$ *del:b* for every relational database $\mathbf{D}$. (If $\mathbf{D}$ is a general first-order formula, defining insertion and deletion is more involved; see [9]). Enumerable sets of elementary transitions are called *transition bases*.

The reader is referred to [4] for a more detailed discussion of elementary updates.

---

[7] Groundedness is imposed for simplicity and because non-ground atoms do not provide new functionality. There is no serious technical problem in handling non-ground atoms in elementary transitions.

4   Model Theory

Just as the syntax is based on two basic ideas—serial conjunction and elementary transitions—the semantics is also based on a small number of fundamental ideas:

- *Transaction Execution Paths*: A transaction causes a sequence of database state changes;

- *Database States*:   A database state is a set of (classical) first-order semantic structures;

- *Executional Entailment*:   Transaction execution is tantamount to truth over a sequence of database states.

Transaction Execution Paths: When the user executes a transaction, the database may change, going from some initial state to some final state. In doing so, the database may pass through any number of intermediate states. For example, execution of the transaction $ins{:}a \otimes ins{:}b \otimes ins{:}c$ takes the database from an initial state $\mathbf{D}$, through the intermediate states $\mathbf{D} + \{a\}$ and $\mathbf{D} + \{a, b\}$, to the final state $\mathbf{D} + \{a, b, c\}$. This idea of a sequence of states is central to our semantics of transactions. It also allows us to model a wide range of constraints. For example, we may require that every intermediate state satisfy some condition, or we may forbid certain sequences of states.

To model transactions, we start with a modal-like semantics, where each state represents a database, and each elementary update causes a transition from one state to another, thereby changing the database.

At this point, however, modal logic and Transaction Logic begin to part company. The first major difference is that unlike modal semantic structures, truth in $\mathcal{TR}$ structures does not hinge on a set of arcs between states. Indeed, $\mathcal{TR}$ structures do not even come with a set of arcs. Instead, in order to model transactions, we focus on *paths*, that is, on sequences of states. Any finite sequence of states is a valid path. Because of the emphasis on paths, we refer to semantic structures in $\mathcal{TR}$ as *path structures*.

Unlike modal structures, truth in path structures is defined on paths, not states. For example, we would say that the path $\mathbf{D}$, $\mathbf{D}+\{a\}$, $\mathbf{D}+\{a, b\}$ satisfies the formula $ins{:}a \otimes ins{:}b$, since it represents an insertion of a followed by an insertion of b. On the other hand, the path $\mathbf{D}$, $\mathbf{D} + \{b\}$, $\mathbf{D} + \{a, b\}$ does *not* satisfy this formula. Instead, it satisfies the formula $ins{:}b \otimes ins{:}a$. We carry the idea of truth on paths to its logical conclusion. Thus, if a path satisfies the formulas ψ and $\neg\psi \vee \phi$, then the path must also satisfy the formula ϕ. Note that a path of length 1 corresponds to a single database state. In this way, $\mathcal{TR}$'s path-based semantics accounts for databases as well as transactions. That is, with just one model-theoretic device, paths, we can give meaning to statements about databases and to statements about transactions.

Database States: Another difference between modal logic and Transaction Logic is in the nature of states. In modal logic, a state is basically a first-order semantic structure, since each state specifies the truth of a set of ground atomic formulas. Such structures are adequate for representing relational databases, but not for representing more general theories, like indefinite databases or general logic programs, which may contain quite complex first-order formulas. We therefore take a more general approach. Since a database is a first-order formula, which has a *set* of first-order models, we define a state to be a *set* of first-order semantic structures. Each state, s, thus corresponds to a particular database—the database having precisely those models that comprise s.

This approach to states provides a lot of flexibility when defining elementary updates. Such flexibility is needed since, for general databases, the semantics of elementary updates is not clear, not even for relatively simple updates like insert and delete. For example, what does it mean to insert an atom b into a database that entails $\neg b$, especially if $\neg b$ itself is not explicitly present in the database? There is no consensus on the answer to this question, and many solutions have been proposed (see [9] for a comprehensive discussion). Similar difficulties exist for deletion. Furthermore, insertions and deletions are not always the best choice for elementary updates, as mentioned earlier.

For these reasons, we take a general approach to elementary updates. For us, an elementary update is a mapping that takes each database $\mathbf{D}_1$ to some other database $\mathbf{D}_2$, where a database is any first-order formula. More generally, an elementary update may be non-deterministic, so it is not just a mapping, but a *binary relation* on databases.[8] Elementary updates are defined axiomatically by a transition base, as outlined in Section 3.

Executional Entailment: Executional entailment is a statement of the form

$$\mathcal{B}, \mathbf{P}, \mathbf{D}_0, \mathbf{D}_1, \ldots, \mathbf{D}_n \models \phi \tag{2}$$

where $\mathcal{B}$ is a transition base, $\mathbf{P}$ is a transaction base, ϕ is a transaction formula, and $\mathbf{D}_0, \mathbf{D}_1, \ldots, \mathbf{D}_n$ is a sequence of databases (first-order formulas).

Informally, (2) is true if transaction ϕ, defined by the transaction base $\mathbf{P}$, is true on the path $\mathbf{D}_0, \mathbf{D}_1, \ldots, \mathbf{D}_n$. This idea ties together the model theory of $\mathcal{TR}$ and the intuitive concept of execution: if (2) is true and the user has issued a transaction $?-\phi$, this results in an execution of this transaction along some path of database states. The path $\mathbf{D}_0, \mathbf{D}_1, \ldots, \mathbf{D}_n$ is one such possible path and $\mathbf{D}_n$ is one of the possible final states of the execution. This concept was illustrated in Section 2 and its formal rendering can be found in [4].

5 Proof Theory

$\mathcal{TR}$ has a sound and complete proof theory. Furthermore, there is a subset of $\mathcal{TR}$, which we call *Horn* $\mathcal{TR}$, that corresponds to classical logic programs and that has an efficient SLD-style proof procedure. Although we cannot give the proof theory adequate coverage in this survey, the following properties of executional entailment form the basis of a "naive" proof theory:[9]

1. If $\mathcal{B}, \mathbf{P}, \mathbf{D}_0, \ldots, \mathbf{D}_n \models \alpha$ and $\mathcal{B}, \mathbf{P}, \mathbf{D}_0, \ldots, \mathbf{D}_n \models \beta$
   then $\mathcal{B}, \mathbf{P}, \mathbf{D}_0, \ldots, \mathbf{D}_n \models \alpha \wedge \beta$.

2. If $\mathcal{B}, \mathbf{P}, \mathbf{D}_0, \ldots, \mathbf{D}_i \models \alpha$ and $\mathcal{B}, \mathbf{P}, \mathbf{D}_i, \ldots, \mathbf{D}_n \models \beta$
   then $\mathcal{B}, \mathbf{P}, \mathbf{D}_0, \ldots, \mathbf{D}_n \models \alpha \otimes \beta$.

---

[8]This is only one source of non-determinism is $\mathcal{TR}$, since, as shown earlier, non-determinism may arise even when all elementary updates are deterministic.

[9]Here, $\mathcal{B}$, $\mathbf{P}$, and $\mathbf{D}_0, \ldots, \mathbf{D}_n$ are as in (2) above, and α and β are transaction formulas.

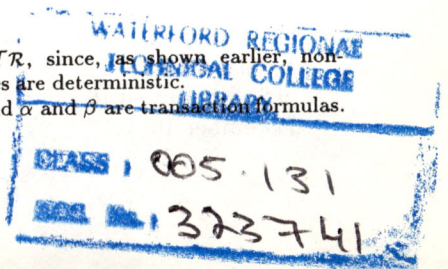

3. If $\alpha \leftarrow \beta$ is in $\mathbf{P}$ and $\mathcal{B}, \mathbf{P}, \mathbf{D}_0, \ldots, \mathbf{D}_n \models \beta$
   then $\mathcal{B}, \mathbf{P}, \mathbf{D}_0, \ldots, \mathbf{D}_n \models \alpha$.

4. If $\langle \mathbf{D}_0, \mathbf{D}_1 \rangle \alpha$ is in $\mathcal{B}$, then $\mathcal{B}, \mathbf{P}, \mathbf{D}_0, \mathbf{D}_1 \models \alpha$.

5. If $\mathbf{D}_0 \models^c \psi$ then $\mathcal{B}, \mathbf{P}, \mathbf{D}_0 \models \psi$,
   where ψ is a first-order formula, and $\models^c$ denotes classical entailment.

We refer the reader to [4] for a thorough treatment of the proof theory.

6 Conclusions

We have reviewed the main ideas underlying Transaction Logic, a novel declarative formalism for specifying and executing actions. A wide range of applications were alluded to, but their full treatment appears elsewhere [4]. These applications include (but are not limited to): view updates in databases, logic programming with "clean" *assert* and *retract*, object-oriented logic programming, temporal constraints among actions, planning robot actions, the frame problem in AI, subjunctive and counterfactual reasoning, program verification, and others.

Acknowledgments

We would like to thank Mariano Consens, Alberto Mendelzon, and Ray Reiter for comments and critique, which inspired many improvements.

We are also gratefully acknowledging productive discussions with Gösta Grahne and Peter Revesz.

References

[1] F. Bancilhon. A logic-programming/Object-oriented cocktail. *SIGMOD Record*, 15(3):11–21, September 1986.

[2] C. Beeri. New data models and languages—The challenge. In *ACM SIGACT-SIGMOD-SIGART Symposium on Principles of Database Systems*, pages 1–15, San Diego, CA, June 1992.

[3] A.J. Bonner and M. Kifer. A general logic of state change. Technical report, CSRI, University of Toronto, 1992. In preparation.

[4] A.J. Bonner and M. Kifer. Transaction logic programming. Technical Report CSRI-270, University of Toronto, April 1992. Revised: December 1992. (This report can be FTP'ed (in binary mode) from the anonymous FTP account at cs.sunysb.edu; file: pub/TechReports/kifer/transaction-logic.dvi.Z)

[5] W. Chen. Declarative specification and evaluation of database updates. In *Intl. Conference on Deductive and Object-Oriented Databases*, volume 566 of *Lecture Notes in Computer Science*, pages 147–166. Springer Verlag, December 1991.

[6] R.E. Fikes and N.J. Nilsson. STRIPS: A new approach to the application of theorem proving to problem solving. *Artificial Intelligence*, 2:189–208, 1971.

[7] D. Harel. **First-Order Dynamic Logic**, volume 68 of *Lecture Notes in Computer Science*. Springer Verlag, 1979.

[8] D. Harel, D. Kozen, and R. Parikh. Process Logic: Expressiveness, decidability, completeness. *Journal of Computer and System Sciences*, 25(2):144–170, October 1982.

[9] H. Katsuno and A.O. Mendelzon. On the difference between updating a knowledge database and revising it. In *Proc. of the 2-nd Intl. Conference on Principles of Knowledge Representation (KR'91)*, pages 387–394, Boston, Mass., April 1991.

[10] M. Kifer, G. Lausen, and J. Wu. Logical foundations of object-oriented and frame-based languages. Technical Report 90/14, Department of Computer Science, SUNY at Stony Brook, July 1990. To appear in J. of ACM.

[11] S. Manchanda and D.S. Warren. A logic-based language for database updates. In J. Minker, editor, *Foundations of Deductive Databases and Logic Programming*, pages 363–394. Morgan-Kaufmann, Los Altos, CA, 1988.

[12] J.M. McCarthy and P.J. Hayes. Some philosophical problems from the standpoint of artificial intelligence. In J.E. Hayes and D. Michie, editors, *Machine Intelligence*, volume 4. Edinburgh University Press, 1974. Reprinted in *Readings in Artificial Intelligence*, 1981, Tioga Publ. Co.

[13] S. Naqvi and R. Krishnamurthy. Database updates in logic programming. In *ACM SIGACT-SIGMOD-SIGART Symposium on Principles of Database Systems*, pages 251–262, March 1988.

[14] N.J. Nilsson. **Principles of Artificial Intelligence**. Tioga Publ. Co., Paolo Alto, CA, 1980.

[15] R. Reiter. Formalizing database evolution in the situation calculus. In *Conf. on Fifth Generation Computer Systems*, 1992.

Aggregate Operations in the Information Source Tracking Method*

Fereidoon Sadri

Department of Computer Science

Concordia University

Montreal, Canada

Abstract

The *Information Source Tracking* method, *IST*, is an approach to the management of uncertain and imprecise data in database systems. In this paper we study the processing of queries involving aggregate operations in the IST method. The problems discussed include producing all possible outcomes of an aggregate query and their probabilities, and determining the probability of a specific outcome. We present algorithms for the evaluation of aggregate queries, and show that some of these problems are intractable.

1   Introduction

The *Information Source Tracking* method, *IST*, is an approach to the management of uncertain and imprecise data in database systems [11]. In this paper we study the processing of queries involving aggregate operations in the IST method.

The main idea behind IST is that database information is supplied, or confirmed, by information sources. The accuracy of data is modeled by the reliability of the contributing information sources. The IST method uses an extended relational model. The identity of contributing information source(s) are stored along with each tuple in the database. Extended relational algebra operations are provided that manipulate data as well as information regarding contributing information sources. In response to a query, the system provides the answer, and also identifies information sources contributing to each answer. More precisely, the IST method identifies the exact conditions under which an answer to a query is valid. Given a quantitative measure of the reliability of information sources, the reliability of answers to queries can be calculated. An SQL interface based on the IST model has been implemented which supports a subset of the SQL query language [4]. In this paper we study how the aggregate operations, *min*, *Max*, *sum*, *count*, and *average*, can be implemented in the IST model.

The rest of this paper is organized as follows. Section 2 is a background review of the IST method, the *alternate worlds semantics* model of the IST, and the reliability calculation algorithms. In Section 3 we introduce aggregate

---

*Supported by grants from the Natural Sciences and Engineering Research Council of Canada (NSERC), and Fonds pour la Formation de Chercheurs et l'Aide a la Recherche (FCAR) of Quebec.

operations in the IST model, and present a brute-force algorithm to calculate all possible answers to an aggregate query and their probabilities. Section 4 is devoted to a discussion of different formulations of the intended meaning of aggregate operations in the IST model, and their complexity. We show that some of these problems are NP-complete, and hence highly unlikely to have an efficient algorithm. In Section 5 we present algorithms for the calculation of expected values of answers to aggregate queries in the IST model. Algorithms for the processing of *min* and *Max* queries are also presented in Section 5. Finally, concluding remarks are presented in Section 6.

2 A Review of the Information Source Tracking Method

The *Information Source Tracking* method, *IST*, was introduced in [11], and a semantic interpretation for IST was presented in [12]. The issue of consistency in the IST method, i.e. how to handle conflicting information supplied by different information sources, was studied in [13]. In [14] the efficiency of query processing and reliability calculation algorithms of IST was studied, and the "Dual IST" method was presented which is more efficient than IST when a large number of information sources supply information to the database. In this section we briefly review some of the concepts from [11, 12]. Interested readers are referred to [11, 12, 13, 14] for detailed discussions.

2.1 Information Source Tracking

The idea behind IST is simple: We record, for each tuple in a relation in the database, the source of the tuple (called the *confirming* or *contributing* information source). Query processing is performed using extended relational algebra operations that manipulate contributing source data in addition to traditional database data. The answer to a query is a relation (similar to a traditional relational database system), but there is also precise information regarding contributing information sources for each tuple in the answer. In this way, we can determine the conditions under which a tuple in the answer is valid. If a quantitative measure of the reliabilities of the information sources is available (supplied by users and/or database administrator), then a quantitative measure of validity can be calculated for each tuple in the answer. In what follows we provide precise definitions of the IST method.

Definitions: The IST model is based upon an extended relational model discussed below. An *extended relation scheme* is a set of attributes $\{A_1, \ldots, A_n, I\}$, where $A_1, \ldots, A_n$ are regular attributes, and I is a special attribute, called the *information source attribute* (*source attribute*, for short). Each attribute A_i has a *domain* of values D_i, $i = 1, \ldots, n$. The domain of the source attribute I, denoted by D_I, is the set of vectors of length k with $-1, 0, 1$ elements, that is, $D_I = \{(a_1 \cdots a_k) \mid a_i \in \{-1, 0, 1\}, \ i = 1, \ldots, k\}$, where k is the number of information sources. An element of D_I is called an *information source vector* (*source vector* for short).

A *tuple* on the (extended) scheme $R = \{A_1, \ldots, A_n, I\}$ is an element of $D_1 \times \cdots \times D_n \times D_I$. We usually write $t@u$ to denote a tuple on the extended scheme

R, where t is the value of the tuple corresponding to the regular attributes $A_1, \ldots, A_n$, and u is the value of the tuple corresponding to the source attribute I. We call t a *pure tuple*, and u is the *source vector* corresponding to t. A *relation instance* (*relation* for short) r on the scheme R is a set of tuples on R.

A source vector u for a tuple $t@u$ identifies sources that contribute to t. Intuitively, t is valid if all sources having a $+1$ entry in u are correct, and all those having a -1 entry in u are incorrect. Usually, each tuple of a stored database relation (sometimes called a *base* relation), is supplied by a single information source. Hence, for base relations, each tuple has a source vector with only one $+1$ element. Once we apply relational algebra operations, for example to produce answers to a query, we will obtain tuples having source vectors with possibly several $+1$ and -1 elements. The extended relational algebra operations are discussed in the next subsection. The -1 entries arise from set difference operation (or the NOT EXISTS construct of SQL). Note that there can be more than one source vector associated with a pure tuple t in a relation, i.e., $t@u_1, \ldots, t@u_p$, $p \geq 1$, can be in r. The interpretation of source vectors is made precise by introducing the *expression* corresponding to a pure tuple t as follows.

First, consider the case where there is a single (extended) tuple $t@u$ in r, where $u = (a_1 \cdots a_k)$. We denote the set of information sources by $S = \{s_1, \ldots, s_k\}$, where k is the number of information sources. The sources $S^+ = \{s_i \mid a_i = 1\}$ are contributing positively to the pure tuple t, while the sources $S^- = \{s_i \mid a_i = -1\}$ are contributing negatively. We also associate with each information source s_i a Boolean variable f_i. The *expression corresponding to t with respect to u*, denoted $e(t@u)$, is written as

$$e(t@u) = \bigwedge_{s_i \in S^+} f_i \bigwedge_{s_j \in S^-} \neg f_j \tag{1}$$

Now, consider the case where $t@u_1, \ldots, t@u_p$ are all the tuples with the pure part t in r, which we write as $t@x \in r$, where $x = \{u_1, \ldots, u_p\}$. The *expression corresponding to t with respect to x*, (*expression corresponding to t* for short), is written as

$$e(t) = e(t@x) = \bigvee_{i=1}^{p} e(t@u_i) \tag{2}$$

We can regard the expression corresponding to a tuple t in a relation r as a propositional logic expression, where $f_1, \ldots, f_k$ represent Boolean variables. A truth assignment $f_i = true$ is interpreted as "information source s_i is correct", otherwise, $f_i = false$ which indicates s_i is incorrect. The truth value of $e(t)$ is a function of the truth values of $f_1, \ldots, f_k$, and indicates whether t is a valid tuple ($e(t) = true$), or an invalid tuple ($e(t) = false$).

The expression corresponding to a tuple t in a relation r can also be used to derive probabilistic information about t, i.e. given probabilities for correctness of sources $s_1, \ldots, s_k$, we can calculate the probability of the validity of t.

2.2 Extended Relational Algebra Operations

In the IST model query processing is achieved using extended relational algebra operations. These extended operations operate on the regular data as their standard counterparts (namely, selection, projection, Cartesian product, natural join, union, and set difference). In addition, the extended operations also operate on source vectors to produce source vectors for the tuples in the result that precisely determine under what conditions the associated tuple is valid. Here we summarize these operations from [11].

The extended relational algebra operations are defined in terms of source vector operations *3OR*, *NEGATION*, and *UNION*.

The 3OR of two non-zero source vectors, $u = (a_1 \cdots a_k)$ and $v = (b_1 \cdots b_k)$ is a source vector $w = (c_1 \cdots c_k)$ obtained using the following table, where $w = 0$ indicates that the whole w vector is zero. A zero source vector corresponds to the logical expression *false*. Note that if we remove the rows having -1 entries from the table, the resulting table corresponds to the logical disjunction (OR) operation. That is why this operation was called 3OR.

a_i	b_i	c_i
-1	-1	-1
-1	0	-1
-1	1	$w = 0$
0	-1	-1
0	0	0
0	1	1
1	-1	$w = 0$
1	0	1
1	1	1

Figure 1. The 3OR operation.

We write $w = u\|v$ to indicate the 3OR operation. For example, if $u = ($ 0 1 -1 0 1 $)$ and $v = ($-1 0 -1 0 1$)$, then $u\|v = ($-1 1 -1 0 1 $)$. Intuitively, the 3OR operation implements the logical conjunction of the expressions corresponding to the source vectors (this has been proven in [11].)

The 3OR of two sets of source vectors, $x = \{u_1, \ldots, u_p\}$ and $y = \{v_1, \ldots, v_q\}$, is calculated pairwise:

$$x\|y = \{u_1\|v_1, \ldots, u_1\|v_q, \ldots, u_p\|v_1, \ldots, u_p\|v_q\}$$

The NEGATION operation on source vectors is defined as follows: Let $u = (a_1 \cdots a_k)$ be a source vector, and let $a_{i_1}, \ldots, a_{i_n}$ be the non-zero elements of u. The NEGATION of u, written $\#(u)$, is a set of source vectors $\{v_{i_1}, \ldots, v_{i_n}\}$ constructed as follows: All the elements of v_{i_j} are zero except its i_jth element, which is $1(-1)$ if $a_{i_j} = -1(1)$. For example if $u = ($ 1 0 -1 1 0 $)$, then

$$\#(u) = \{ (\text{-}1\ 0\ 0\ 0\ 0), (0\ 0\ 1\ 0\ 0), (0\ 0\ 0\ \text{-}1\ 0) \}.$$

The NEGATION of a set of source vectors $x = \{u_1, \ldots, u_p\}$ is calculated as follows:

$$\#(x) = \#(u_1)\| \ldots \|\#(u_p)$$

The UNION operation for source vectors is the same as the classical set theory operation: Let $x = \{u_1, \ldots, u_p\}$ and $y = \{v_1, \ldots, v_q\}$ be sets of source vectors, then $x \cup y = \{u_1, \ldots, u_p, v_1, \ldots, v_q\}$, where duplicate source vectors, if any, are removed.

Now we can summarize the extended relational algebra operations: Extended selection, projection, and union are similar to their regular counterparts:

$$
\begin{aligned}
\sigma_C(r) &= \{t@u \mid t@u \in r, \text{ and } t \text{ satisfies condition } C\} \\
\Pi_X(r) &= \{t[X]@u \mid t@u \in r\} \\
r \cup s &= \{t@u \mid t@u \in r \text{ or } t@u \in s\}
\end{aligned}
$$

Note that an implicit UNION operation takes place for source vectors with the same pure component in the above operations. We shall also note that the information source attribute I is not visible to users, and can not be referenced (e.g. in the condition of a selection or in the attribute set of a projection).

Intersection, Cartesian product, and natural join are defined using the 3OR operation for source vectors:

$$
\begin{aligned}
r \cap s &= \{t@(u_1 \| u_2) \mid t@u_1 \in r \text{ and } t@u_2 \in s\} \\
r \times s &= \{(t_1.t_2@(u_1 \| u_2)) \mid t_1@u_1 \in r, \text{ and } t_2@u_2 \in s\} \\
r \bowtie s &= \{(t_1 \otimes t_2@(u_1 \| u_2)) \mid t_1@u_1 \in r, t_2@u_2 \in s, \text{ and } t_1 \text{ and } t_2 \text{ join } \}
\end{aligned}
$$

where $t_1.t_2$ indicates the concatenation of t_1 and t_2, and $t_1 \otimes t_2$ indicates the join of t_1 and t_2, i.e. the concatenation of t_1 and t_2 with the removal of duplicate values of common attributes. Two tuples t_1 and t_2 join if they have the same values for the common attributes. Note that t_1 and t_2 are *pure* tuples and do not contain values for the information source attribute I. In other words, we should not try to match the information source vectors when joining.

Finally, set difference uses NEGATION and 3OR of source vectors:

$$
\begin{aligned}
r - s = \{t@x \mid \quad &t@x \in r, \text{ and the pure tuple } t \text{ does not appear in } s, \text{ or,} \\
&t@y \in r, t@z \in s, \text{ and } x = y \| (\# z)\}
\end{aligned}
$$

2.3 The Alternate Worlds Semantics

The *alternate worlds model* was presented in [12] to provide a semantic interpretation for IST. The idea is similar to the notions of "representation", "possibility functions", "alternate worlds", and "possible worlds" used by researchers in databases and artificial intelligence [1, 3, 6, 7, 9, 10]. It was shown in [12] that the extended relational algebra operations of IST are *precise* under the alternate worlds interpretation. The reliability calculation algorithms were also shown to be correct under this interpretation. Here we briefly review the alternate worlds semantics.

An extended relation *represents* a set of (regular) relations. This set of regular relations is called the *alternate world* of the extended relation. We give precise definitions below.

Definitions: Given a relation r on the (extended) scheme R, r can be written as $r = \{t_1@x_1, \ldots, t_n@x_n\}$, where $x_1, \ldots, x_n$ are sets of source vectors. We define r^* as a function from the set of subsets of information sources S to the set of (regular) relations Rel on the scheme $R - \{I\}$, that is,

$$r^* : 2^S \to Rel \tag{3}$$

Let $Q \subseteq S$ be a set of information sources. Assign truth value "true" to sources in Q, and "false" to other sources. (We will denote this truth assignment by $truth(Q)$.) Then,

$$r^*(Q) = \{t_i \mid e(t_i) = true \text{ under } truth(Q)\} \tag{4}$$

where $e(t_i)$ is the expression corresponding to t_i in r.

An extended relation r *represents* the function r^*. The set of (regular) relations $r^*(Q)$, $Q \subseteq S$, is called the *alternate world* of r. Informally, an extended relation r represents the set of (regular) relations consisting of those tuples that would be valid if the information sources in Q were correct and all other information sources were incorrect, for all $Q \subseteq S$.

Example 1: Consider the relation *employee* of Figure 2.

Employee	Salary	I
a	40,000	1 0
b	60,000	0 1

Figure 2. The *employee* relation.

The alternate world of *employee* consists of four relations, the empty relation $r_1 = \phi$, corresponding to the empty set of information sources, plus relations r_2, r_3, and r_4 of Figure 3, corresponding to $\{s_1\}$, $\{s_2\}$, and $\{s_1, s_2\}$, respectively.

Employee	Salary
a	40,000

Employee	Salary
b	60,000

Employee	Salary
a	40,000
b	60,000

Figure 3. Relations r_2, r_3, and r_4

In [12] we prove that extended relational algebra operations introduced in [11] are *precise* under the alternate worlds semantics. That is, informally, the extended operations applied to extended relations produce exactly the same result as the regular operations applied to the alternate world of the corresponding extended relations.

2.4   Reliability Calculation

In the IST model users (or database administrator) can provide reliability figures for information sources. The *reliability* of a source s_i is defined as the probability that data confirmed by s_i is correct, and is denoted by p_i. The query processing in a database system based on IST is carried out using extended relational algebra operations. Once an answer is obtained for a query, the reliability of each tuple in the answer can be calculated as a function of the contributing information sources reliabilities.

Two algorithms for the calculation of the reliabilities of the tuples in the answer to a query were presented in [11] and proven correct under alternate worlds semantics in [12]. Here, we briefly review Algorithm 2 from [11].

The algorithm is based on the conversion of source vectors into *disjunctive normal form*. For example a source vector (1 0 0) is equivalent to the set of source vectors { (1 1 1), (1 -1 1), (1 1 -1), (1 -1 -1) } Let $t@\{v_1, \ldots, v_q\}$ be all the tuples with pure component t, where v_i's are in disjunctive normal form. The reliability of t, denoted by $re(t)$, is calculated as:

$$re(t) = re(t@v_1) + \cdots + re(t@v_q) \tag{5}$$

where, for a single source vector u,

$$re(t@u) = \prod_{s_i \in S^+(u)} p_i \prod_{s_i \in S^-(u)} (1 - p_i) \tag{6}$$

where $S^+(u)$ and $S^-(u)$ are the set of information sources contributing to $t@u$ positively and negatively, respectively. That is, for $u = (a_1 \cdots a_k)$,

$$
\begin{aligned}
S^+(u) &= \{s_i \mid a_i = 1, i = 1, \ldots, k\} \\
S^-(u) &= \{s_i \mid a_i = -1, i = 1, \ldots, k\}
\end{aligned}
$$

3 Aggregate Operations in IST

Aggregate operations, such as *min*, *Max*, *sum*, *count*, and *average* in SQL, are frequently needed in many applications. In a regular database, where no uncertainty exists, the processing of queries involving aggregate operations is straightforward. The algorithms for these operations have a linear time performance in the size of the relation involved (except when an index is available, where some operations, such as *min* and *Max*, can be performed more efficiently.)

The situation becomes much more complicated in the presence of uncertain and imprecise data. In this section we discuss the meaning of the aggregate operations in the IST model, and present a brute-force algorithm for processing such operations.

Our starting point will be the alternate worlds semantics of the IST model. Recall that if k information sources $s_1, \ldots, s_k$ contribute to an extended relation r, then the alternate world of r consists of up to 2^k regular relations. Each subset Q of the set of information sources, $Q \subseteq \{s_1, \ldots, s_k\}$, defines a regular relation represented by r, but some of these regular relations may be identical. A possible interpretation of the result of an aggregate operation on an extended relation r is the list of the possible results of the operation carried out on the regular relations represented by r, together with their probabilities. More precisely, we define the result of an aggregate operation *agg* on an extended relation r with respect to an attribute A as a function agg^* from the set of subsets of $S = \{s_1, \ldots, s_k\}$ to values, $agg^* : 2^S \rightarrow R$, where

$$agg_A^*(Q) = agg_A(r^*(Q))$$

for all $Q \subseteq S$, where agg_A applied to a regular relation is the classical aggregate operation, and $r^*(Q)$ is the regular relation represented by r corresponding to $Q \subseteq S$.

Example 2: Consider the extended relation *employee* of Figure 2. The relations in the alternate world of *employee* consists of the empty relation $r_1 = \phi$

and the relations r_2, r_3, and r_4 shown in Figure 3. The query $sum_{salary}(employee)$, or in SQL

select sum(salary) from employee

can be evaluated against the four regular relations r_1 to r_4 in the alternate world of r. The answer would be 0, 40,000, 60,000, and 100,000 respectively.

Given reliability figures for the information sources, we can associate a probability with each regular relation in the alternate world of an extended relation [12]. These probabilities can be associated, in a straightforward manner, with the results of an aggregate operation on these regular relations. For example, if the reliabilities of the two information sources in the above example were 90% and 80%, respectively, then the probabilities associated with the answers, 0, 40,000, 60,000, and 100,000, would be 2%, 18%, 8%, and 72% respectively.

3.1 An Algorithm for Aggregate Operations in the IST Model

A brute-force algorithm to enumerate the answers of an aggregate operation on the relations in the alternate world of an extended relation by obtaining the alternate world relations and processing the aggregate operation on each of them is clearly inefficient. There are an exponential number of relations (exponential in the number of information sources) in the alternate world of an extended relation in the worst case, and the brute-force algorithm will have an exponential time complexity. In fact, the size of the answer, which is exponential in the worst case eliminates any hopes of finding an efficient (linear or at least polynomial) algorithm. Note that the number of tuples in an extended relation can be linear in the number of information sources, which means the size of the answer is exponential in the size of the relation. Further, we will prove in the next section that even some simplified problems involving aggregate operations in the IST model are NP-complete and hence unlikely (unless P = NP) to have efficient algorithms. In what follows, we briefly describe an algorithm to enumerate all possible answers to an aggregate query and their probabilities with the help of an example. The algorithm is based on the expansion of the information source vectors to standard forms discussed in [11]. For example, a vector (0 1 0) will be expanded to the set {(-1 1 -1), (1 1 -1), (-1 1 1), (1 1 1)}.

Example 3: Let us expand every tuple in the *employee* relation of Figure 2, and group the tuples according to the source vectors:

Employee	Salary	I	
b	60,000	-1	1
a	40,000	1	-1
a	40,000	1	1
b	60,000	1	1

Figure 4. The expanded *employee* relation.

Obviously, each group corresponds to one alternate world relation. The aggregate operation can be applied to each group separately to obtain the answers. We obtain for our example:

sum	I	
60,000	-1	1
40,000	1	-1
100,000	1	1

Figure 5. The sum of salaries relation.

The probability associated with each answer can be obtained directly from the associated source vectors [11]. Any source vector combination that does not appear in the expanded relation corresponds to the empty relation in the alternate world.

4   Other Formulations, and Intractability Results

As we saw in the previous section providing all possible answers to an aggregate query in the IST model results in algorithms with an exponential time complexity. In this section we will first discuss various questions for aggregate operations, and then study the complexity for some of them. We will show that some queries that may seem simple in the first sight turn out to be NP-complete, and hence it is unlikely that an efficient algorithm exists for them. In the following $aggr_A(r)$ designates the operation $aggr$, one of the usual aggregate operations, on the attribute A of the extended relation r.

Instead of listing all possible results of an aggregate operation, we might be interested in the following questions:

1. Given a constant c, what is the probability associated with the result of the aggregate operation to be equal to c. For example, in the employee relation of previous sections, we may ask the question "What is the probability for the sum of salaries to be 100,000?" The answer would be 72% for our running example.

2. Find the expected value of the result. For our running example, the expected value of sum of salaries is obtained as

$$0 \times .02 + 40,000 \times 0.18 + 60,000 \times 0.08 + 100,000 \times 0.72 = 84,000$$

In some cases we would be interested to obtain a "normalized" expected value. That is, we only consider non-empty relations in the alternate world as meaningful, and distribute the probability associated with the empty relation over the non-empty ones. This can be accomplished by dividing the probabilities associated with non-empty relation by their sum (which is equal to one minus the probability of the empty relation). For our example, the normalized expected value of sum of salaries is $84,000/0.98 = 85,714$.

4.1 Intractability Results

In this section we will show that the first problem above is NP-complete for aggregate operations *sum*, *count*, and *average*. In fact, we show the result for a simpler problem, which we will call problem P1, specified below.

Problem P1-SUM.

Given an extended relation r, determine whether the probability of $sum_A(r) = c$ is non-zero, where c is a constant, and A is an attribute of r.

Theorem 1: Problem P1-SUM is NP-complete.

Proof: Given an extended relation r, we can non-deterministically guess a subset Q of the information sources, obtain the corresponding regular relation $r^*(Q)$ in the alternate world of r, and check to see whether $sum_A(r^*(Q)) = c$. Hence the problem P1-SUM is in NP. The proof of completeness is by reducing the three satisfiability (3SAT) problem [2, 5] to P1-SUM. Let $C = \{c_1, c_2, \ldots, c_m\}$ be an instance of the 3SAT problem, where each c_i is a disjunctive clause containing three literals over the set of Boolean variables $U = \{u_1, u_2, \ldots, u_n\}$. We will construct an extended relation r over the scheme $R = \{A, B, I\}$ with $3 \times m$ tuples. There are n information sources $s_1, s_2, \ldots, s_n$ corresponding to the Boolean variables. The reliability of each information source is 50% (any value other than 0 and 100% is acceptable). Each clause c_i gives rise to 3 tuples in r, one for each literal in c_i. If a literal L in c_i is a (non-negated) variable u_k, then the source vector of the corresponding tuple in r has a +1 for s_k and zeros for all other information sources. If the literal is a negated variable, then the corresponding source vector has a -1 for the corresponding information source, and zeros for the rest. The value of the attribute A is the same for all the tuples, equal to 1. The value of the attribute B for each tuple generated by a clause c_i is set to i. Hence, for each $1 \leq i \leq m$ there are 3 tuples in r with their B-value equal to i. This construction is clearly polynomial in the size of the 3SAT instance.

We now claim that the probability of $sum_A(r) = m$ is non-zero if and only if C is satisfiable. It is simple to see that $sum_A(r) = m$ is non-zero iff at least one regular relation in the alternate world of r contains m tuples, which can happen iff all the pure tuples in r are valid under the truth assignment $truth(Q)$ for a subset Q of the information sources. The same truth assignment applied to the Boolean variables designates a satisfying assignment for the 3SAT instance C. □

The problems P1-COUNT and P1-AVERAGE are similar to P1-SUM except that the aggregate operation is *count* and *average* respectively. These problems are also NP-complete. The proof is similar to the proof for P1-SUM. We will state the theorem and just sketch the proofs below.

Theorem 2: The P1-COUNT and P1-AVERAGE problems are NP-complete.

Proof: For P1-AVERAGE the extended relation r is constructed as it was in the case of P1-SUM, except that the A attribute does not have the same value for all tuples. For example, we can make the 3 tuples corresponding to the clause c_1 have an A-value of 2, and the remaining tuples have an A-value of 1. Then $average_A(r) = (m + 1)/m$ has a non-zero probability if and only if the 3SAT instance C is satisfiable.

For P1-COUNT the extended relation needs only the B attribute, and

$count(r) = m$ has a non-zero probability if and only if the 3SAT instance C is satisfiable. □

5   Algorithms

In the previous sections we showed that the problem of listing all answers to an aggregate query in the IST model has an exponential time complexity. Further, we proved that the simpler question of determining the probability of the answer being equal to a given value is NP-complete for *sum*, *count*, and *average* operations, and hence it is highly unlikely (unless P = NP) that an efficient algorithm can be found for these problems. In this section we present algorithms for some of the remaining problems.

5.1   Determining the Expected Value of Aggregate Queries

The expected value of the *sum* and *count* operations can be calculated directly (rather than enumerating alternate world relations.) This was the second problem on our list in the previous section, and hence we will call it problem P2.

Algorithm P2-SUM

Given an extended relation $r = \{t_1@x_1, t_2@x_2, \ldots, t_n@x_n\}$, where t_i is a pure tuple, and x_i is the set of information source vectors corresponding to t_i, the expected value of $sum_A(r)$ can be calculated as

$$\sum_{i=1}^{n} t_i(A) \times re(t_i) \tag{7}$$

where $re(t)$ is the reliability of tuple t calculated by one of the algorithms of [11] (A summary of one of the algorithms was given in Section 2.4.)

Theorem 3: Algorithm P2-SUM correctly calculates the expected value of $sum_A(r)$.

Proof: The expected value of $sum_A(r)$, by definition, is

$$\sum_{Q \subseteq S} sum_A(r^*(Q)) \times P(Q) \tag{8}$$

where S is the set of information sources, r^* is the function represented by r (hence $r^*(Q)$ is the regular relation in the alternate world of r corresponding to $Q \subseteq S$, and $P(Q)$ is the probability associated with Q (and with $r^*(Q)$). Note that

$$P(Q) = \prod_{s_i \in Q} p_i \prod_{s_i \notin Q} (1 - p_i)$$

Equation 8 can be written as

$$\sum_{Q \subseteq S} \sum_{t \in r^*(Q)} t(A) \times P(Q) \tag{9}$$

or

$$\sum_{t@x\in r} t(A) \times \sum_{t\in r^*(Q)} P(Q) \tag{10}$$

where x is the set of source vectors corresponding to the pure tuple t in r.

Now, we note that [12]

$$re(t) = \sum_{r^*(Q)\ni t} P(Q)$$

and hence Equation 10 simplifies to Equation 7. □

The P2-COUNT problem, i.e. finding the expected value of $count(r)$ of an extended relation r, is similar to P2-SUM. In fact, $count$ can be implemented as the sum by adding an attribute A with a value of 1 to all the tuples, and then obtaining $sum_A(r)$. Below we will only give the algorithm. The proof of correctness follows from that of P2-SUM.

Algorithm P2-COUNT.

Given an extended relation $r = \{t_1@x_1, t_2@x_2, \ldots, t_n@x_n\}$, where t_i is a pure tuple, and x_i is the set of information source vectors corresponding to t_i, the expected value of $count_A(r)$ can be calculated as

$$\sum_{i=1}^{n} re(t_i) \tag{11}$$

Normalized Expected Values.

As discussed in the previous section, we might be interested in a *normalized* expected value of an aggregate operation, where the empty relation (if existent) in the alternate world on the extended relation of interest is regarded as irrelevant. To obtain a normalized expected value, we need the probability associated with the empty relation. The following algorithm can be used to obtain this probability.

Algorithm to compute the probability of the empty relation.

The input to the algorithm is an extended relation $r = \{t_1@x_1, \ldots, t_n@x_n\}$. Let $\mathcal{Q}$ be the set of subsets of information sources giving rise to the empty relation, that is

$$\mathcal{Q} = \{Q \mid r^*(Q) = \Phi\} \tag{12}$$

We can compute a source vector set that characterizes $\mathcal{Q}$ as follows:

$$x_\phi = \#x_1 \| \#x_2 \| \cdots \| \#x_n \tag{13}$$

where $\#$ and $\|$ are the source vector operations negation and 3OR. The probability of the empty relation can be calculated from x_ϕ in the same manner that the probability of a tuple associated with x_ϕ is calculated (see Section 2.4). Let us denote this probability by p_ϕ. The normalized expected value is obtained by dividing the (non-normalized) expected value by $1 - p_\phi$.

It is easy to see why Equation 13 correctly characterizes the set Q, and we will only sketch the proof here. The expression corresponding to x_ϕ is true iff all the expressions corresponding to $x_1, \ldots, x_n$ are false, in which case all tuples $t_1, \ldots, t_n$ are invalid (and hence, we have an empty relation.)

Expected Value of the *average* **Operation.**

A simple equation similar to Equations 7 and 11 can not be obtained for the *average* operation. We might use the following definition for an approximate expected average, bearing in mind that this value is generally not equal to the actual expected average.

$$\text{approx-exp-}avg_A(r) = \frac{\text{exp-}sum_A(r)}{\text{exp-}count(r)} \tag{14}$$

An efficient algorithm to calculate expected average (or proving the problem to be NP-complete) requires further investigation.

5.2   *Max* and *min* operations

In this section we present an algorithm to determine, for a constant c, the probability of $Max_A(r) = c$ (or $min_A(r) = c$). As we proved in Section 4, this problem, which we called the P1 problem, is NP-complete for *sum*, *count*, and *average* operations. We will specify the algorithm for the *Max* operation. The corresponding algorithm for the *min* operation can be obtained with slight modifications.

Algorithm P1-Max: The probability of $Max_A(r) = c$.

Obviously, if c does not appear in r as an A-value, then the probability of $Max_A(r) = c$ is zero. In the following, we assume that $c = t(A)$ for at least one pure tuple $t \in r$. As usual, assume $r = \{t_1@x_1, \ldots, t_n@x_n\}$. We first project r over A, and sort the result according to the A-values. (Note that in IST the information source attribute I is invisible to the users, hence the scheme of the result will be $\{A, I\}$.) Let $r' = \{a_1@y_1, \ldots, a_m@y_m\}$ be the resulting sequence, where $a_1 > a_2 > \cdots > a_m$. Assume $c = a_j$ for some $1 \leq j \leq m$. For each A-value a_i we can calculate a set of information source vectors characterizing the relations in the alternate world of r in which a_i is the Maximum. Let z_i denote this set of vectors for a_i. Then the probability of $Max_A(r) = c$ can be obtained from z_j in the same manner that the probability of a tuple associated with z_j is calculated (see Section 2.4).

$$z_i = y_i \, || \, \#(\cup_{k=1}^{i-1} y_k) \tag{15}$$

where $\#$ and $||$ are the IST source vector negation and 3OR operations, and $\cup$ is the IST union operation (which is the same as the classical union.)

Theorem 4: Given a constant c, Algorithm P2-Max correctly determines the probability of $Max_A(r) = c$.

Proof: We need to show that z_i correctly characterizes the relations in the alternate world of r in which a_i is the Maximum A-value. Consider the expression corresponding to z_i, $e(z_i)$. Let $Q \subseteq S$ be a subset of information sources such that $e(z_i)$ is *true* under $truth(Q)$. Let $r^*(Q)$ be the regular relation in the alternate world of r corresponding to Q. We claim that (i) a_i appears in $r^*(Q)$, and (ii) No $a_k > a_i$ appears in $r^*(Q)$. These follow from the construction of z_i, Equation 15. We have shown that the source vector 3OR operation implements the logical conjunction of the expressions corresponding to source vectors, and the source vector negation operation implements the logical negation [11]. Since $e(z_i)$ is $true$ under $truth(Q)$, then so is $e(y_i)$. Hence a_i appears in $r^*(Q)$. Similarly, $e(y_k)$ is $false$ under $truth(Q)$ for $1 \leq k < i$, and hence no $a_k > a_i$ appears in $r^*(Q)$. □

Example 4: Consider the following extended relation $sample$, which is already ordered according to the A-values:

A		I	
80	1	-1	0
60	1	0	1
60	1	1	-1
50	0	1	-1
30	-1	1	1
30	1	0	-1

Figure 6. The $sample$ relation.

To find the probability of $Max_A(sample) = 50$ we need to calculate

$$z = \{(0\ 1\ \text{-}1)\} \parallel \#\{(1\ \text{-}1\ 0), (1\ 0\ 1), (1\ 1\ \text{-}1)\}$$

obtaining $z = (\text{-}1\ 1\ \text{-}1)$. If, for example, the reliabilities of the information sources s_1, s_2, and s_3 were 90%, 80%, and 70%, respectively, we would obtain a probability of 2.4% for $Max_A(sample) = 50$. □

Algorithm P1-Max can also be used to enumerate the possible values of $Max_A(r)$ and their probabilities for an extended relation r in the decreasing order. It is easy to show that

$$\#(\cup_{k=1}^{i}(y_k)) = \#(\cup_{k=1}^{i-1}(y_k)) \parallel \#y_i$$

which provides an iterative algorithm to obtain the sequence of $z_1, z_2, \ldots$ using Equation 15. This approach can be efficient in applications where a few of the possible values is needed (as opposed to listing all possible values, which is exponential in the number of information sources in the worst case.)

6   Conclusions and Future Work

We discussed the processing of aggregate operations min, Max, sum, count, and $average$ in the Information Source Tracking method. Three types of questions were addressed: Enumerating all possible answers and their probabilities, determining the probability of a given answer, and finding the expected value of an aggregate query. We showed that the first problem is intractable, and the second is NP-complete for sum, $count$, and $average$. Algorithms were presented for expected values of sum, and $count$ queries, and for determining the probability of a given answer to a Max or min query.

Some other questions about aggregate queries merit further investigation. For example in some applications we are interested in the most likely answer to an aggregate query, i.e. the answer with the highest probability. Algorithms for the efficient processing of *average* queries also need further studies.

References

[1] J. Biskup, A Foundation of Codd's Relational Maybe Operations, ACM Transactions on Database Systems, 8(4), 1983, 608-636.

[2] S.A. Cook, The Complexity of Theorem Proving Procedures, Proc. 3rd ACM Symp. on Theory of Computing, 1971,151-158.

[3] L. DeMichiel, Resolving Database Incompatibility: An Approach to Performing Operations over Mismatched Domains, IEEE Trans. on Knowledge and Data Engineering, 1(4), December 1989, 485-493.

[4] B. Doyon, Reliability of Answers to an SQL Query, Project Report, Department of Computer Science, Concordia University, May 1990.

[5] M.R. Garey and D.S. Johnson, **Computers and Intractability, A Guide to the Theory of NP-Completeness**, Freeman Press, 1979.

[6] A.M. Keller and M. Winslett-Wilkins, On the Use of an Extended Relational Model to Handle Changing Incomplete Information, IEEE Trans. on Software Engineering, SE-11:7, July 1985, 620-633.

[7] K-C. Liu and R. Sunderraman, Indefinite and Maybe Information in Relational Databases, ACM Trans. on Database Systems, 15(1), March 1990, 1-39.

[8] K-C. Liu and R. Sunderraman, A Generalized Relational Model for Indefinite and Maybe Information, IEEE Trans. on Knowledge and Data Engineering, 3(1), March 1991, 65-77.

[9] D. Maier, **The Theory of Relational Databases**, Computer Science Press, 1983.

[10] Nils J. Nilsson, Probabilistic Logic, Artificial Intelligence, 28 (1986), 71-87.

[11] F. Sadri, Reliability of Answers to Queries in Relational Databases, IEEE Trans. on Knowledge and Data Engineering, 3(2), June 1991, 245-251.

[12] F. Sadri, Modeling Uncertainty in Databases, IEEE Int. Conference on Data Engineering, May 1991, 122-131.

[13] F. Sadri, Integrity Constraints in the Information Source Tracking Method, IEEE Trans. on Knowledge and Data Engineering, to appear.

[14] F. Sadri, Information Source Tracking, Manuscript, September 1991. Submitted for publication.

An Incremental Concept Formation Approach for Learning from Databases

Rokia Missaoui and Robert Godin

Département de Mathématiques et d'Informatique,

UQAM, Montréal, Canada

Abstract

Based on the Galois lattice theory, we propose a concept formation approach to discover new concepts and implication rules from data. The Galois lattice of a binary relation between a set of objects and a set of properties (descriptors) is a *concept hierarchy* in which each node represents a subset of objects with their common properties.

In this paper, we present some efficient algorithms for generating rules from the Galois lattice, and for learning characteristic and classification rules. The rules are either in conjunctive or disjunctive form. An incremental algorithm for rule generation is also proposed. When an update occurs in the data, it generates rules by considering only the new data and the set of rules produced before the update. Because of the nature of these rules, the decision procedure used for reasoning about functional dependencies in relational databases can be directly adapted to implication rules.

1 Introduction

Third generation database systems are expected to handle data, objects and rules, manage a broader set of applications [6], and deal with various kinds of queries such as intensional ones which are evaluated using the semantics of the data [23]. One of the most important issues to be addressed to this end involves the way to discover and exploit the semantics of the data and utilize them in making inferences. In databases (DB), there are two kinds of information: extensional information (data) which represents real world objects, and intensional information which reflects the meaning, the structure (in terms of properties) and the relationships between properties and/or objects. As pointed out by Parsaye *et al* [24] and Frawley *et al* [9], many organizations have more data than they can analyze, and therefore, tools are needed to automatically discover patterns and rules from databases.

Research about the discovery of rules and concepts from large databases is relatively recent and is ranked among the most promising topics in the field of DBs for the 1990s [26]. According to [9], knowledge discovery is "the nontrivial extraction of implicit, previously unknown, and potentially useful information from data." Knowledge discovery techniques are unfortunately not well spread in database applications. There are at least two reasons for this. One is the fact that DBs are generally complex, voluminous, noisy and continually changing. Two is the fact that the overhead due to the application of discovery techniques may be high. That is why researchers in this area [25] recommend that discovery algorithms for database applications be *incremental*, sufficiently *efficient* to have at most a quadratic growth with respect to the size of input, and *robust* enough to cope with noisy data.

The system RX [2] is one of the early works in knowledge discovery. It uses artificial intelligence techniques to guide the statistical analysis of medical collected data. Borgida and Williamson [3] uses machine learning techniques to detect and accommodate exceptional information that may occur in a database. The IXL (Induction on Extremely Large databases) system [16,24] combines machine learning and statistics to extract patterns and rules from large databases. Cai *et al* [4] presents an induction algorithm which extracts classification and characterization rules from relational databases by performing a step by step generalization on individual attributes. Classification rules discriminate the concepts of one class from that of the others, while characteristic rules characterize a class independently from the other classes. In [21], statistical analysis techniques are used to analyze the contents of a relational database and discover a part of its semantics. In [15], the discovery process is incremental and includes two consecutive steps: conceptual clustering and rule generation using the classification obtained at the first step. Ioannidis *et al* [17] uses two machine learning algorithms, *viz.* COBWEB and UNIMEM [10], to generate concept hierarchies from queries addressed to a database.

The main purpose of this paper is to present algorithms for generating implication rules from the Galois (concept) lattice structure of a binary relation. This article extends our previous work on knowledge discovery [22]. Our approach is similar to the work done by [15] since it is incremental and is based on a conceptual clustering procedure. However, the classification produced by [15] is a tree rather than a lattice. Like in [4], our approach helps learn characteristic rules (*i.e.* data summarization) as well as classification rules. The rules are either in conjunctive or disjunctive form.

The remainder of this paper is organized as follows. In the next section we give a background on the concept lattice theory and its relationship with machine learning techniques. Section 3 gives definitions for implications rules. Algorithms for rule generation are presented in Section 4. Finally, a brief discussion on further refinements is proposed.

2   The concept lattice

2.1   Definition

From the context $(\mathcal{O}, \mathcal{D}, \mathcal{R})$ describing a set $\mathcal{O}$ of objects, a set $\mathcal{D}$ of properties and a binary relation $\mathcal{R}$ (Table 2.1) between $\mathcal{O}$ and $\mathcal{D}$, there is a unique ordered set which describes the inherent lattice structure defining natural groupings and relationships among the objects and their properties (Figure 1). This structure is also known as concept lattice [28] or Galois lattice [1]. In the following we will use both terminologies interchangeably. The notation $x\mathcal{R}x'$ will be used to express the fact that an element x from $\mathcal{O}$ is related to an element x' from $\mathcal{D}$. Each element of the lattice $\mathcal{L}$ derived from the context $(\mathcal{O}, \mathcal{D}, \mathcal{R})$ [28] is a couple, noted (X, X'), composed of an object set X of the power set $\mathcal{P}(\mathcal{O})$ and an attribute (or descriptor) set $X' \in \mathcal{P}(\mathcal{D})$. Each couple (called *concept* by Wille) must be a complete couple with respect to $\mathcal{R}$, which means that the following two properties are satisfied:

(i) $X' = f(X)$ where $f(X) = \{x' \in \mathcal{D} \mid \forall x \in X, x\mathcal{R}x'\}$.

(ii) $X = f'(X')$ where $f'(X') = \{x \in \mathcal{O} \mid \forall x' \in X', x\mathcal{R}x'\}$.

X is the largest set described by the attributes found in X'. From this point of view, it can be considered as a kind of a maximally specific description [19]. The couple of functions (f, f') is a *Galois connection* between $\mathcal{P}(\mathcal{O})$ and $\mathcal{P}(\mathcal{D})$ and the Galois lattice $\mathcal{L}$ for the binary relation is the set of all complete couples [1] with the following partial order.
Given $C_1 = (X_1, X'_1)$ and $C_2 = (X_2, X'_2)$, $C_1 \leq C_2 \Leftrightarrow X'_1 \subset X'_2$. There is a dual relationship between the X and X' sets in the lattice, *i.e.*, $X'_1 \subset X'_2 \Leftrightarrow X_2 \subset X_1$ and therefore, $C_1 \leq C_2 \Leftrightarrow X_2 \subset X_1$.
The partial order is used to generate the graph in the following way: there is an edge from C_1 to C_2 if $C_1 < C_2$ and there is no other element C_3 in the lattice such that $C_1 < C_3 < C_2$. In that case, we say that C_1 is covered by C_2. The graph is usually called a Hasse diagram and the precedent covering relation means that C_1 is parent of C_2. By convention, when drawing a Hasse diagram, the edge direction is downwards. Given, $\mathcal{C}$, a set of elements from the lattice $\mathcal{L}$, $inf(\mathcal{C})$ and $sup(\mathcal{C})$ will denote respectively the greatest lower bound (or *meet*) and the lowest upper bound (or *join*) of the elements in $\mathcal{C}$.

A filter [1] is a nonvoid subset $\mathcal{J}$ of a lattice $\mathcal{L}$ with the properties:

(i) $\forall a \in \mathcal{J}, \forall x \in \mathcal{L}, x \geq a \Rightarrow x \in \mathcal{J}$;

(ii) $\forall a \in \mathcal{J}, \forall b \in \mathcal{J} \Rightarrow a \wedge b \in \mathcal{J}$.

The set $\mathcal{L}(\alpha)$ of all elements of the lattice $\mathcal{L}$ such that $\alpha \in \mathcal{L}$ and $x \geq \alpha$ is called the principal filter of $\mathcal{L}$ generated by α. The concept of ideal is dual to the concept of filter. Since the Galois lattice is in fact a double lattice: one for descriptors and one for objects, filters can be expressed either in terms of descriptors or objects.

Many algorithms have been proposed for generating the elements of the lattice but only Bordat's algorithm constructs the Hasse diagram [12] which is necessary for the considered applications. Furthermore, none of these algorithms is incremental, and all the objects and their attributes have to be known in advance to build the lattice. In [11] we present an $O\|\mathcal{O}^2\|$ incremental algorithm for updating the concept lattice when new objects are added to the relation. A large experimental application has revealed that adding a new object may be done in time proportional to the number of objects on the average. When there is a fixed upper bound on the number of properties related to an object, which is the case in practical applications, the worst case analysis of the algorithm confirms the experimental observations of linear growth with respect to the number of objects. Surprisingly, our current experiments on four algorithms for lattice construction show that, in most cases, our incremental algorithm is the most efficient and is always the best asymptotically.

2.2   A Machine learning approach

The concept lattice is a form of *concept hierarchy* where each node represents a subset of objects (extent) with their common properties (intent) [1,7,28]. The

Hasse diagram of the lattice represents a generalization/specialization relationship between the concepts. Therefore, building the lattice and Hasse diagram corresponding to a set of objects, each described by some properties, can be used as an effective tool for symbolic data analysis and knowledge acquisition [13,29].

The task of inducing a concept hierarchy in an incremental manner is called *incremental concept formation* [10]. Concept formation is similar to conceptual clustering which also builds concept hierarchies [20]. However, the former approach is partially distinguished from the latter by the fact that the learning is incremental. Concept formation falls into the category of *unsupervised learning* also called learning from observation [5] since the concepts to learn are not predetermined by a teacher, and the instances are not pre-classified with respect to these concepts. As opposed to *explanation-based learning* methods [8], this approach falls into the class of *empirical learning* [20] since no background knowledge is needed.

For the purposes of illustration, a part of the well-known relation describing animals [15] will be used.

Table 2.1 The input relation.

Objects	Attributes				
	F	R	E	M	S
Tiger	f_1	r_1	e_1	m_1	s_1
Horse	f_2	r_1	e_3	m_1	s_1
Sheep	f_2	r_1	e_3	m_1	s_0
Penguin	f_3	r_2	e_1	m_0	s_1
Frog	f_3	r_2	e_1	m_0	s_2
Dog	f_1	r_1	e_2	m_1	s_1

The attributes and their values have the following meaning:
$F=$ Feet
   $f_1=$claw; $f_2=$hoof; $f_3=$web.
$R=$Ears
   $r_1=$ external; $r_2=$ middle.
$E=$Eats
   $e_1=$ meat; $e_2=$ grain; $e_3=$grass.
$M=$Gives milk
   $m_0=$ no milk; $m_1=$milk.
$S=$Swims
   $s_0=$unable; $s_1=$able; $s_2=$well.

The corresponding concept lattice is given in Figure 1. For details about the algorithm that builds the lattice, see [11,12].

3 Learning rules from the concept lattice

In addition to be a technique for classifying and defining concepts from the data, the concept lattice may be exploited to discover dependencies among the

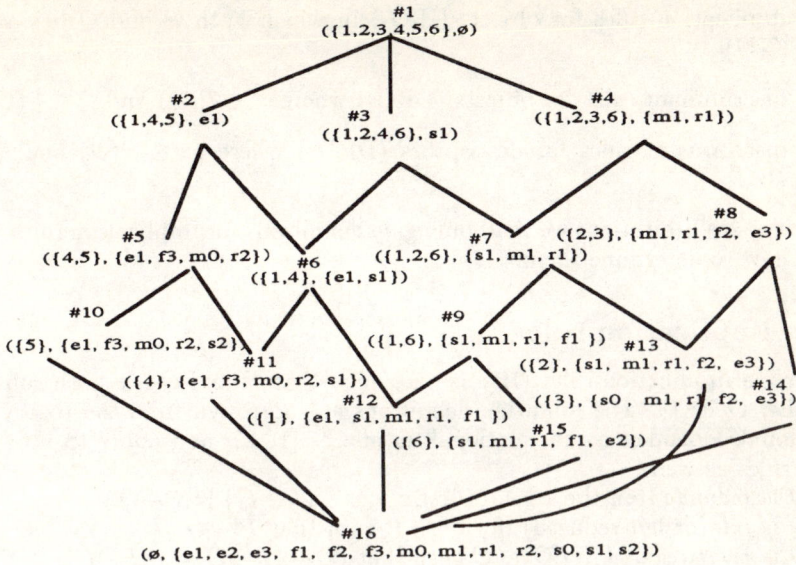

Figure 1: The Concept lattice.

objects and the properties. The process may be undertaken in two different ways, depending on the peculiarities of the DB under consideration and the needs of the users: (i) scan the whole lattice or part of it in order to generate a set of rules that can be later used in a knowledge-based system, (ii) browse the lattice to check if a given rule holds.

In the first case, the learning process is as follows.

Input.   A relation or a view of the database.

Output.   (i) The corresponding concept lattice,
              (ii) a set of conjunctive implication rules.

Method

Step 1. Construct the concept lattice of the binary relation.

Step 2. Use Algorithm 4.1 or 4.2 to derive conjunctive rules from the lattice.

Step 3. Remove redundant rules using the nonredundant cover algorithm [18].

In Section 4, we also present an incremental algorithm which, when given a set of rules relative to the lattice $\mathcal{L}$, a description of the new object x^* to be inserted, and the new lattice $\mathcal{L}'$ (obtained after adding the object x^* to the input relation), computes the new set of rules.

In the following we use $P, Q, R, \cdots Z$ to denote sets of properties, while we use lower-case letters to name atomic properties. The notation abc is a simplification of the notation $\{a, b, c\}$. In the sequel, we shall take the freedom of using either the logical notation or the set-oriented notation, depending on the context under consideration.

The general format of a rule is $P \rightarrow Q$, where P and Q represent either a set of objects or a set of properties. Four cases can be considered:

(i) implication rules for descriptors (IRDs) in which both P and Q belong to $\mathcal{P}(\mathcal{D})$

(ii) implication rules for objects (IROs) in which both P and Q belong to $\mathcal{P}(\mathcal{O})$

(iii) discriminant rules for objects (DROs) where $P \in \mathcal{P}(\mathcal{D})$ and $Q \in \mathcal{P}(\mathcal{O})$

(iv) discriminant rules for descriptors (DRDs) where $P \in \mathcal{P}(\mathcal{O})$ and $Q \in \mathcal{P}(\mathcal{D})$.

For space limitations we shall only give definitions for implication rules and show how to determine them.

3.1 Implication rules

We define implication rules (IR) as ones such that P and Q are both subsets of either $\mathcal{O}$ or $\mathcal{D}$. The following definitions are borrowed from the theory on functional dependencies in relational databases [18,27] and apply to implications rules as well.

$P{\rightarrow}Q$ is *redundant* in the set Σ of IRDs if $\Sigma - \{P{\rightarrow}Q\} \models P{\rightarrow}Q$

$P{\rightarrow}Q$ is *full* (or left-reduced) if $\not\exists P' \subset P$ such that $P'{\rightarrow}Q$

$P{\rightarrow}Q$ is *right-reduced* if $\not\exists Q' \subset Q$ such that $(\Sigma - \{P{\rightarrow}Q\}) \cup \{P{\rightarrow}Q'\} \equiv \Sigma$

$P{\rightarrow}Q$ is *elementary* if it is full and $\|Q\| = 1$ and $Q \not\subset P$

The *closure* P^+ of a set P according to Σ is defined by: $P^+ = P \cup \{Q \mid Z \subseteq P^+$ and $Z{\rightarrow}Q \in \Sigma\}$.

3.1.1 Conjunctive implication rules

Definition 1. The *conjunctive* implication rule for *descriptors* (IRD) between two subsets D and D' of $\mathcal{P}(\mathcal{D})$, denoted by $D{\rightarrow}D'$, means that if a non-empty set of objects is defined by all the properties found in D, then it is necessarily defined by the whole set D' of properties.

Proposition 1. $D{\rightarrow}D'$ is a conjunctive IRD $\Leftrightarrow [[(O'', D'') = inf\{(X, X') \in \mathcal{L} \mid D \subset X'$ and $X \neq \emptyset\}] \Rightarrow D' \subset D'']$. $\qquad\square$

In other words, the rule $D{\rightarrow}D'$ holds if and only if the smallest concept (with respect to descriptors) containing D as a part of its intent is also described by D'.

Proof

$\Rightarrow$ If $D{\rightarrow}D'$ is derived from the node described by the couple (O'', D''), it means that the objects in $\mathcal{O}$ have the properties D and D', and therefore $D \cup D' \subseteq D''$. In particular, $D' \subset D''$.

$\Leftarrow$ Whenever the couple (O'', D'') is the smallest concept containing D, it also contains D'. This corresponds exactly to the definition of the IRD: $D{\rightarrow}D'$.

Example 1. From the lattice shown in Figure 1, one can generate the IRD $f_1{\rightarrow}m_1 \wedge r_1 \wedge s_1$ since the first encountered node containing the property f_1, which is node #9, contains also the properties m_1, r_1, s_1. However, the IRD $s_1{\rightarrow}m_1$ is not true because node #3 is described by the property s_1 alone.

Definition 2. The *conjunctive* implication rule for *objects* (IRO) between O and O', denoted by $O{\rightarrow}O'$, means that if a non-empty set of properties is associated with the objects in O, then it is also associated with the objects in O'. For example, the rule $dog \rightarrow \{bulldog, poodle\}$ means that bulldogs and poodles have at least the properties attached to dogs, *i.e.* they are dogs with possibly additional characterizations. The following proposition is the dual of proposition 1.

Proposition 2. $O \rightarrow O'$ *is a conjunctive IRO* $\Leftrightarrow [[(O", D") = sup\{(X, X') \in \mathcal{L} \mid O \subset X \text{ and } X' \neq \emptyset\}] \Rightarrow O' \subset O"]$. $\quad\square$

In other words, $O \rightarrow O'$ if and only if the biggest node (with respect to descriptors) containing O as a part of its extent is also described by O'.

Definition 3. A property p is *independent* if it belongs to the intent X' of either $inf(\mathcal{L})$ when $X' \neq \emptyset$, or one of its children when the intent of $inf(\mathcal{L})$ is empty. For example, the properties e_1, s_1, m_1, and r_1 are independent (see Figure 1). *Dependent* properties are therefore properties that subsume at least one independent property. Two properties are *equivalent* if they have the same closure. *Existence* implication rules are rules in which the premise includes only dependent elements. *Composite* rules are those in which the premise includes at least one independent element. In a symmetrical way, independent objects can be defined. The significance of these notions will become clear later.

3.1.2 Disjunctive implication rules

Disjunctive implication rules are rules such that either their left-hand side (LHS) or their right-hand side (RHS) contains the disjunctive expression $Q_1 \vee \cdots \vee Q_m$. There is a mapping between conjunctive and disjunctive rules. The conjunctive IRD $d_j \rightarrow Q$ can be computed from the right-hand disjunctive IRD $d_j \rightarrow Q_1 \vee \cdots \vee Q_m$ by setting Q to the attributes common to $\{Q_1 \cdots Q_m\}$. The left-hand disjunctive IRD $Q_1 \vee \cdots \vee Q_m \rightarrow d_i$ means that $Q_1 \cdots Q_m$ are the alternative properties which subsume d_i, and can be computed from the set of conjunctive IRDs (see Algorithm 4.5).

3.2 Characteristic and classification rules

As mentioned earlier, *classification* rules discriminate the concepts of one class (*e.g.* a carnivore) from that of the others, while *characteristic* rules characterize a class independently from the other classes. The first kind is a sufficient condition of the class under consideration while the second type is a necessary condition of the class (see [4] for more details).

Implication rules can express these two kinds of rules. For example, the RHS disjunctive IRD $d_j \rightarrow Q_1 \vee \cdots \vee Q_m$ may be useful for defining the characteristic rule for objects having the property d_j, while the LHS disjunctive IRD $Q_1 \vee \cdots \vee Q_m \rightarrow d_i$ can be used to define the classification rule for objects with the property d_i. *e.g.*, the classification rule for animals having claws (see Figure 1) is $e_2 \rightarrow f_1$ while the characteristic rule for this kind of animals is $f_1 \rightarrow m_1 r_1 s_1$.

4 Implication rule determination

In [14,29], the authors deal with the problem of extracting rules from the concept lattice structure. However, they do not propose any algorithm to determine those rules. In this section we propose a set of algorithms for rule generation. For ease of exposition, we limit ourselves to IRDs. However, owing to the symmetry of the lattice structure, the definitions and algorithms can be adapted without difficulty to IROs.

Based on proposition 1 defined before, the obvious method for rule generation that immediately comes to mind is to systematically generate at each node $N = (X, X')$ the power set of X', and for each set P in $2^{X'}$, make sure that its value is not included in the intent of the parent nodes of N. The rules generated by this algorithm are either *existence* rules or *composite* ones.

Algorithm 4.1

Input: A lattice $\mathcal{L}$.

Output: The whole set Σ of conjunctive IRDs: $P{\rightarrow}Q$.

begin

$\Sigma := \emptyset$;

For each node $N = (X, X') \in \mathcal{L}$ **do**

    begin

        $\Delta := \emptyset$; /* the set of IRDs generated from the current node */

        If $X \neq \emptyset$ and $\|X'\| > 1$ **then**

        For each non empty set $P \in \{\mathcal{P}(X') - X'\}$ **do**

            If $\nexists\, M = (Y, Y')$ parent of N such that $P \subseteq Y'$ **then**

                If $\nexists\, P'{\rightarrow}Q \in \Delta$ such that $P' \subset P$ **then**

                    $\Delta := \Delta \cup \{P{\rightarrow}X' - P\}$

                endIf

            endIf

        endFor

        endIf

        $\Sigma := \Sigma \cup \Delta$

    end

endFor

return(Σ)

end

Complexity analysis

As detailed in [12], when there is an upper bound k on the number of descriptors per object, the lattice grows linearly with respect to the cardinality of the set $\mathcal{O}$ of objects. Therefore, the outer *For* loop takes $O(\|\mathcal{O}\|)$ time. For almost all nodes $N = (X, X')$ in $\mathcal{L}$, we need to compute the power set $\mathcal{P}(X')$ and compare each element in it with the intent of the parents of N. Based on the assumption of an upper bound k, the number of iterations of the inner *For* loop is $O(1)$, and the number of descendants (and ancestors) of a node is $O(\|\mathcal{O}\|)$ in the worst case (and $O(log(\|\mathcal{O}\|))$ for a large experiment [13]). Therefore, the time complexity of Algorithm 4.1 is $O(\|\mathcal{O}\|^2)$ in the worst case, and more likely $O(\|\mathcal{O}\| * log(\|\mathcal{O}\|))$.

Remarks

(i) Even though the *If* tests help eliminate redundant rules produced at a given step of the outer *For* loop, some redundant ones may persist because they are produced by two different iterations of this loop. Redundant rules may be removed, using the polynomial time algorithm for nonredundant cover determination [18].

(ii) There may be cycles in the resulting set of IRDs (*e.g.* both $e_1 m_1 r_1 \rightarrow f_1$ and $f_1 \rightarrow s_1 m_1 r_1$ hold).

Example 2. The IRD: $e_1 m_1 r_1 \rightarrow s_1 f_1$ is generated from node #12 (Figure 1), and can be simplified later into $e_1 m_1 \rightarrow f_1$ since m_1 and r_1 are equivalent (see node #4), and $f_1 \rightarrow m_1 r_1 s_1$ holds from node #9.

A second algorithm for generating conjunctive rules gives a subset of the whole set of IRDs discovered by Algorithm 4.1. This subset corresponds to *existence* rules that are full but not necessarily right-reduced. Algorithm 4.2 uses a slightly modified description of nodes in $\mathcal{L}$. Each node N, instead of being a couple (X, X') is a triple (X, X', X'') where X and X' have the same meaning as earlier, and X'' is the set of properties encountered for the first time in the node N.

Algorithm 4.2

Input: A modified version of nodes in $\mathcal{L}$ where $N = (X, X', X'')$.

Output: The set Σ of conjunctive *existence* IRDs: $P \rightarrow Q$, and the set Φ of classes of equivalent properties

begin

$\Sigma := \emptyset; \Phi := \emptyset; P := \emptyset;$

For each node $N = (X, X', X'') \in \mathcal{L}$ **do**

    begin

        If $\|X''\| > 1$ **then**

            $\Phi := \Phi \cup \{X''\}$

        endIf

        If $X \neq \emptyset$ and $X'' \neq \emptyset$ and $X' \neq X''$ **then**

            $\Sigma := \Sigma \cup \{X'' \rightarrow (X' - X'')\}$

        endIf

        $P := P \cup X''$

        If $P = D$ **then return**(Σ, Φ)

        endIf

    end

endFor

return(Σ, Φ)

end

Complexity analysis

The number of iterations of the *For* loop is $\|\mathcal{L}\|$ which is $O(\|(\mathcal{O})\|)$ as shown earlier. Therefore, the time complexity of Algorithm 4.2 is $O(\|(\mathcal{O})\|)$ and hence, lower than the time complexity of Algorithm 4.1. However, Algorithm 4.2 needs slightly more space to store the lattice nodes.

Example 3. Based on the lattice example, Algorithm 4.2 generates a set of IRD, which once the right part is reduced, leads to

$\Sigma := \{f_3 m_0 r_2 {\rightarrow} e_1, e_3 f_2 {\rightarrow} m_1 r_1, f_1 {\rightarrow} m_1 r_1 s_1, s_0 {\rightarrow} e_3 f_2, s_2 {\rightarrow} f_3 m_0 r_2, e_2 {\rightarrow} f_1\}$. It also computes the set Φ which is equal to $\{m_1 r_1, f_3 m_0 r_2, e_3 f_2\}$. The reader may notice that the rule $e_1 m_1 r_1 {\rightarrow} s_1 f_1$ produced by Algorithm 4.1 is missing from the output of Algorithm 4.2 because it is a composite rule.

To avoid the repetitive process of determining the set Σ of implication rules from scratch each time a new object is introduced in the input relation, we propose an incremental algorithm with the same function as Algorithm 4.2. Algorithm 4.3 computes the new set Σ' of existence IRDs $P {\rightarrow} Q$ by retaining those rules in the old set Σ that remain consistent after the insertion of the new object x^*, and by adding the rules extracted from the principal filter $\mathcal{L}'(\alpha)$ where α is the smallest node (in terms of objects) in which the new object x^* appears in the new lattice $\mathcal{L}'$. To this end, three subsets are extracted from Σ:
(i) The set I of rules for which the condition $P \cap f^*(\{x^*\}) = \emptyset$ holds. It corresponds to the set of rules that remain consistent after the insertion of the new object x^*;
(ii) the set G in which rules from Σ verify the condition $P \cap f^*(\{x^*\}) \subset P$ which indicates that some properties in the premise P are no longer equivalent when x^* is inserted, and therefore $P - (P \cap f^*(\{x^*\})){\rightarrow}(P \cap f^*(\{x^*\}))$ holds while $(P \cap f^*(\{x^*\})){\rightarrow}P - (P \cap f^*(\{x^*\}))$ is not true any more. The set K is used to store the former rule;
(iii) the set J in which rules verify the conjunction $P \subseteq f^*(\{x^*\}) \wedge (Q - f^*(\{x^*\})) \neq \emptyset$. This set contains rules that must be discarded from the new set Σ'.

Proposition 3. *The set Σ' is given by:* $\Sigma' = I \cup K \cup \{$*the IRDs generated from the nodes in* $\mathcal{L}'(\alpha)\}$. $\square$

The following incremental algorithm generates existence rules using the same principle as Algorithm 4.2. It can be adapted to produce the whole set of existence and composite rules as in Algorithm 4.1.

Algorithm 4.3

Input: The set Σ of existence IRDs before the insertion of the new element x^* defined by $f^*(\{x^*\})$.
    The Galois lattice $\mathcal{L}'$ for the new binary relation.

Output: The new set Σ' of existence IRDs.

begin

Step (1) Compute the filter $\mathcal{L}'(\alpha)$

  If $\mathcal{L}'(\alpha)$ does not contain a new node then /* *i.e.* $\|\mathcal{L}\| = \|\mathcal{L}'\|$ */

   return(Σ)

  else $\Sigma' := \emptyset$.

  endIf

Step (2) Retain rules that remain consistent after the insertion of x^*

  For each IRD: $P {\rightarrow} Q \in \Sigma$ **do**

    $Temp := P \cap f^*(\{x^*\})$

> **If** $Temp = \emptyset$ **then**
>
> $\Sigma' := \Sigma' \cup \{P \rightarrow Q\}$
>
> **else**
>
>   **If** $\text{Temp} \subset P$ **then**
>
> $\Sigma' := \Sigma' \cup \{(P - Temp) \rightarrow Temp\}$
>
>   **endIf**
>
> **endIf**

endFor

Step (3) Generate the rules from the filter $\mathcal{L}'(\alpha)$

For each node $N = (X, X', X") \in \mathcal{L}'(\alpha)$ **do**

> **If** $X \neq \emptyset$ and $X" \neq \emptyset$ and $X' \neq X"$ **then**
>
> $\Sigma' := \Sigma' \cup \{X" \rightarrow (X' - X")\}$
>
> **endIf**

endFor

return(Σ')

end

Complexity analysis

The first and last steps take $O(\|\mathcal{O}\|)$ time. Step 2 needs at most $\|\Sigma\|$ iterations, and more precisely $\|\mathcal{D}\|$ iterations because there are at most as many existence rules as descriptors. In the worst case, $\|\mathcal{D}\|$ is $O(\|\mathcal{O}\|)$. Therefore, the time complexity is $O(\|\mathcal{O}\|)$.

Example 4. Let us compute the set of IRDs when the new object to be inserted in Table 2.1 is the element #7 describing a pig by the set $\{f_2, r_1, m_1, e_2, s_1\}$. Based on the incremental algorithm, we need to have two kinds of input: the lattice corresponding to the new relation, and the set Σ of rules generated from all but the seventh object in that input relation.

$\Sigma = \{f_3 m_0 r_2 \rightarrow e_1, e_3 f_2 \rightarrow m_1 r_1, f_1 \rightarrow m_1 r_1 s_1, s_0 \rightarrow e_3 f_2, s_2 \rightarrow f_3 m_0 r_2, e_2 \rightarrow f_1\}$.

Algorithm 4.3 will produce the following.

$\mathcal{L}'(\alpha) := \{(\{1,2,3,4,5,6,7\}, \emptyset), (\{1,2,4,6,7\}, s_1), (\{1,2,3,6,7\}, m_1 r_1),$
$(\{1,2,6,7\}, m_1 r_1 s_1), (\{2,3,7\}, m_1 r_1 f_2), (\{6,7\}, m_1 r_1 s_1 e_2), (\{2,7\}, m_1 r_1 s_1 f_2),$
$(\{7\}, m_1 r_1 s_1 f_2 e_2)\};$

$J := \{e_2 \rightarrow f_1\};$

$G := \{e_3 f_2 \rightarrow m_1 r_1\};$

$K := \{e_3 \rightarrow f_2\};$

$F := \{f_3 m_0 r_2 \rightarrow e_1, f_1 \rightarrow m_1 r_1 s_1, s_0 \rightarrow e_3 f_2, s_2 \rightarrow f_3 m_0 r_2\};$

$\Sigma' := \Sigma - G - J \cup K \cup F$, where F is generated from $\mathcal{L}'(\alpha)$.

We have proposed so far algorithms for generating rules in conjunctive forms. In the following we present procedures aimed at detecting rules in (exclusive) *disjunctive* forms as well.

Algorithm 4.4

Input: A descriptor d_j in $\mathcal{D}$, and a lattice $\mathcal{L}$.

Output: A disjunctive RHS rule of the form $d_j \rightarrow Q_1 \vee \cdots \vee Q_m$.

begin

$RHS := \emptyset$;
  For each parent node N_i of $sup(\mathcal{L})$ **do**

      If $d_j \subseteq X'(N_i)$ **then** /* $X'(N_i)$ stands for the intent of Ni */
        $RHS := RHS \cup (X'(N_i) - \{d_j\})$
      endIf
  endFor
return($d_j \rightarrow RHS$)
end

Algorithm 4.5
Input: A descriptor d_i in $\mathcal{D}$, and a set Σ of conjunctive IRDs.
Output: The disjunctive LHS rule $Q_1 \vee \cdots \vee Q_m \rightarrow d_i$.
begin
$Old := \emptyset$; $New := d_i$;
  While $Old \neq New$ or $\Sigma \neq \emptyset$ **do**

    begin
    $Old := New$
     For each $\{P \rightarrow Q\} \in \Sigma$ **do**
       If $\exists S \in New$ such that $Q \subseteq S$ **then**
       begin
       $\Sigma := \Sigma - \{P \rightarrow Q\}$
       $New := New \cup \{P \cup (S - Q)\}$
      end
      endIf
     endFor
    end
  endWhile
return($\{New - \{d_i\}\} \rightarrow d_i$)
end

    For example, if $d_j = f$ and $\Sigma = \{a-> b; bc-> d; k-> e; d-> e; e-> f\}$, then the algorithm will produce $\{e, d, k, bc, ac\}$.

5   Conclusion

We have proposed an approach based on the concept lattice structure to discover concepts and rules related to the objects and their properties. This approach has been tested on many data sets found in the literature and has been found to be as efficient and effective as some works related to knowledge mining [4,25]. For example, all rules that can be generated by algorithms in [4,15] are also determined by our algorithms. Experiments on real-life applications are currently conducted.

    Our further research aims at: (i) generalizing the Galois lattice nodes structure to allow richer knowledge representation schemes such as conceptual graphs, (ii) dealing with complex objects, (iii) and testing the potential of these ideas in different application domains such as software reuse, database design, and intensional query answering.

Acknowledgments

This research has been supported by NSERC (the Natural Sciences and Engineering Research Council of Canada) under grants No OGP0041899, OGP0009184, and EQP0092688, and by FCAR Funds under grant No 91-NC-0446.

References

[1] Birkhoff, G., **Lattice Theory**, 3rd ed. 1967, Providence, Rhode Island, American Mathematical Society.

[2] Blum, R.L., "Discovery Confirmation and Incorporation of Causal Relationships from a Large Time-oriented Clinical Data Base: The RX Project," *Computers Biomedical Research*, 15:164-187, 1982.

[3] Borgida, A. and Williamson, K.E., "Accommodating Exceptions in Databases, and Refining the Schema by Learning from them," *Proc. 11th Conf. On Very Large Data Bases*, 1985, Stockholm, 72-81.

[4] Cai, Y., Cercone, N. and Han, J., "Attribute-Oriented Induction in Relational Databases", in *Knowledge Discovery from Database*, G. Piatetsky-Shapiro and W.J. Frawley, (Ed.), 1991, AAAI Press/The MIT Press, Menlo Park, Calif., 213-228.

[5] Carbonell, J.G., "Introduction: Paradigms for Machine Learning," in *Machine Learning: Paradigms and Methods*, J.G. Carbonell, (Ed.), 1990, The MIT Press: Cambridge, Mass., 1-9.

[6] Committee for Advanced DBMS Function, "Third Generation Database System Manifesto," *SIGMOD RECORD*, 19(3):31-44, 1990.

[7] Davey, B.A. and Priestley, H.A., **Introduction to Lattices and Order**, 1990, Cambridge: Cambridge University Press, 248.

[8] Ellman, T., "Explanation-Based Learning: A Survey of Programs and Perspectives," *ACM Computing Surveys*, 21(2):163-222, 1989.

[9] Frawley, W.J., Piatetsky-Shapiro, G. and Matheus, C.J., "Knowledge Discovery in Databases: An Overview," in *Knowledge Discovery in Databases*, G. Piatetsky-Shapiro and W.J. Frawley, (Ed.), 1991, AAAI Press/The MIT Press, Menlo Park, Calif., 1-27.

[10] Gennari, J.H., Langley, P. and Fisher, D., "Models of Incremental Concept Formation," in *Machine Learning: Paradigms and Methods*, J. Carbonell, (Ed.), 1990, MIT Press, Amsterdam, The Netherlands, 11-62.

[11] Godin, R., Missaoui, R. and Alaoui, H., "Incremental Algorithms for Updating the Galois Lattice of a Binary Relation," Tech. Rep. #155, Dept. of Comp. Science, UQAM, Sept. 1991.

[12] Godin, R., Missaoui, R. and Alaoui, H., "Learning Algorithms Using a Galois Lattice Structure," *Proc. Third Int. Conf. on Tools for Artificial Intelligence*, 1991, San Jose, Calif., IEEE Computer Society Press, 22-29.

[13] Godin, R., Missaoui, R. and April, A., "Experimental Comparison of Galois Lattice Browsing with Conventional Information Retrieval Methods," To appear in *International Journal of Man-Machine Studies*, 1992.

[14] Guigues, J.L. and Duquenne, V., "Familles Minimales d'Implications Informatives Résultant d'un Tableau de Données Binaires," *Mathématiques et Sciences Humaines*, 95:5-18, 1986.

[15] Hong, J. and Mao, C., "Incremental Discovery of Rules and Structure by Hierarchical and Parallel Clustering," in *Knowledge Discovery in Databases*, G. Piatetsky-Shapiro and W.J. Frawley, (Ed.), 1991, AAAI Press/The MIT Press, Menlo Park, Calif., 177-194.

[16] IntelligenceWare, **IXL: The Machine Learning System**, 1988, IntelligenceWare, Los Angeles.

[17] Ioannidis, Y.E., Saulys, T. and Whitsitt, A.J., "Conceptual Learning in Database Design," *ACM Trans. on Information Systems*, 10(3):265-293, 1992.

[18] Maier, D., **The theory of Relational Databases**, 1983, Rockville, Md.: Computer Science Press.

[19] Michalski, R., Carbonell, J., and Mitchell, T., **Machine Learning: An Artificial Intelligence Approach**, 1983, Tioga Publishing Company.

[20] Michalski, R.S. and Kodratoff, Y., "Research in Machine Learning: Recent Progress, Classification of Methods, and Future Directions," in *Machine Learning: An Artificial Intelligence Approach*, Y. Kodratoff and R.S. Michalski, Editor. 1990, Morgan Kaufmann: San Mateo, CA, pp. 1-30.

[21] Missaoui, R., "Extracting Knowledge from Data," *Proc. Int. Symp. on Information Theory and Its Application*, 1990, Waikiki, Hawaii, 239-242.

[22] Missaoui, R. and Godin, R., "An Expert System for Discovering and Using the Semantics of Databases," *Proc. The World Congress on Expert Systems*, 1991, Orlando, Florida, Pergamon Press, 1732-1740.

[23] Motro, A., "Using Integrity Constraints to Provide Intensional Answers to Relational Queries," *Proc. 15th Int. Conf. On Very Large Data Bases*, 1989. Amsterdam, The Netherlands, 237-246.

[24] Parsaye, K., *et al*, **Intelligent Databases: Object-Oriented, Deductive, Hypermedia Technologies**, 1989, New York, John Wiley & Sons.

[25] Piatetsky-Shapiro, G. and Frawley, W.J., ed. **Knowledge Discovery in Databases**, 1991, AAAI Press/The MIT Press, Menlo Park, Calif., 525p.

[26] Silberschatz, A., Stonebraker, M. and Ullman, J., "Database Systems: Achievements and Opportunities," *CACM*, 34(10):110-120, 1991.

[27] Ullman, J.D., *Principles of Database and Knowledge Base Systems*, Vol. I & II, 1988-89, Computer Science Press.

[28] Wille, R., "Restructuring Lattice Theory: an Approach Based on Hierarchies of Concepts," in *Ordered Sets*, I. Rival (ed.), 1982, Reidel, Dordrecht-Boston, 445-470.

[29] Wille, R., "Knowledge Acquisition by Methods of Formal Concept Analysis," in *Data Analysis, Learning Symbolic and Numeric Knowledge*, E. Diday, (ed.), 1989, Nova Science Pub., New York, 365-380.

The Tecton Proof System*

Deepak Kapur[1], David R. Musser[2] and Xumin Nie[1]

[1]Institute for Programming and Logics
Computer Science Department
State University of New York
Albany, New York 12222

[2]Computer Science Department
Rensselaer Polytechnic Institute
Troy, New York 12180

Abstract

The Tecton Proof System is a new verification system designed to support construction of large and complex proofs, using novel user interface methods and extensive automation. We first describe the main features of the user interface, including the use of tabular formats for ordinary logical formulas and Hoare formulas, graphical proof representations, and hypertext links between related parts of large proofs. In the area of proof automation, we describe the inference mechanisms used by the Tecton inference engine and the integration of a decision procedure for a subclass of Presburger Arithmetic into the inference mechanisms. Through its combination of user interface features and automated deduction capabilities, Tecton provides the kind of support necessary for building libraries of verified software and hardware components.

1 Introduction

The Tecton Proof System is a new verification system designed to support construction of large and complex proofs of properties of computation both in hardware and software. A main goal of Tecton is to aid the user in finding proofs and in understanding proofs in order to reuse parts of them, for the purpose of building libraries of verified software or hardware components [18]. To achieve this goal, Tecton provides a simple command language, a structured internal representation of proofs, and a visual representation using a hypertext system, all of which are designed to help organize and clarify the structure of large proofs. A hypertext system, Knowledge Management System (KMS) [1], is the basis of Tecton's front-end for user interactions and displaying graphical representations of proofs. For automation of many proof steps, Tecton uses inference mechanisms such as reduction, case analysis, generalization, and induction from the Rewrite Rule Laboratory (RRL) [13, 14]. Into these capabilities we have recently integrated a decision procedure for a subclass of Presburger arithmetic [20]. The decision procedure is provided because of the primary importance of integers in the mathematics of computation.

---

*Partially supported by National Science Foundation Grants CCR–8906678 and CDA-8805910.

2 Main features of Tecton

In Tecton, a proof is represented as a goal/subgoal tree, allowing easy identification of both the structure of the proof (how goals relate to each other) and the details of how each inference step depends on other information given previously (such as axioms and other theorems) [6].

Tecton can explore different paths of inference steps in searching for a proof, both in its automatic mode and with interactive guidance from the user using the command language. All such paths are recorded in the forest of proof trees maintained by the system, so that it is easy to compare different partial or complete proof attempts for length, clarity, or dependence on assumptions.

The visual representation of proofs combines a graphical representation of proof trees with hypertext links connecting different parts of the visual representation. The visual representation is presented on a series of *pages,* which allows the representation to be displayed on a workstation screen or printed on paper in essentially identical form (no reformatting is required). Several techniques are used to make proof trees relatively compact, including extensive use of references to information stored in tables that are displayed on each proof page.

The interface to Tecton is menu-driven, with most features selectable using a mouse. In combination with the hypertext links connecting different parts of the proof forest, this kind of interface allows much more rapid interaction and access to a large amount of information than is possible with older teletype style interfaces.

Tecton makes a natural extension of tree-structured proofs to represent proofs of properties of programs [8]. Proof goals may be Hoare formulas as well as ordinary logical formulas, and Hoare-style proof rules for programming language constructs are applied to produce subgoals [17]. This process is repeated until the leaves of the proof tree are ordinary logical formulas (to which inference rules of ordinary first-order logic are then applied). The stage of subgoal generation in which Hoare-rules are applied can be done fully automatically; it is equivalent to what is currently done in other program verification systems by a so-called "verification condition generator," but has the advantage that the original program constructs and inductive assertions appear (in abbreviated form) in the proof tree, so that problems with the code or assertions that lead to unprovable subgoals can much more easily be tracked down.

Tecton has a built-in decision procedure for a subclass of Presburger arithmetic to provide additional capability for integers. This procedure is incorporated into the inference mechanisms of the Tecton inference engine, unlike the stand-alone procedures presented in the literature [20]. This built-in procedure eliminates the need to explicitly state some axioms for integers, such as transitivity axioms, the use of which is hard to control. Proofs obtained using the procedure are more compact and natural.

These features result in a system that is useful both for educational purposes and for moderate-to-large-scale proof efforts. The appendices contain examples of actual Tecton output, illustrating how proof trees and information tables are displayed. Appendix A contains the proof of a typical lemma about integer division. The proof in Appendix B is for the (partial) correctness of an efficient quotient-remainder algorithm. Other examples with much longer proofs include an efficient square root algorithm, the Takuchi function, and a prime factorization algorithm. These proofs make extensive use of the integer decision procedure. A few examples of simple algorithms that manipulate abstract data types, such as concatenation of queues, have also been done, and we have recently begun to experiment with specifications and proofs about some of the generic algorithms in [18].

3   Tecton user interface

The task of verifying the correctness or other semantic properties of computer programs or hardware designs often involves large, complex proofs, requiring the statement and proof of many lemmas and theorems. We believe that this task will become truly practical only when machine assistance can be effectively used even at the earliest stages of stating conjectures and attempting proofs.

In books on logic, a formal proof is defined as a sequence of formulas with justifications for each formula. A "pure" proof involves two types of justifications: (i) a formula is an instance of an axiom schema, or (ii) a formula is obtained by a particular rule of inference applied on other preceding formulas in the sequence. In practice, such "pure" proofs from first principles tend to be very long, complex, tedious, and difficult to understand. Consequently, one rarely finds such proofs in the literature. Instead, proofs are hierarchically structured using derived rules of inference and meta-theorems, which in addition to axiom schemas and rules of inference, are freely used as justifications. In order to present or understand a proof, the structure of a proof becomes crucial. Most complex proofs typically require human organization. Developing good proofs is an art much like writing good programs.

Computer generated proofs have an additional problem of opaqueness because, typically, a computer proof is the result of an exhaustive search process (built into the heuristics or strategy used by a theorem prover intertwined with human guidance). For understanding such proofs, it is all the more essential that proof structure is highlighted.

Ensuring that a computation indeed realizes a given specification is an iterative process. During the process of finding a proof, typically bugs are uncovered in a specification or in a program or hardware design implementing a computation. Most of the time, proof attempts exist in a partially completed state, and the user spends most of his or her effort trying to comprehend the current state of the attempt in order to guide the system towards a complete proof [16]. Multiple goals with incomplete proofs typically coexist, and it may sometimes be useful to maintain several distinct attempts to prove the same goal. It is thus important that a verification system provide facilities to maintain theorems and lemmas and to visualize and manage proofs. Furthermore, due to the complexity of verification systems, information on how to use them should be readily available on-line.

Most verification systems do not provide adequate tools to deal with these issues. The structure of the proofs is buried in a style of linear representations most suitable for texts. The theorems and lemmas used in proofs are not readily available with the proofs and have to be looked up in an often large list of mostly irrelevant theorems and lemmas. Most systems still use a teletype style interface.

We believe that hypertext technology [3, 4] provides an excellent set of tools for dealing with these problems. The basic idea of hypertext is to associate objects in a database with windows, or with text or icons within windows, and to provide links between objects. Proofs are non-linear objects that lend themselves naturally to linked representation—different parts of the proofs can be linked together and we can examine the proofs by following the links. References to theorems and lemmas can also be represented by links to the appropriate entries in the database of theorems and lemmas, which in turn can refer to their proofs. The graphical capability of hypertext systems can provide a larger vocabulary and allow more suitable formats for displaying symbols and formulas. Links and procedural attachment capabilities in hypertext systems support design and implementation of an efficient and convenient user interface; they can of course also be used to structure on-line documentation.

The user interface of Tecton is implemented in a commercial hypertext system, Knowledge Management System (KMS) [1]. The functions of the user interface are to process commands and to present proofs graphically. It uses:

- tabular formats for logical formulas and programs, in order to provide compact and readable representations;

- tree diagrams on the screen or in a printed report to present the structure of proofs (how formulas used in the proof are related to each other and to program parts);

- hypertext links for additional structuring of large proofs, as well as for on-line documentation;

- action items for mouse-driven command entry.

The design of the Tecton user interface follows closely the style of the KMS user interface, based on the direct manipulation paradigm and the three-button mouse [1]. In a sense, the user interface is an extension of KMS functionality using its Action Language. On-line documentation has also been created and structured with hypertext links to provide semantic information on individual commands.

3.1 Tabular formats and symbols

Logical formulas are used in Tecton to express relationships. "Ordinary" logical formulas are used to express static relationships between mathematical objects such as numbers or boolean values or members of some other abstract data type. But Tecton also employs "Hoare formulas" [8], which specify the dynamic behavior of computer programs by relating program parts to ordinary logical formulas.

Logical formulas are usually expressed in Tecton as tables. Ordinary logical formulas are displayed as two column tables. For example, the basic "laws of equality" can be expressed as

	$x = x$
$x = y$	$y = x$
$x = y$	$x = z$
$y = z$	

In such a table each row represents an implication. Here the second row represents $x = y \supset y = x$. If there is more than line in a table entry, the conjunction of the lines is taken. Thus the third row represents $x = y \wedge y = z \supset x = z$. If an entry is blank, it is the same as if it contained the boolean value *true*. Thus the first entry represents $x = x$ (since this is same as $true \supset x = x$).

A Hoare formula is expressed in Tecton as a three column table. Each entry in the middle column represents a statement S of a given programming language, and the left and right column entries represent a precondition and postcondition for the statement. The precondition and postcondition are expressed in the same format as the left and right columns of Tecton format for ordinary formulas. Preconditions and postconditions are also called (program) *assertions.* The meaning of a row of the table is that if the precondition holds before the statement is executed, and the execution of the statement terminates, then the postcondition holds afterward. (Implicit in this description is a notion of "program state" and of a programming language statement producing a new program state.) For example, the Hoare formula

$x > y$	$x := x + 1$	$x > y + 1$
$z = a$ $z > 0$ $x = 1$	while $z \neq 0$ do $x := x * y$ endwhile	$x = y^a$

is the conjunction of two Hoare formulas, the first about an assignment statement $x := x + 1$ and the second about a while statement.

Frequently in Tecton formula tables we use symbols to stand for subformulas. Use of symbols helps reveal the structure of proofs and makes the proof representation more compact, since often the same formula appears in many different places within a proof. In particular, Tecton introduces a symbol for each rewrite rule and a symbol for each program construct. Symbols for formulas are introduced as necessary when formula tables are displayed and are reused whenever possible. To relate symbols with what they stand for, Tecton uses three kinds of tables, called *Program Tables*, *Rule Tables* and *Parts Tables*.

Program Tables (see Appendix B for an example) introduce symbols for program parts and assertions about the parts. They are produced from a straight text version of the program prepared by the user on a KMS frame. The user has to supply symbols for program assertions and loop invariants. Tecton generates symbols for program statements and for branching conditions of conditional and while statements, and displays the program and assertions in a tabular format. In general a Program Table contains rows that alternate between one column, containing program fragments, and two columns, containing assertions, which are ordinary logical formulas. The ordinary logical formulas above and below a program part in the table act as a precondition and postcondition for the part, respectively.

A Rule Table lists in a formula table all the rewrite rules used in the inferences on the current page. We represent a rewrite rule as a logical formula

A_1 ... A_n	$L = R$

The equality $L = R$ is used as rewrite rule to replace an instance of L by the corresponding instance (same substitution for variables) of R, whenever the corresponding instances of $A_1, \ldots, A_n$ hold. This is a *conditional rewrite rule* (unconditional if there are no assumptions A_i).

A Parts Table, though it looks very similar to a Rule Table, is not actually a formula table, since some of its row entries may be just terms rather than formulas. Also, variables in Parts Table entries stand only for themselves, whereas variables in Rule Table formulas are implicitly universally quantified. Entries in a Parts Table are introduced as necessary when formula tables are displayed and are reused whenever possible.

3.2 Proof representation

Tecton represents proofs as *proof trees*. One way to think of proof trees is in terms of the more general notion of trees used in expressing the structure of problem solutions. We start with a problem to be solved, called a goal, and proceed by breaking the problem down into simpler problems (subgoals), such that if solutions of all of the subgoals can be found, there is a well-defined way of combining those solutions into a solution of the goal. Each such division into subgoals is called a *solution step*, or *solution strategy*.

3.2.1 Problem solution trees

It is well known that we may want to try different solution strategies on the same problem, probably because the previous strategies did not produce a solution, or because we might not be satisfied with the complexity of the solution. This fact motivates the formulation of problem solution trees as finite trees with two kinds of nodes: (i) goal (or subgoal) nodes; and (ii) solution step nodes. Each goal has a finite number, possibly zero, of solution steps as its children, and each solution step has a finite number, possibly zero, of goals as its children. The children of a goal represent different alternatives for a first step toward solving the goal problem. The children of a solution step represent subgoals such that there is a way to combine solutions of the subgoals into a solution of the goal.[1] Thus a problem solution tree has the form shown in Figure 1.

3.2.2 Proofs as problem solution trees

Getting back now to proof trees, the kind of problem to be solved in this case is to show that a formula is valid. We express a goal by just writing the formula whose validity is in question, using the tabular format previously described. By a solution step we now mean an "inference mechanism" that produces a finite number, possibly zero, of subgoals such that if each subgoal formula is valid, then so is the parent goal. In the example given in Appendix B, the goal is to show that the Hoare formula about the procedure body is valid, and *composition* is an inference mechanism that divides this problem into the

---

[1] Such a tree is sometimes called an "and/or" tree since information from the children of a solution step is "and-ed" together, while information from the children of a goal is "or-ed" together.

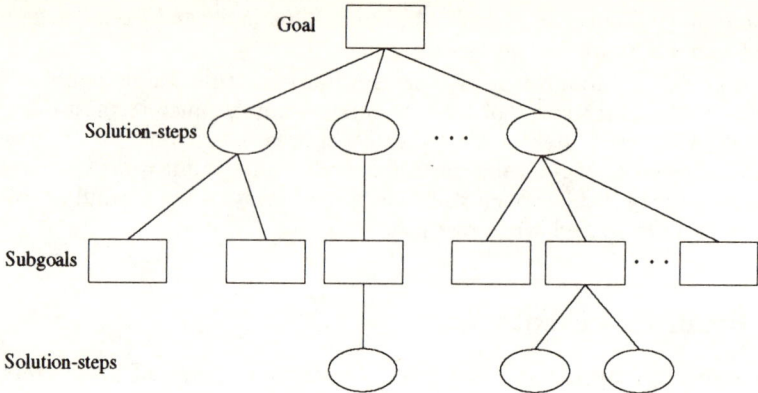

Figure 1: Problem Solution Tree Format

two subgoals that are Hoare formulas about the first and second halves of the
procedure body. [2]

Because of some special characteristics of proof trees, the format Tecton uses
to display proof trees is a little different from that indicated in Figure 1. Since
it is common for proof goals to have only one child, we save space by placing
the inference node directly below its parent and omitting the line connecting
it to its parent. We also omit the enclosing circle, just using the text item
that names the inference mechanism and perhaps some parameters used in
the mechanism. If there are more than one children of a goal we duplicate
the goal node on another page and show an alternative inference in the same
position as the one on the first page, directly below the goal. A hypertext link
to the alternate is placed on the first page next to the inference text item. An
example is the item "o Sibling on page3" on page2 of the example proof report
in Appendix A. Note that page3 (see the second page of Appendix A) also has
a hypertext link, above the goal formula node, back to the page with the first
alternative. If there were more than two children, there would also be another
"sibling" link next to the inference node on page3.

The layout of the subgoals of an inference is also a little unusual (see Figure 2). This format is used for two reasons. First, since goals are often expressed with long text items, a format that easily accommodates such items is
desirable. Second, a frequently used inference mechanism is "reduce," which
produces only one subgoal. In this case the subgoal is aligned directly below
the parent goal; no horizontal space is lost to indentation, as might be the case
with more conventional tree layouts.

If there is not enough space on the current page to display all the subgoal
formula nodes below an inference node, a *continuation marker* is created in
place of the inference node, textually indicating on which page the subgoals
will be displayed and linked to that page (see Appendix B). Continuation
markers are created on demand as the proof proceeds. On the new page, an
item is created which links with and textually indicates the page from which

---

[2]Perhaps this mechanism should be called "decomposition." However, the inference mechanisms for Hoare formulas are named for the main program structure connective in the statement part of the Hoare formula; in this case, statement composition.

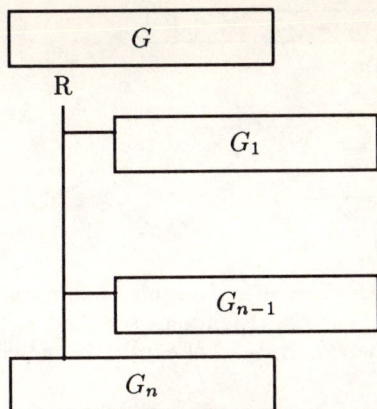

Figure 2: Goal-subgoal Layout in Tecton Proof Trees

the new page is continued.

A user can use the sibling and continuation links to browse through the proofs quickly and to examine different parts of the proofs.

4 Tecton inference engine

We describe the inference rules supported by Tecton. These rules are classified into two categories: (i) Hoare inference rules, which deal with Hoare formulas, and (ii) inference rules for first order formulas.

4.1 Hoare logic

Hoare formulas are used to express properties of programs, by relating program statements to assertions expressed in first order logic. Hoare inference rules are systematically used to reduce a Hoare formula goal into subgoals with simpler program constructs, until subgoals are eventually produced that are first order logic formulas. We omit the discussion on the syntax and semantics of Hoare logic and only list a few Hoare inference rules. In addition to the rules given below, there are inference rules for other linguistic constructs such as *declare* and *release* statements, *abort* statement, *null* statement, nondeterministic choice statement and *exchange statement*. Interested readers can consult [10] for details.

4.1.1 Assignment

Let $x_1, \ldots, x_n$ be distinct simple identifiers and $P_{e_1,\ldots,e_n}^{x_1,\ldots,x_n}$ stand for the result of simultaneously substituting each e_i for all free occurrences of x_i in P. The inference rule for assignment statment is

$$\boxed{Q \mid x_1, ..., x_n := e_1, ..., e_n \mid P}$$

assignment

$$\boxed{Q \mid P^{x_1,...,x_n}_{e_1,...,e_n}}$$

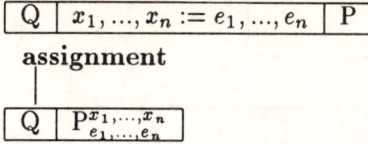

4.1.2 Composition

Let R be an first order formula. The rule of composition is shown below on the left. In case when S_2 is an assignment statement, the rule is shown below on the right, where R is P^x_e. Instead of explicitly showing both subgoals, we show only the first,

$$\boxed{Q \mid S_1 \mid P^x_e}$$

since the second is trivially reduced by the assignment rule to the tautology $P^x_e \supset P^x_e$.

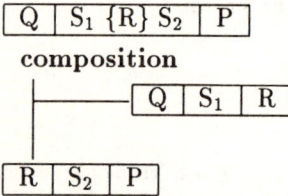

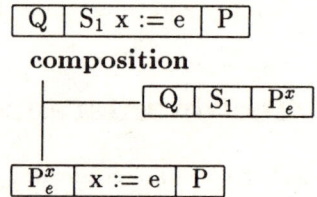

$$\boxed{Q \mid S_1 \; \{R\} \; S_2 \mid P}$$

composition

$$\boxed{Q \mid S_1 \mid R}$$

$$\boxed{R \mid S_2 \mid P}$$

$$\boxed{Q \mid S_1 \; x := e \mid P}$$

composition

$$\boxed{Q \mid S_1 \mid P^x_e}$$

$$\boxed{P^x_e \mid x := e \mid P}$$

4.1.3 Conditional

We show below the inference rules for both the one-branch conditional statement and the two-branch conditional statement.

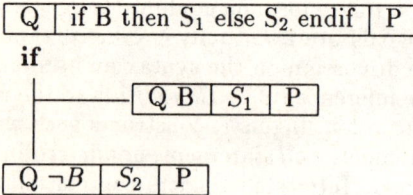

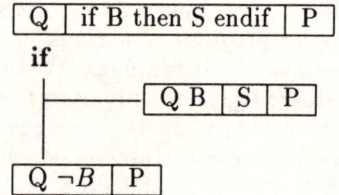

$$\boxed{Q \mid \text{if } B \text{ then } S_1 \text{ else } S_2 \text{ endif} \mid P}$$

if

$$\boxed{Q \; B \mid S_1 \mid P}$$

$$\boxed{Q \; \neg B \mid S_2 \mid P}$$

$$\boxed{Q \mid \text{if } B \text{ then } S \text{ endif} \mid P}$$

if

$$\boxed{Q \; B \mid S \mid P}$$

$$\boxed{Q \; \neg B \mid P}$$

4.1.4 While statement

Let I be the "loop invariant", an assertion which states relationships that hold among the variables on each iteration. Below is the inference rule for the *while* statement.

```
┌───┬─────────────────────────┬───┐
│ I │ while B do S endwhile   │ P │
└───┴─────────────────────────┴───┘
```
while
```
                    ┌───┬───┬───┐
├───────────────────│ I B │ S │ I │
│                   └───┴───┴───┘
│
│   ┌──────┬───┐
└───│ I ¬B │ P │
    └──────┴───┘
```

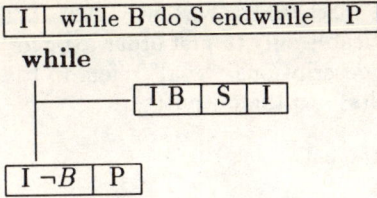

4.2 Inference Mechanisms

A proof system for first order logic is typically defined to have only a few inference rules, such as *modus ponens*

$$A, A \supset B \vdash B.$$

In principle, proofs could be done using only these rules. But most proofs would have to be uncomfortably large if constructed out of such simple building blocks. In order to reduce the size of proofs, it is convenient to allow the use of *derived rules of inference*, which are rules of the form

$$A_1, \ldots, A_n \vdash B \quad (n \geq 1)$$

where there exists a basic proof tree[3] with B at its root and $A_1, \ldots, A_n$ at the leaves. The use of such a rule thus merely abbreviates the corresponding proof tree to a tree with nodes only for B, leaves $A_1, \ldots, A_n$, and the inference node (referencing the derived rule) in between. A derived inference rule is analogous to a macro used in programming to generate a larger piece of code.

Tecton goes further in proof abbreviation than just using derived rules of inference. In a Tecton proof tree an inference node may refer either to an inference rule or a derived inference rule or to an *inference mechanism*.

- an *inference mechanism* is an algorithm that takes a formula as input and produces as output a sequence of formulas, such that there exists a basic proof tree whose root is labeled with the input formula and whose leaves are labeled with the output formulas or with axioms or lemmas.

- The children of an inference node labeled with the name of inference mechanism M are labeled with the formulas that M outputs when given the parent node formula as input; the inference node itself is labeled with the name of M and references to any axioms and lemmas used.

Corresponding to any particular use of an inference mechanism is a derived rule of inference; one might say that the mechanism generates derived rules "on the fly."

---

[3] A basic proof tree is a finite tree in which each node is labeled with a formula and for each non-leaf node there is an inference rule such that the children of the node are labeled by the premises of the rule and the node itself is labeled with the conclusion of rule.

The following are the main inference mechanisms currently used in Tecton. All of the inference mechanisms are applicable only to first order logic formulas, not to Hoare formulas. In the following descriptions, "goal" refers to the input formula to the mechanism and "subgoal(s)" to the output(s).

4.2.1 Reduction

One of the most important inference mechanisms used in Tecton is *reduce*, an algorithm that makes a sequence of rewrites using rewrite rules, producing as its output the final formula of the rewrite sequence. The rewrite rules used are unconditional or conditional rules corresponding to proper axioms or lemmas. In a first order logic with equality, rewriting is justifiable by a basic proof tree, since the laws of equality (reflexivity, symmetry, transitivity, substitution) are axioms or theorems of the logic.

Rewrite rules are formed by Tecton using a term ordering to determine which side of an equation to take as the left hand side of a rule. The ordering used is called *lexicographic recursive path ordering* (lrpo) [5]. Additional rewrite rules may be generated by Tecton using a variant of the Knuth-Bendix procedure (Tecton includes implementations of several variants).

Also built into *reduce* are transformations and simplifications based on the logical axioms used by Tecton. Use of these transformations is *not* indicated on the inference node.

In case the resulting formula produced by *reduce* is *true*, there is no subgoal of the reduce inference node, and it is labeled as *finish* instead.

Note that reduction includes the important case of applying another theorem as a lemma. A theorem is converted into a rewrite rule and an inference node cites the rule number and the theorem itself appears in the Rules table on the current page.

4.2.2 Case analysis and splitting

If the special predicate *cond* appears in a goal, then the *case* mechanism applies, producing subgoals based on the first argument of *cond*, which is a boolean value. There are two subgoals, one in which the first argument is replaced by *true* and the other in which the first argument is replaced by *false*.

The *split* mechanism eliminates boolean operators, $\vee$ and $\wedge$, in the goals by generating necessary subgoals. For example, given a goal

$$\begin{array}{|c|c|} \hline \mathcal{A} & C_1 \\ & C_2 \\ & \ldots \\ & C_n \\ \hline \end{array}$$

the split mechanism produces n subgoals

$$\begin{array}{|c|c|} \hline \mathcal{A} & C_i \\ \hline \end{array}$$

for $i = 1, \ldots, n$.

4.2.3 Induction

Tecton uses the *cover set induction* mechanism [21]. Consider a subterm occurring in a goal G. Consider the definition, by equations, of the outermost function symbol of the subterm. Left sides of the rules in the definition constitute a cover set.

Suppose that terms $t_1, \ldots t_k$ constitute a cover set for performing induction on subterm $f(x_1, \ldots, x_n)$, where each t_i has f as its outermost symbol. In general, $k + 2$ subgoals should be[4] generated using a well-founded ordering $\prec$:

1. Induction subgoals: corresponding to each t_i, there is a subgoal G_i generated from the goal G where $f(x_1, \ldots, x_n)$ is replaced by t_i with an induction hypothesis as an additional hypothesis for the subgoal. That is, G_i is obtained from $G(f(x_1, \ldots, x_n))$, producing $G(t_i') \supset G(t_i)$, where $t_i' \prec t_i$. The case when $G(t_i')$ is true is the basis step. In general, there can be as many induction hypotheses as needed insofar as the subterms used in place of t_i are smaller than t_i w.r.t. $\prec$.

2. Completeness: There should be a subgoal for proving that this is a complete cover set for f. That is, the union of the sets of ground instances of $t_1, \ldots, t_k$ is equivalent to the set of ground instances of $f(x_1, \ldots, x_n)$, when x_i are substituted by constructor ground terms of the type of x_i.

3. Well-foundedness: There should be another subgoal $t_1' \prec t_1$ and ... and $t_k' \prec t_k$. Often, t_i' is a subterm from the right-hand side of the rule defining f whose left side is t_i. Since these rules are oriented using lexicographic recursive path ordering (lrpo) we can finish this subgoal by saying that the proof follows from lrpo.

4.2.4 Generalization

The *generalize* mechanism looks for common subterms appearing on the two sides of an equational goal or in the assumptions and conclusions of a goal. It produces a subgoal in which these subterms are replaced by distinct variables. For example, in Appendix A, the goal

$$\boxed{((y * (x/y)) + rem(x, y)) = x \quad | \quad (y * ((x + y)/y)) + rem(x, y) = x + y}$$

(*div* is denoted as "/") is generalized into

$$\boxed{((y * (x/y)) + z) = x \quad | \quad (y * ((x + y)/y)) + z = x + y}$$

by replacing $rem(x, y)$ by a new variable z. In general, more than one subterm may be generalized at the same time.

It should be noted that generalization, unlike the other inference mechanisms used in Tecton, can produce an invalid formula as a subgoal even when the goal is valid. When this happens it is necessary to try an alternative generalization or other inference steps.

The generalization mechanism is used inside cover-set induction mechanism of Tecton to automatically generate lemmas which may or may not be valid.

---

[4]Currently Tecton only generates the induction subgoals, not the completeness and well-foundedness subgoals.

If a lemma obtained as a generalization cannot be proved (i.e. the prover fails to prove it), then Tecton automatically backtracks and makes another proof attempt.

4.3 Linear arithmetic decision procedure

We have built into the reduction mechanism a decision procedure for a subclass of *Presburger arithmetic*, because of the primary importance of integers in the mathematics of computer programming. The built-in procedure eliminates the need to explicitly state some axioms for integers such as transitivity axioms for inequality relations.

Roughly speaking, Presburger formulas are those that can be built up from integer constants, integer variables, addition, multiplication by constants, the usual arithmetical relations ($<, \leq, >, \geq, =$), and the first-order logical connectives. The subclass decided consists of Presburger formulas that, when placed in prenex form, contain only universal quantifiers. The decision problem on this class of Presburger formulas has been considered before [20], mostly in isolation. Boyer and Moore incorporated a similar rational-based procedure into their heuristic theorem prover [2]. Our implementation is heavily influenced by the work of Boyer and Moore. In particular, we became aware of many difficult issues by studying [2].

We call the procedure the *linear procedure*. The linear procedure and the reduction mechanism use each other as mutually recursive procedures. The linear procedure may use the reduction mechanism to derive additional relations among integer terms; the reduction mechanism may call the linear procedure to establish the conditions of a conditional rewrite rule before the rule can be applied. This close interaction makes our procedure different from and more useful than stand-alone procedures.

The linear procedure also interacts with other parts of the inference engine by exchanging integer equality terms between them. If the linear procedure derives an integer equality [15], it will pass the equality to the Tecton inference engine. Any equality among integer terms derived by the equational reasoning component of Tecton inference engine is also passed to the linear procedure. This interaction by equality sharing is an extremely powerful method to combine different decision procedures [19] and has made the linear procedure more useful.

5 Concluding remarks

In this paper we have described some of the novel features of the Tecton Proof System in the areas of "proof visualization" and proof automation. By proof visualization techniques we mean ways of expressing mathematical proofs about computations that make the proofs more easily comprehensible. By simplifying and organizing the way programs, assertions, and proofs are expressed—using tables, graphics, and a combination of cross-indexing and hypertext techniques—Tecton does, we believe, greatly improve the readability of specifications and proofs. In the area of proof automation, we have described the main inference mechanisms including Hoare proof rules, reduction, case analysis and splitting, induction, generalization, and a linear arithmetic decision procedure that is well integrated into the other mechanisms.

Tecton is an experimental proof system. As we use it for constructing large complex proofs, we expect it to evolve. The main extensions we believe are crucial to overall success of such a system are

- A *high level specification language.*

- A *proof command language* for interactively guiding the construction of large, complex proofs, allowing the user to keep control of proof development while making effective use of the automated deduction capabilities of the system.

- A *program modeling language* capable of modeling crucial features in production programming languages, such as Ada and C++, for building libraries of generic software components: encapsulation, templates/generics, and class inheritance.

- *Data base facilities* for storing, indexing, and retrieving large collections of specifications, designs, programs, axioms, theorems, and proofs.

Relative to the first area, we have recently completed a design of the syntax and semantics of a Tecton language for describing and using abstract concepts in formal software development and hardware design. The language, based in part on a much earlier but incomplete description of a high-level specification language (with the same name and goals) [11, 12], and some of the main proof issues are illustrated in [9] with an extended example of a behavioral and structural description of a carry-lookahead adder circuit, with the circuit realization given in terms of a generic parallel-prefix circuit. We have also implemented and are currently experimenting with a simple proof command language.

Acknowledgments

Raj Agarwal, Michael Seager, and Changqing Wang have assisted in the implementation of Tecton, particularly of the program parser, Hoare formula generator, and program table displayer. Chuck Kacmar first called our attention to the KMS system and encouraged us in early discussions of our goals.

References

[1] R.M. Akscyn, D.L. McCracken, E.A. Yoder. "KMS: A Distributed Hypermedia System for Managing Knowledge in Organizations," *Comm. ACM*, 31(7):820-835 (1988).

[2] R.S. Boyer and J.S. Moore, "Integrating Decision Procedures into Heuristic Theorem Provers: A Case Study of Linear Arithmetic," *Machine Intelligence*, 11:83-157 (1988).

[3] *Communications of the ACM*, 31(7) (July 1988).

[4] J. Conklin, "Hypertext: An Introduction and Survey," *IEEE Computer*, 2(9):17-41 (1987).

[5] N. Dershowitz, "Termination of rewriting", *J. Symbolic Computation*, 3:69-116 (1987).

[6] R.W. Erickson and D.R. Musser, "The AFFIRM Theorem Prover: Proof Forests and Management of Large Proofs," *5th Conference on Automated Deduction, Lecture Notes in Computer Science*, Vol. 87, Springer-Verlag, New York, 1980.

[7] M.A. Ellis and B. Stroustrup, **The Annotated C++ Reference Manual**, Addison-Wesley, 1990.

[8] C.A.R. Hoare, "An Axiomatic Basis for Computer Programming," *Comm. ACM*, 12(10):576-583 (1969).

[9] D. Kapur and D.R. Musser, **Tecton: A Framework for Specifying and Verifying Generic System Components**, Rensselaer Polytechnic Institute Computer Science Department TR 92-20 (1992).

[10] D. Kapur, D.R. Musser and X. Nie, "The Tecton Proof System: Introduction and User's Guide", Institute for Programming and Logic, State University of New York (1991).

[11] D. Kapur, D.R. Musser, and A.A. Stepanov, "Operators and algebraic structures," *Proc. of Conference on Functional Programming Languages and Computer Architecture*, Portsmouth, NH (1981).

[12] D. Kapur, D.R. Musser, and A.A. Stepanov, "Tecton: A Language for Manipulating Generic Objects," *Proc. of Program Specification Workshop, University of Aarhus, Denmark*, (1981), *Lecture Notes in Computer Science*, Springer-Verlag, Vol. 134 (1982).

[13] D. Kapur and H. Zhang, **RRL: A Rewrite Rule Laboratory—User's Manual**, General Electric Corporate Research and Development Report, Schenectady, NY (1987).

[14] D. Kapur and H. Zhang, "An Overview of RRL (Rewrite Rule Laboratory)," *Proc. of Third International Conf. of Rewriting Techniques and Applications*, Chapel Hill, NC (1989).

[15] T. Käufl, "Reasoning about Systems of Linear Inequalities," *Proc. of 9th International Conf. on Automated Deduction*, 563-572, Argonne, ILL (1988).

[16] R.A. Kemmerer, "Verification Assessment Study Final Report", Vol. 1-5, National Computer Security Center, Fort George G. Meade, MD.

[17] D.R. Musser, **Elements of a Pragmatic Approach to Program Verification**, Rensselaer Polytechnic Institute Computer Science Department TR 89-24 (1989).

[18] D.R. Musser and A.A. Stepanov, **The Ada Generic Library: Linear List Processing Packages**, Springer-Verlag Compass Series (1989).

[19] G. Nelson and D.C. Oppen, "Simplification by Cooperating Decision Procedures," *ACM Trans. on Programming Languages and Systems*, 1(2):245-257 (1979)

[20] R.E. Shostak, "A Practical Decision Procedure for Arithmetic with Function Symbols", *Journal of ACM*, 26(2):351-360 (1979)

[21] H. Zhang, D. Kapur, and M.S. Krishnamoorthy, "A Mechanizable Induction Principle for Equational Specifications," *Proc. of Ninth International Conference on Automated Deduction (CADE-9)*, Argonne, ILL (1988).

A   Proof of a lemma about integer division

A proof of a typical lemma about integer division is shown. Note the hypertext link to an alternate proof attempt, "∘ Sibling on page3". The destination of that link is shown on the following page. This proof attempt is generated because a generalization of the goal fails. Another generalization is tried which succeeds and gives the proof.

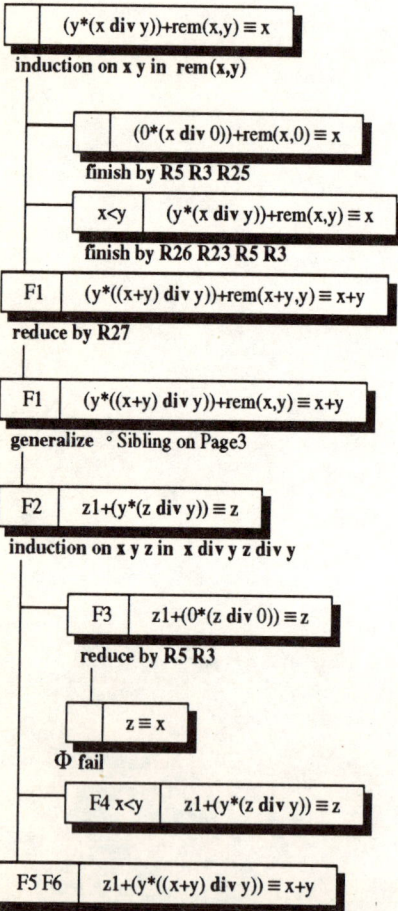

Page2

| | $(y*(x \text{ div } y))+\text{rem}(x,y) \equiv x$ |

induction on **x y** in **rem(x,y)**

| | | $(0*(x \text{ div } 0))+\text{rem}(x,0) \equiv x$ |

finish by R5 R3 R25

| | x<y | $(y*(x \text{ div } y))+\text{rem}(x,y) \equiv x$ |

finish by R26 R23 R5 R3

| F1 | $(y*((x+y) \text{ div } y))+\text{rem}(x+y,y) \equiv x+y$ |

reduce by R27

| F1 | $(y*((x+y) \text{ div } y))+\text{rem}(x,y) \equiv x+y$ |

generalize ∘ Sibling on Page3

| F2 | $z1+(y*(z \text{ div } y)) \equiv z$ |

induction on **x y z** in **x div y z div y**

| | F3 | $z1+(0*(z \text{ div } 0)) \equiv z$ |

reduce by R5 R3

| | | $z \equiv x$ |

Φ fail

| | F4 x<y | $z1+(y*(z \text{ div } y)) \equiv z$ |

| F5 F6 | $z1+(y*((x+y) \text{ div } y)) \equiv x+y$ |

Rules

R3		$x+0 \equiv x$
R5		$x*0 \equiv 0$
R23	x<y	$x \text{ div } y \equiv 0$
R25		$\text{rem}(x,0) \equiv x$
R26	x<y	$\text{rem}(x,y) \equiv x$
R27		$\text{rem}(y+x,y) \equiv \text{rem}(x,y)$

Parts

F1		$((y*(x \text{ div } y))+\text{rem}(x,y))=x$
F2		$((y*(x \text{ div } y))+z1)=x$
F3		$(z1+(0*(x \text{ div } 0)))=x$
F4		$(z1+(y*(x \text{ div } y)))=x$
F5		$(z1+(y*((x1+y) \text{ div } y)))=(x1+y)$
F6	F7	$z1+(y*(x \text{ div } y)) \equiv x$
F7		$(z1+(y*(x1 \text{ div } y)))=x1$

Page3 ∘ Continued from Page2

F1	$(y*((x+y) \text{ div } y))+\text{rem}(x,y) \equiv x+y$

generalize

F2	$z+(y*((x+y) \text{ div } y)) \equiv x+y$

induction on x y in x div y

F3	$z+(0*((x+0) \text{ div } 0)) \equiv x+0$

finish by reformulation

F4 x<y	$z+(y*((x+y) \text{ div } y)) \equiv x+y$

finish by R24 R6 R23 R5 R3

F5 F6	$z+(y*((x+y+y) \text{ div } y)) \equiv x+y+y$

split on ∨

¬F4 F5 ¬0=y	$z+(y*((x+y+y) \text{ div } y)) \equiv x+y+y$

finish by R24 R6

F5 ¬0=y	$z+(y*((x+y+y) \text{ div } y)) \equiv x+y+y$

Φ **finish by R24 R6**

Rules

R3		$x+0 \equiv x$
R5		$x*0 \equiv 0$
R6		$x*\text{add1}(y) \equiv x+(x*y)$
R23	x<y	$x \text{ div } y \equiv 0$
R24	¬0=y	$(y+x) \text{ div } y \equiv \text{add1}(x \text{ div } y)$

Parts

F1		$((y*(x \text{ div } y))+\text{rem}(x,y))=x$
F2		$((y*(x \text{ div } y))+z)=x$
F3		$(z+(0*(x \text{ div } 0)))=x$
F4		$(z+(y*(x \text{ div } y)))=x$
F5		$(z+(y*((x+y) \text{ div } y)))=(x+y)$
F6	F4	$z+(y*((x+y) \text{ div } y)) \equiv x+y$

B Quotient algorithm

We show the proof for the partial correctness of an efficient quotient algorithm. This page contains the Program table for the quotient algorithm and part of the Hoare logical proofs. All the lemmas used are provable from definitions of natural numbers. Appendix A shows proof of one such lemma. Proofs of all lemmas take Tecton 15 pages.

Page17

| Q | D1 A1 A2 {I} W1 A5 A6 {I1} W2 | R |

composition

| Q | D1 A1 A2 | I |

assignment

| Q | D1 A1 | F1 |

assignment

| Q | D1 | F2 |

declare

| y>0 x≥0 | $y=(y*2^0)$ $0\geq0$ $x\geq0$ |

Φ **Continue on Page 22**

| I | W1 A5 A6 {I1} W2 | R |

composition

| I | W1 A5 A6 | I1 |

assignment

| I | W1 A5 | F3 |

° **Continue on Page 18**

| I1 | W2 | R |

° **Continue on Page 19**

Parts

F1
| | $z=(y*2^0)$ $0\geq0$ $x\geq0$ |

F2
| | $y=(y*2^0)$ $0\geq0$ $x\geq0$ |

F3
| | $z=(y*2^n)$ $x=((0*z)+r)$ $r\geq0$ $z>r$ $n\geq0$ |

Program table:

	procedure fast_quotient (x,y,q,r) **alters** q,r; **parameters** (x,Z), (y,Z), (q,Z), (r,Z);
Q	$x \geq 0$
	$y > 0$
D1	**declare** (n, Z, 0), (z, Z, y);
A1	z := y;
A2	n := 0;
I	$z = y * 2^n$
	$n \geq 0$
	$x \geq 0$
B1	**while** z ≤ x **do**
A3	z := z * 2;
A4	n := n + 1;
W1	**endwhile;**
A5	r := x;
A6	q := 0;
I1	$z = y * 2^n$
	$x = q * z + r$
	$r \geq 0$
	$z > r$
	$n \geq 0$
B2	**while** n ≠ 0 **do**
A7	z := z div 2;
A8	n := n - 1;
A9	q := q * 2;
B3	**if** r ≥ z **then**
A10	q := q + 1;
A11	r := r - z;
C1	**endif;**
W2	**endwhile;**
R	$0 \leq r$
	$r < y$
	$x = q * y + r$
	endprocedure

This page continues the proof for the quotient algorithm.

Page18 ∘ Continued from PAGE17

I	W1 A5	F1

assignment

I	W1	F2

while

z=(y*2^n) z>x x≥0 n≥0	z=(y*2^n) x=((0*z)+x) x≥0 z>x n≥0

split on ∧

z=(y*2^n) z>x x≥0 n≥0	x=((0*z)+x)

finish by reformulation

I B1	A3 A4	I

assignment

I B1	A3	F3

assignment

z=(y*2^n) x≥z x≥0 n≥0	(z*2)=(y*2^{n+1}) n+1≥0 x≥0

Φ **Continue on Page23**

Parts

F1	z=(y*2^n) x=((0*z)+r) r≥0 z>r n≥0
F2	z=(y*2^n) x=((0*z)+x) x≥0 z>x n≥0
F3	z=(y*2^{n+1}) n+1≥0 x≥0

74

This page continues the proof for the quotient algorithm.

Page19 ◦ Continued from PAGE17

I1	W2	R

while

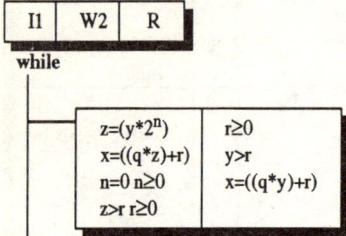

$z=(y*2^n)$	$r\geq0$
$x=((q*z)+r)$	$y>r$
$n=0$ $n\geq0$	$x=((q*y)+r)$
$z>r$ $r\geq0$	

Φ **Continue on Page24**

I1 B2	A7 A8 A9 C1	I1

if

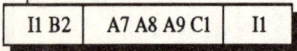

I1 B2	A7 A8 A9 (B3) A10 A11	I1

assignment

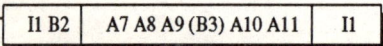

I1 B2	A7 A8 A9 (B3) A10	F1

assignment

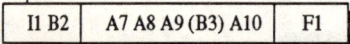

I1 B2	A7 A8 A9 (B3)	F2

assume

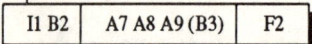

I1 B2	A7 A8 A9	B3⊃F2

assignment

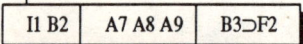

I1 B2	A7 A8	B3⊃F3

◦ **Continue on Page20**

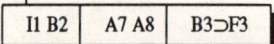

I1 B2	A7 A8 A9 (¬ B3)	I1

◦ **Continue on Page21**

Parts

F1	$z=(y*2^n)$
	$x=((q*z)+(r-z))$
	$r-z\geq0$
	$z>r-z$
	$n\geq0$
F2	$z=(y*2^n)$
	$x=(((q+1)*z)+(r-z))$
	$r-z\geq0$
	$z>r-z$
	$n\geq0$
F3	$z=(y*2^n)$
	$x=((((q*2)+1)*z)+(r-z))$
	$r-z\geq0$
	$z>r-z$
	$n\geq0$

This page continues the proof for the quotient algorithm. Note that we show two pages of the actual output (page20 and page22).

Page20 ∘ Continued from PAGE19

I1 B2	A7 A8	B3⊃F1

assignment

I1 B2	A7	B3⊃F2

assignment

$z=(y*2^n)$	$(z \text{ div } 2)=(y*2^{n-1})$
$x=((q*z)+r)$	$x=((((q*2)+1)*(z \text{ div } 2))+(r-(z \text{ div } 2)))$
$r \geq z \text{ div } 2$	$r-(z \text{ div } 2) \geq 0$
$n \neq 0 \; n \geq 0$	$z \text{ div } 2 > r-(z \text{ div } 2)$
$z > r \; r \geq 0$	$n-1 \geq 0$

Φ **Continue on Page25**

Parts

F1	$z=(y*2^n)$
	$x=((((q*2)+1)*z)+(r-z))$
	$r-z \geq 0$
	$z > r-z$
	$n \geq 0$
F2	$z=(y*2^{n-1})$
	$x=((((q*2)+1)*z)+(r-z))$
	$r-z \geq 0$
	$z > r-z$
	$n-1 \geq 0$

Page22 ∘ Continued from PAGE17

$y>0 \; x \geq 0$	$y=(y*2^0)$
	$0 \geq 0$
	$x \geq 0$

split on ∧

	$y>0 \; x \geq 0$	$0 \geq 0$

finish by reformulation

$y>0 \; x \geq 0$	$y=(y*2^0)$

Φ **finish by R10 R29 R6 R5 R3**

Rules

R3	$x+0 \equiv x$
R5	$x*0 \equiv 0$
R6	$x*\text{add1}(y) \equiv x+(x*y)$
R10	$x>y \equiv y<x$
R29	$x^0 \equiv \text{add1}(0)$

This page continues the proof for the quotient algorithm.

Page21   ∘ Continued from PAGE19

I1 B2	A7 A8 A9 ($\neg$ B3)	I1

assume

I1 B2	A7 A8 A9	$\neg$ B3$\supset$I1

assignment

I1 B2	A7 A8	$\neg$ B3$\supset$F1

assignment

I1 B2	A7	$\neg$ B3$\supset$F2

assignment

$z=(y*2^n)$	$(z \textbf{ div } 2)=(y*2^{n-1})$
$x=((q*z)+r)$	$x=(((q*2)*(z \textbf{ div } 2))+r)$
$z \textbf{ div } 2 > r$	$r \geq 0$
$n \neq 0$ $n \geq 0$	$z \textbf{ div } 2 > r$
$z > r$ $r \geq 0$	$n-1 \geq 0$

Φ **Continue on Page26**

Parts

F1	$z=(y*2^n)$
	$x=(((q*2)*z)+r)$
	$r \geq 0$
	$z > r$
	$n \geq 0$
F2	$z=(y*2^{n-1})$
	$x=(((q*2)*z)+r)$
	$r \geq 0$
	$z > r$
	$n-1 \geq 0$

This page contains the proofs of some verification conditions. Again we show two pages of the actual output (this time page23 and page24).

Page23 ∘ Continued from PAGE18

$z=(y*2^n)$	$(z*2)=(y*2^{n+1})$
$x{\geq}z$ $x{\geq}0$	$n+1{\geq}0$
$n{\geq}0$	$x{\geq}0$

split on ∧

$z=(y*2^n)$	$n+1{\geq}0$
$x{\geq}z$ $x{\geq}0$	
$n{\geq}0$	

finish by reformulation

$z=(y*2^n)$	$(z*2)=(y*2^{n+1})$
$x{\geq}z$ $x{\geq}0$	
$n{\geq}0$	

Φ **finish by R2 R1 R4 R30 R6 R17 R5 R3**

Rules

R1	$1 \equiv add1(0)$
R2	$2 \equiv add1(add1(0))$
R3	$x+0 \equiv x$
R4	$x+add1(y) \equiv add1(x+y)$
R5	$x*0 \equiv 0$
R6	$x*add1(y) \equiv x+(x*y)$
R17	$x*(y+z) \equiv (x*y)+(x*z)$
R30	$x^{add1(y)} \equiv x*x^y$

Page24 ∘ Continued from PAGE19

$z=(y*2^n)$	$r{\geq}0$
$x=((q*z)+r)$	$y>r$
$n=0$ $n{\geq}0$	$x=((q*y)+r)$
$z>r$ $r{\geq}0$	

split on ∧

$z=(y*2^n)$	$x=((q*y)+r)$
$x=((q*z)+r)$	
$n=0$ $n{\geq}0$	
$z>r$ $r{\geq}0$	

finish by R29 R6 R5 R3 R10

$z=(y*2^n)$	$y>r$
$x=((q*z)+r)$	
$n=0$ $n{\geq}0$	
$z>r$ $r{\geq}0$	

Φ **finish by R29 R6 R5 R3**

Rules

R3	$x+0 \equiv x$
R5	$x*0 \equiv 0$
R6	$x*add1(y) \equiv x+(x*y)$
R10	$x>y \equiv y<x$
R29	$x^0 \equiv add1(0)$

78

This page contains the proofs of more verification conditions.

Page25 ∘ Continued from PAGE20

$z=(y*2^n)$	$(z \text{ div } 2)=(y*2^{n-1})$
$x=((q*z)+r)$	$x=((((q*2)+1)*(z \text{ div } 2))+(r-(z \text{ div } 2)))$
$r \geq z \text{ div } 2$	$r-(z \text{ div } 2) \geq 0$
$n \neq 0 \ n \geq 0$	$z \text{ div } 2 > r-(z \text{ div } 2)$
$z>r \ r \geq 0$	$n-1 \geq 0$

split on ∧

$z=(y*2^n)$	$n-1 \geq 0$
$x=((q*z)+r)$	
$r \geq z \text{ div } 2$	
$n \neq 0 \ n \geq 0$	
$z>r \ r \geq 0$	

finish by reformulation

$z=(y*2^n)$	$z \text{ div } 2>r-(z \text{ div } 2)$
$x=((q*z)+r)$	
$r \geq z \text{ div } 2$	
$n \neq 0 \ n \geq 0$	
$z>r \ r \geq 0$	

finish by R14 R10 R47 R43 R45 R2 R44 R46

$z=(y*2^n)$	$r-(z \text{ div } 2) \geq 0$
$x=((q*z)+r)$	
$r \geq z \text{ div } 2$	
$n \neq 0 \ n \geq 0$	
$z>r \ r \geq 0$	

finish by reformulation

$z=(y*2^n)$	$x=((((q*2)+1)*(z \text{ div } 2))+(r-(z \text{ div } 2)))$
$x=((q*z)+r)$	
$r \geq z \text{ div } 2$	
$n \neq 0 \ n \geq 0$	
$z>r \ r \geq 0$	

finish by R10 R14 R1 R43 R45 R2 R44 R6 R17 R46 R5 R3

$z=(y*2^n)$	$(z \text{ div } 2)=(y*2^{n-1})$
$x=((q*z)+r)$	
$r \geq z \text{ div } 2$	
$n \neq 0 \ n \geq 0$	
$z>r \ r \geq 0$	

Φ finish by R10 R14 R43 R45 R44 R2 R1

Rules

R1		$1 \equiv add1(0)$
R2		$2 \equiv add1(add1(0))$
R3		$x+0 \equiv x$
R5		$x*0 \equiv 0$
R6		$x*add1(y) \equiv x+(x*y)$
R10		$x>y \equiv y<x$
R14		$x \neq y \equiv (true \oplus x=y)$
R17		$x*(y+z) \equiv (x*y)+(x*z)$
R43	$rem(z,x)=0$	$(y*z) \text{ div } x \equiv y*(z \text{ div } x)$
R44	$0<y \ \neg 0=x$	$x^y \text{ div } x \equiv x^{y-add1(0)}$
R45	$\neg 0=y \ \neg 0=x$	$rem(x^y,x) \equiv 0$
R46	$0<x$	$(y*F1^{x-add1(0)})+(y*F1^{x-add1(0)}) \equiv y*F1^x$
R47	$y \geq z$	$y-z<x \equiv y<x+z$

Parts

F1		$add1(add1(0))$

This page finishes the proof of the partial correctness of the quotient algorithm.

Page26 ∘ Continued from PAGE21

$z=(y*2^n)$	$(z \text{ div } 2)=(y*2^{n-1})$
$x=((q*z)+r)$	$x=(((q*2)*(z \text{ div } 2))+r)$
$z \text{ div } 2 > r$	$r \geq 0$
$n \neq 0 \ n \geq 0$	$z \text{ div } 2 > r$
$z > r \ r \geq 0$	$n-1 \geq 0$

split on ∧

$z=(y*2^n)$	$n-1 \geq 0$
$x=((q*z)+r)$	
$z \text{ div } 2 > r$	
$n \neq 0 \ n \geq 0$	
$z > r \ r \geq 0$	

finish by reformulation

$z=(y*2^n)$	$x=(((q*2)*(z \text{ div } 2))+r)$
$x=((q*z)+r)$	
$z \text{ div } 2 > r$	
$n \neq 0 \ n \geq 0$	
$z > r \ r \geq 0$	

finish by R14 R10 R43 R44 R34 R38 R2 R45

$z=(y*2^n)$	$(z \text{ div } 2)=(y*2^{n-1})$
$x=((q*z)+r)$	
$z \text{ div } 2 > r$	
$n \neq 0 \ n \geq 0$	
$z > r \ r \geq 0$	

Φ finish by R14 R10 R43 R45 R44 R2 R1

Rules

R1		$1 \equiv \text{add1}(0)$
R2		$2 \equiv \text{add1}(\text{add1}(0))$
R10		$x > y \equiv y < x$
R14		$x \neq y \equiv (\text{true} \oplus x = y)$
R34	$\text{rem}(x,y)=0$	$y*(x \text{ div } y) \equiv x$
R38	$\text{rem}(z,x)=0$	$\text{rem}(y*z,x) \equiv 0$
R43	$\text{rem}(z,x)=0$	$(y*z) \text{ div } x \equiv y*(z \text{ div } x)$
R44	$0 < y \ \neg 0 = x$	$x^y \text{ div } x \equiv x^{y-\text{add1}(0)}$
R45	$\neg 0 = y \ \neg 0 = x$	$\text{rem}(x^y,x) \equiv 0$

Modeling Time in Information Systems*

V.S. Alagar

Computer Science Department

Concordia University

Montreal, Quebec, Canada H3G 1M8

1   Introduction

The design of time dependent information systems must adopt a model of time that corresponds to time in nature. Our own experiences and awareness of time stimulate us to invent models, theories and concepts of time so as to capture both chronological past and unborn future. Clearly, subjective and objective views are mixed in our efforts in inventing time models.

The distinct impressions about the uneven flow of time and our cognitive interpretations of such impressions are subjective and cannot be formalised. Formal measurements can be applied to only a scientific concept of time which includes physical observation and measurements, mathematical formalism and logical analysis. However, an absolute objectivity in any view of time cannot be claimed—unless the observer is completely detached from the universe wherein time flows. Therefore it is desirable to build an (objective) abstract model of time based on a minimal set of subjective impressions. The following short list of subjective experiences of time seem sufficient for a good approximate formalisation of time in information systems.

[E_1] Time is a continuum; it is endlessly divisible and is not a succession of states.

[E_2] Time denotes change and evolution which in turn create disorder from order.

[E_3] Humans have the ability to judge occurrences of events based on intervals of time.

[E_4] Information is usually lost with the passage of time. Time memory is imprecise and approximate.

[E_5] It takes some interval of time to achieve temporal orientation (a framework where events can be relatively ordered).

One of the areas in artificial intelligence, known as qualitative physics, is concerned with reasoning about continuous change to physical situations. Some typical problems are predicting the outcome of a pan of water placed on a

*This research was supported by a grant from the Natural Sciences and Engineering Research Council of Canada and in part by a grant from the Fonds pour Formation de Chercherus et l'Aide à la Recherche of Quèbec.

stove (will it boil before the pan shatters), planning the activities of an autonomous vehicle (say, a robot) and reasoning about the possible motions of objects amidst obstacles and fixed barriers. Clearly we need to bring in a continuous model of time (E_1) to support the concepts here.

Information systems must maintain internal and external consistencies. For example, database systems must deal with outdated information. If data is not deleted when updates are made, the database model will force many tuples to have the same key and in turn this causes severe problems during subsequent operations of the system. However, if data is deleted when updates are made, during the future life of the system only those information that are true at the time of retrieval will be accessible. Here is an instance where we need to devise methods to restrict the disorderly growth (E_2) of information systems.

In a variety of situations there is difficulty in making predictions about an extended period of time in the future. For example, if a software is completed and put into operation today, can we predict whether it will still be operational 10 days later? 10 months later? or 10 years later? There is a notion here that goes beyond simple persistence of facts. The length of time into the future seems to have a bearing on the prediction. Completely deterministic systems for which there are well defined laws of change and initial conditions can be predicted with great accuracy into the future. However, in commonsense reasoning, a complete set of deterministic laws is rarely achieved. So, predictions over a short period of time are more reliable (and can be efficiently computed) over longer ones. An analogous situation arises when stating the preconditions for the outcome of an action. In principle, the number of preconditions for an action can be infinite. This implies a trade-off between the accuracy of prediction and the complexity of computing that prediction. These are the situations that calls for modeling imprecise and approximate information over the time domain (E_4).

In everyday experience, one comes across statements such as "the events for the month of July are ...", "in the event I solved the problem, I deserve a prize", "in the event that robot fails to monitor the water level reservoir will overflow" and "there are several parallel events in olympics". Event is defined in Webster's Dictionary as "the fundamental entity of observed physical reality represented by a point designated by three coordinates of place and one of time in the space-time continuum postulated by the theory of relativity". These definitions convey the meaning that an event is a collection of actions, a condition as well as any observed physical reality. Most importantly "events" are expressed in terms of time duration and change. It is also clear that the subjective world views events not in isolation but as complicated bundles, in which connections of different kinds exist among events. In the context of information systems, there are at least three types of events that have interesting connections:

1 Environmental events. An event of this type belongs to the "observing system". An observing system consists of the experimental apparatus and includes also human observers. Some examples of environmental events are "dialling the digits in a telephone", "sensor signal transmission to a robot" and "clicking the mouse". These examples suggest that an environmental event initiates an internal system process and triggers a chain of events within the system.

2 System events. An event of this type belongs to the "observed system". An

observed system, due to the fact that it is embedded in an environment, must have a formalism in which all observations may be clearly specified so that the experiments on the system can be performed by any one in the environment properly equipped with the instruments in the environment. Moreover, every observation should remain formally verifiable based on the logic of the formalism and the results of the observation should be capable of being reproduced by any one using the apparatus in the environment. A system event causes other system events or enables environmental events to happen. Some examples of system events are, "parse user's query", "commit changes to database", "send the signal that there is temporal inconsistency" and "wait until receiving a signal".

3 **Transition event.** An event of this type is a temporal marking in time and may denote instantaneous state changes. In reality, a transition event is an infinitesimally small durational event. Hence there may be system events that are transition events and there may be environmental events that are also transition events. However, any particular transition event can belong to only one of (system, environment) and not both.

Events in the first two types are durational, may occur repeatedly (infinitely many times) and may demand minimum (maximum) delays between successive occurrences. For example, the event "a database transaction is submitted" is an environmental durational event that may occur periodically with non-uniform frequency. The event "a database transaction is committed" is a system event and whose maximum duration is dependent on the internal implementation details; the frequency of occurrence of this event cannot be controlled by the system designer. These considerations should convince the reader that both E_3 and E_5 must be accounted for in a formalism dealing with time dependent information.

This paper attempts to compare two formalisms which are believed to account for the subjective principles E_1 to E_5; this is done in the next two sections. Section 4 presents the conclusions and comments on the related ongoing research work.

2 Functional Formalism

In [?] Alagar and Ramanathan designed a functional formalism for describing and analyzing the time dependent behaviour of real-time concurrent systems. This formalism introduces a pure behavior model capturing only the time dependent properties of the system being modeled. The times associated with various event occurrences and not the sites of the occurrences are taken to specify and analyze the system behavior. Thus the notion of machine state is absent in the formalism making it purely *applicative*. The fundamental premise of this formalism is that every event occurring in the system is *durational*; that is, environmental events and system events are durational events. The expressive power of this formalism has been brought out through the formal specification and correctness proof for problems taken from robotics (automated assembly, navigation controller) [?], hardware (arbiter design) [8], real-time database (concurrency control) [9] and temporal databases [10]. Below, the formalism is briefly reviewed.

2.1   Durational Event Model

Having taken the notion of interval as primitive, the model allows significant imprecision, uncertainty of information and permits reasoning based on decomposition of intervals (and hence events). Moreover, the model separates the observing system from the observed system using the same formalism: under the passage of time an observer watches the initiation and termination of event occurrences as they happen in the system. The formalism accounts for transition events by letting infinitesimally small intervals to be associated with such events.

An event $e \in E$ can occur any number of times during the life of the system. In order to remain observable, e can occur only a finite number of times within a finite period of time. Consequently, event histories can be characterized by two infinite time sequences—the initiation and termination times—which do not have limit points in any finite segment of the time domain. For a fixed e, the time sequences are denoted by $\text{TIME}_1(e)$, $\text{TIME}_2(e)$ which are monotonic non-decreasing functions from $\overline{N}$ to $\overline{R}$. They satisfy the axioms and are related by a bijective mapping as stated below:

$$[A_1]\ \text{TIME}_j(e)(n) \geq 0, n > 0, j = 1, 2.$$

Every non-zeroth occurrence has non-negative initiation and termination times.

$$[A_2]\ \text{TIME}_j(e)(0) = -\infty, j = 1, 2$$

$$[A_3]\ \text{TIME}_j(e)(+\infty) = +\infty, j = 1, 2.$$

The system has a beginning; however, it need not terminate. When the system does not exist no event could have taken place and consequently the zeroth occurrence must have happened at time $-\infty$.

$$[A_4]\ \text{TIME}_2(e)(n) \geq \text{TIME}_1(e)(n), \forall e \in E, n \in \mathcal{N}.$$

An observer cannot observe the completion of an event occurrence before the initiation of that occurrence.

This, combined with the facts that durations of event occurrences are (in general) unequal and each time function is monotonic non-decreasing, requires the introduction of a bijective mapping to match corresponding initiation and completion times of any particular event occurrence.

This is defined by $P_e : \overline{N} \to \overline{N}$, with $P_e(0) = 0$, $P_e(\infty) = \infty$ such that the composite function $\text{CTIME}_2(e) = \text{TIME}_2(e) \cdot P_e$ is not monotonic. The intervals $[\text{TIME}_1(e)(n), \text{CTIME}_2(e)(n)]$ define the occurrence of e, $n \geq 0$.

Example 1. An observer records the initiations and termination of phone calls as follows:

$$\text{TIME}_1(phone\text{-}call) \leftrightarrow (1, 2, 3, 4, 5, ...)$$

$$\text{TIME}_2(phone\text{-}call) \leftrightarrow (5, 7, 10, 12, 18, ...)$$

The observer records only the observation times. Now, the first phone call may have happened for 6 units of time, the second for 3 units of time, etc. To get a more precise knowledge, the bijective function should be given. Let $P_e : \mathcal{N} \to$

$\mathcal{N}$ be defined as: $P_e(1) = 2, P_e(2) = 1, P_e(3) = 5, P_e(4) = 3, P_e(5) = 4$. The intervals associated with the first, second, ..., fifth occurrences of the event *phone-call* are: [1,7], [2,5], [3,18], [4,10], [5,12]. So, the duration of the first call is 6 units of time, the duration of the second is 3 units of time, etc.

Temporal information in a database can be easily defined based on this formalism; see Ramanathan [?] for details. For reasoning and transaction purposes, the formalism defines an algebraic structure of events. This in turn leads to several implementations for representing events (intervals) and for interpreting compound events in terms of simpler events.

2.2   Basic events and Algebra of events

In addition to the event names in E, other events that are common to many information systems are easy to define in the formalism. For example, ASSIGN : $V \rightarrow E$ is a function which creates the event $ASSIGN(v)$ for every variable $v \in V$. During the history of the system, each variable $v \in V$ may assume different values from a domain DOM. The expressions $TIME_1(ASSIGN(v))(k)$ and $CTIME_2(ASSIGN(v))(k)$ denote the start and completion times of the k-th assignment to v, a value from DOM.

A nice feature of the formalism is that only a small set of primitive functions on E are necessary to specify complex systems such as robotics and database; that is, application dependent functions are easy to define on top of these functions. For example, transaction events and their dependence (causal and real-time) are discussed in [?]; see also Ramanathan [10] in this volume.

Comparison (temporal) between events is done using their corresponding time functions. To facilitate such comparisons, two relations are defined on the event set E. The relation $\leq$ (precedence) defined on E induces a lattice structure on E: $e \leq f$ if $[TIME_1(e) \geq TIME_1(f)] \wedge [CTIME_2(e) \leq CTIME_2(f)]$. The relation $\rightarrow$ (follows) defined on E induces an irreflexive poset on E: $e \rightarrow f$ if $[CTIME_2(f) \leq CTIME_2(e)]$.

Events can be compared by shifting times of initiations; subevents of an event e can be introduced by extracting monotonic non-decreasing subsequence of the time sequence associated with e. Composite events can be defined by merging time sequences. For example, the event $hold = (hold_c + hold_d)$ is a composite event created from simple (or composite) events $hold_c + hold_d$ which has the property that *hold* is initiated whenever $hold_c$ is initiated or whenever $hold_d$ is initiated and the observed termination time of *hold* is the corresponding observed termination time of $hold_c$ or $hold_d$. See [?] for theorems that characterize the conditions under which the temporal relation of individual events are preserved in the composite events created by them.

Causal dependency between any two events is defined using conditional events, where a conditional event is a logical event. A conditional event triggers a class of events whose initiations and terminations occur at the times when the designated predicate in the condition becomes true. Denoting by $[e|C]$ a class of events which begin whenever e finishes and C is true, the composite event $[e|C_1] + [f|C_2]$ denotes the set $\{g|g = e' + f', \ e' \in [e|C_1], \ f' \in [f|C_2]\}$.

Quantitative aspects of a system can be measured by *counters*. Counter functions are inverses of the time functions which give the number of initiations (terminations) strictly before (including) time t. Historical information can be modeled by defining functions for the most recent initiation or completion times of events before (or after) a time t. Note that durational model and the functional formalism with its ability to compose functions, define higher order and recursive functions which are very powerful to express changes explicitly, the attributes that change and the attributes that cause changes. See Ramanathan [9,10] for a rigorous application to temporal database formalization.

3 Allen's Temporal Logic

Allen's temporal logic formalism [?] is an extension of first-order classical logic to specify and reason about events, actions and their relationship. The notion of time in this formalism is the same as in the functional model described in section 2; that is, time is a continuum which can be decomposed into subtimes. Therefore, time intervals rather than time points are primitive. Another point of conformity with the functional model is the notion of events taking time; that is, events are durational.

The primary motivation for introducing this formalism by Allen was to model and reason about actions in the context of natural language processing, certain areas of Artificial Intelligence (planning) and "qualitative physics". An attempt is made in this section to show that the formalism has sufficient expressive power that can be exploited and applied to the specification of time dependent information systems.

An information system models a real word that is domain-specific and intuitive. The modeled objects evolve over time and hence must be describable in terms of their *static* and *dynamic* aspects. The static aspects are captured by *properties* that remain invariant over stretches of time. The dynamic aspects are captured by *occurrences* which describe the structure, behavior and interactions.

3.1 Formalism and Examples

There are four types of objects in the typed first-order predicate calculus formalism: Time-Interval, Property, Domain objects, Occurrence. While discussing a specific information system, say the database of students, *students, courses, teachers* are domain objects. A small number of primitive predicates exists in the logic to specify time dependent properties and compare time intervals. The predicate HOLDS(p,t) asserts that property p holds (i.e.: is true) during the time interval t. The predicates expressing the basic relations between time intervals and their semantics are as follows:

Let t_0, t_1 denote the lower and upper end points of a temporal interval t, with the property $t_0 < t_1$.

- EQUAL(s,t) : $(t_0 = s_0) \wedge (t_1 = s_1)$

- OVERLAPS(s,t) : $(s_0 < t_0) \wedge (t_0 \leq s_1) \wedge (s_1 < t_1)$

- MEETS(s,t) : $t_1 = s_0$

- DURING(s,t) : $((t_0 \leq s_0) \wedge (t_1 > s_1)) \vee ((t_0 < s_0) \wedge (t_1 \geq s_1))$.

- BEFORE(s, t) : $s_1 < t_0$

- STARTS(s, t) : $(s_0 = t_0) \land (s_1 < t_1)$

- FINISHES(s, t) : $(t_0 < s_0) \land (s_1 = t_1)$

Considering the inverse of the relations expressed by the above six predicates, there are a total of thirteen ways in which any two temporal intervals can be related. It is also possible to generate other relationships by computing the predicates arising from the transitive closure of these thirteen relations. It is easy to verify that all these relationships can be expressed in the functional model formalism described in section 2.

The intention of the HOLDS predicate is to express persistence: HOLDS(p, t) is true if and only if the property p holds during t.

$$\forall t'(\text{HOLDS}(p, t) \land \text{IN}(t', t) \rightarrow \text{HOLDS}(p, t')),$$
where
$$\text{IN}(u, v) \leftrightarrow (\text{DURING}(u, v) \lor \text{STARTS}(u, v) \lor \text{FINISHES}(u, v)).$$

The term *occurrence* denotes an object type in the logic. Objects of this type can be classified into *events* and *processes*. Process denotes a non-terminating action with no expected effect. Events denote actions with termination and outcome. A distinguishing feature between events and processes is that one can count the number of times an event occurs, but one cannot count the number of times a process occurs. This subtle distinction between terminating and non-terminating events is taken care of in the functional formalism by letting time intervals of arbitrary length and events of infinite duration. Moreover, the counters in the functional model count the number of initiations and the number of terminations, but not the number of event happenings.

The predicate OCCUR takes an event e and a time interval t and is true only if the event e happened during the entire interval t. That is,
$$\text{OCCUR}(e, t) \land \text{IN}(s, t) \rightarrow \sim \text{OCCUR}(e, s)$$
All events for which OCCUR predicate can be applied are the durational events of the functional formalism. To express the requirement that Mary was employed in a project $\mathcal{P}$ during an interval of time t, we first construct the event $e = employed(\text{Mary}, \mathcal{P})$ and then write the predicate OCCUR(e, t). Here *employed* is a function, Mary and $\mathcal{P}$ are domain objects.

The predicates HOLDS, OCCUR and those defined on time intervals can be combined in several ways to express complex requirements. The predicate
$$\text{HOLDS\_FROM}(p, s, t) \triangleq (\sim \text{HOLDS}(p, t) \land \text{HOLDS}(p, s) \land \text{MEETS}(s, t))$$
express the requirement that p does not hold during the interval t, but holds in the interval s following t. The following predicate expresses the claim that p holds during the interval t but not in any interval s following t:
$$\text{HOLDS\_TO}(p, t) \triangleq \forall s \cdot (\text{HOLDS}(p, t) \land \sim \text{HOLDS}(p, s) \land \text{MEETS}(s, t))$$
A version that expresses the maximality of the interval t for property p is
$$\text{HOLDS\_FOR}(p, t) \triangleq (\text{HOLDS}(p, t) \land \sim (\exists s \cdot (\text{HOLDS}(p, s) \land \text{IN}(s, t))))$$
Combining these two predicates, the assertion that t is maximal for property p and no extension of t can have property p is expressed by HOLDS_TO$(p, t) \land$ HOLDS_FOR(p, t).

Some more useful supplementary predicates are:

$$\text{OCCUR\_ATEND}(e,t) \triangleq \exists\, s \cdot (\text{OCCUR}(e,s) \wedge \text{DURING}(s,t) \wedge \text{FINISHES}(s,t))$$
$$\text{OCCUR\_ATBEGIN}(e,t) \triangleq \exists\, s \cdot (\text{OCCUR}(e,s) \wedge \text{DURING}(s,t) \wedge \text{START}(s,t))$$

For time delays $\epsilon, \delta > 0$,

$$\text{HOLDS\_DURING}(p,t,s) \triangleq \text{HOLDS}(p,t) \wedge \text{DURING}(t,s)$$
$$\text{HOLDS\_WITHIN}(p,\epsilon,\delta,t) \triangleq \exists\, t' \cdot (\text{HOLDS}(p,t') \wedge (t_1 + \epsilon \le t'_0) \wedge (t_1 + \delta \ge t'_0))$$
$$\text{OCCUR\_DURING}(e,t,s) \triangleq \text{OCCUR}(e,t) \wedge \text{DURING}(t,s)$$
$$\text{OCCUR\_IN}(e,t,\delta) \triangleq \exists\, t' \cdot (\text{OCCUR}(e,t') \wedge (t'_0 = t_1 + \delta))$$
$$\text{OCCUR\_WITHIN}(e,\epsilon,\delta,t) \triangleq \exists\, t' \cdot (\text{OCCUR}(e,t') \wedge (t_1 + \epsilon \le t'_0) \wedge (t_1 + \delta \ge t'_0))$$

The requirement that "Mary was moved to project Q during time interval t" is inherently incomplete and yet it can be expressed in the logic as $\text{OCCUR}(g,t)$, where $g = moved(\text{Mary,Q})$. Notice that all domain specific functions such as *employed*, *moved* are of type (NAME X PROJECT $\rightarrow$ E), where E is the set of all event names; see functional formalism.

Analogous to subevents, repeating events, composite and concurrent events of the functional formalism, new events using primitive events can be defined in Allen's formalism. For example, the class of events of repeating an event twice is defined as:

$$\text{OCCUR}(\text{TWICE}(e),t) \triangleq \exists\, u,v \cdot (\text{IN}(u,t) \wedge \text{IN}(v,t) \wedge \sim \text{EQUAL}(u,v) \wedge$$
$$\text{OCCUR}(e,v) \wedge \text{OCCUR}(e,v)).$$

The (and) composition of two simultaneous events e, f during an interval t is the event g such that $\text{OCCUR}(g,t) \triangleq \text{OCCUR}(e,t) \wedge \text{OCCUR}(f,t)$. The (or) composition of any two events e, f can also be defined as $\text{OCCUR}(g,t') \triangleq \text{OCCUR}(e,t) \vee \text{OCCUR}(f,s)$ where $t' = t$ if $g = e$, $t' = s$, if $g = f$.

Processes are different from events in Allen's logic: if a process p is occurring over an interval t then p must also be occurring over at least one subinterval of t. The predicate OCCURRING is used for processes:

$$\text{OCCURRING}(p,t) \rightarrow \exists s \cdot (\text{IN}(s,t) \wedge \text{OCCURRING}(p,s)).$$

If an event e occurred, then it was occurring:

$$\text{OCCUR}(e,t) \rightarrow \text{OCCURRING}(e,t).$$

During the history of a system, certain events happen continuously while some others happen in piecewise continuous manner. The assertion 'whistle blows for a duration of 5 seconds following the instant at which water level in a reservoir reaches x meters' can be stated as follows:

$$\forall\, t(\text{OCCURRING}(\text{has\_level}(x),t) \rightarrow \text{HOLDS}(\text{blow\_whistle},s) \wedge$$
$$(t_1 = s_0 \wedge s_1 = s_0 + 5))$$

This assertion is valid in general situations wherein water level may increase or decrease due to the continuous flow-in and flow-out of water in a reservoir. Suppose we want to assert 'John's salary rose last year' in the context of a temporal database update. The truth of this statement cannot vary continuously over time; there are stretches of time when it may not be true.

Let has_salary: NAME X SAL $\rightarrow$ E denote a function which associates with a pair (name, salary) an event in E. With respect to the current interval of time t, there exists a past interval s such that the salary of John during s exceeds the salary of John during t:

$$\forall \, t \, \exists \, s \cdot (\text{HOLDS}(has\_salary(\text{John}, x), s) \rightarrow \text{HOLDS}(has\_salary(\text{John}, y), t) \wedge$$
$$\text{BEFORE}(s, t) \wedge (y > x)) \, .$$

It seems that every process is an event occurrence e which can be decomposed into subevents not all of which are of the same type e. However, events and processes are closely related. For example, let $failing(x)$ denote the event that software x is showing defects. Then, the assertion OCCURRING($failing(x)$,t) states that software x is found defective during the period t. In practice, defects are exposed when software is used in some context. If $failed \, (y, x)$ is the predicate that x (failed) showed defects when used by y, then during the period t of usage,

$$\text{OCCUR}(failed(y, x), t) \rightarrow \text{OCCURRING}(failing(x), t)$$

Allen's logic provides predicates for asserting causality of events and generating actions by agents. The predicate ECAUSE(e, s, f, t) is true only if event e occurring during s causes event f to occur during t. An event can cause events to occur only in future and not in the past.

$$\text{ECAUSE}(e, s, f, t) \rightarrow \text{IN}(t, s) \vee \text{BEFORE}(s, t) \vee \text{MEETS}(s, t) \vee$$
$$\text{OVERLAPS}(s, t) \vee \text{EQUAL}(s, t) \, .$$

The assertion 'the alarm rings 1 second after depressing the button and stops ringing 2 seconds after the button is released' can be specified as follows:

$$\forall \, s \cdot (\text{ECAUSE}(depress\_button, s, sound\_alarm, t) \wedge$$
$$(t_0 = s_0 + 1) \wedge (t_1 = s_1 + 2)).$$

A class of actions are introduced by the function ACAUSE(agent,occurrence) which produces the action of the agent causing the occurrence. Both the agent and the action are occurring over the same interval t.

$$\text{OCCURRING}(\text{ACAUSE}(\text{agent,occurrence}), t) \rightarrow \text{OCCURRING}(\text{occurrence}, t).$$

The function ACAUSE : AGENT_OBJECTS X OCCURRENCE $\rightarrow$ E, where E is the set of events is a *performance*; the function
ACAUSE : AGENT_OBJECTS X OCCURRENCE $\rightarrow$ P, where P is the set of processes is an *activity*. Since events take place over entire intervals,

$$\text{OCCURRING}(\text{ACAUSE}(\text{agent,event}), t) \rightarrow \text{OCCUR}(\text{event}, t).$$

Sequential and concurrent activities can be expressed using the constructors for composite events; that is, composition of activities is an activity. The composite event obtained by composing an activity and a performance is a performance. The events in a composite event may themselves be independent (no causality), or not composite (atomic) or not cotemporal.

A wide range of rich composite events arise when the events constituting a composite event are themselves dependent of each other. Such composite events have the expressive power to model transactions and triggered actions in information systems. The dependence relationship between two actions is of five kinds [?]: 1) the actions are cotemporal; 2) one action is part of the other; 3) the occurrence of one causes the occurrence of the other; 4) it is a requirement of the application domain; 5) one is defined (in the formalism) in terms of the other. The predicate GENERATES(a, b, t) takes actions a, b and time interval t to indicate whether or not b is generated during time t due to the occurrence of action a. That is, the predicate is true only if action a generates action b during time t. Notice that the specification is incomplete in the sense that the exact nature of dependence is not part of the predicate. It is also implicit that event a is happening *now*, the current interval of time.

The dual of composing events is the process of decomposing actions into subactions. In the area of Artificial Intelligence, there are examples of actions that cannot be decomposed into subactions. The class of actions that can only be defined in terms of the agent's beliefs and intentions are not decomposable. However, the creation of a pragmatic real-time information development methodology should start with the modeling of domain-specific concepts and key intuitive concepts of time. This model includes the beliefs and intentions of the system users and consequently all actions and their formal relationships cannot be decomposed beyond the modeled information.

Finally, a list of constructs for specifying real-time database requirements is given below:

Triggered actions. Triggered actions are necessary to indicate that certain critical actions must be taken in the system to respond to the actions causing the trigger. Three types of triggers can be considered:

1) A class of actions which begin whenever an action a finishes and a property p is true. Let t denote the interval during which a is happening. The assertion for generated action b is

$$\forall t \, \exists t' \cdot (\text{OCCUR}(a, t) \wedge \text{HOLDS}(p, t') \wedge \text{FINISHES}(t, t') \wedge \\ \sim \text{OCCUR}(e, t') \rightarrow \text{GENERATES}(a, b, t'))$$

2) A class of actions which start whenever an action a starts and some predicate p is true is given by the assertion

$$\forall t \, \exists t' \cdot (\text{OCCUR}(a, t) \wedge \text{HOLDS}(p, t') \wedge \text{STARTS}(t', t) \rightarrow \text{GENERATES}(a, b, t'))$$

3) A class of actions which start within a time period ϵ after the termination of an action a provided p is true at the termination of a is given by the assertion.

$$\forall t \, \exists t' \cdot (\text{OCCUR}(a, t) \wedge \text{BEFORE}(t, t') \wedge \exists s \cdot (\text{MEETS}(s, t) \wedge \\ \text{HOLDS}(p, s)) \rightarrow \text{GENERATES}(a, b, t') \wedge (t'_0 = t_1 + \epsilon))$$

Periodic Events. An event e is periodic if each occurrence of e happens exactly after ϵ time period from the previous occurrence of e. Periodic events are useful to specify clocks and monitors. We have to assume that there is an invariant property p for e.

$$\forall\, t, t', t'' \cdot (\text{HOLDS}(p, t) \wedge \text{OCCUR}(e, t') \wedge \text{DURING}(t', t) \rightarrow \text{OCCUR}(e, t'') \wedge \text{MEETS}(t', t'') \wedge (t_0'' = t_1' + \epsilon))$$

Bounded Response Events. In safety critical applications, response to an action should be generated within a finite (prespecified) time period. If event a occurs during interval t and b denotes the response event for a then the assertion that b occurs within bounded time $\delta(> 0)$ is

$$\forall\, t\, \exists\, t'(\text{OCCUR}(a, t) \wedge \text{BEFORE}(t, t') \rightarrow \text{GENERATES}(a, b, t') \wedge (t_0' \leq t_1 + \delta))$$

Temporal Consistency. In real-time distributed databases ensuring the consistency of shared variables is essential (and time critical). If the consumption rate of values is faster than the observation and reading rate of the latest values from external sources, then only the most recent value can be used for the next consumption. Similarly, database must update the values of variables before a consumer may access the most recent values for consumption. Such temporal consistency constraints are somewhat easier to specify in the functional formalism than in Allen's logic.

Let $e_i = update(v_i)$, $i = 1, 2, \cdots, n$ be the events defining update actions on a set of database variables $v_1, v_2, \cdots, v_n$. Let us assume for the sake of discussion here that $g = f(v_1, v_2, \cdots, v_n)$, and $g_k = f_k(v_1, v_2, \cdots, v_n)$, $k = 1, 2, \cdots$, where g_k is the value of the function computed on the k-th set of values of the variables. Clearly, g_k cannot be computed when the k-th updates on all the $v_i s$ are not completed. Let t_i, $1 = 1, 2, \cdots, n$ denote the time intervals corresponding to the k-th set of update actions e_i; that is, $\text{OCCUR}(e_i, t_i)$, $i = 1, 2, \cdots, n$ hold. The property that the k-th value of v_i is computed is true for an interval of time immediately following t_i; that is, $\text{HOLDS}(has\_value(v_i), t_i') \wedge \text{MEETS}(t_i', t_i)$. Therefore, for a fixed k, and for each update action e_i

$$\text{OCCUR}(e_i, t_i) \rightarrow \exists\, t' \cdot (\text{HOLDS}(has\_value(v_i), t_i') \wedge \text{MEETS}(t_i', t_i)).$$

Let t denote the interval for which the right end point is maximum of the right end points of $t_1, \cdots, t_n$. Then, there is an interval s meeting t during which g_k has the k-th value:

$$\exists\, s \cdot (\text{HOLDS}(has\_value(g_k), s) \wedge \text{MEET}(s, t)).$$

The converse of this problem is to determine the number of updates computed on all the variables before t, the reference; if this number is j, then the value of g during interval t is g_j. Expressing such quantitative measures in Allen's logic is quite difficult; see [10] for a functional expression.

3.2   Semantics of Objectcharts—An application

This section describes briefly the ongoing research activity of our research group in developing a formal semantics of Objectcharts [5] and model checking based on it. Allen's logic with its first order formalism and its ability to model durational events has sufficient expressive power to model reactive systems. The alarmclock example of Harel [6] is taken to illustrate what we are attempting to do. A full version of a paper with formal semantics and complexity of model checking for Objectcharts is under preparation [?].

An Objectchart diagram is a simple extension of Statechart diagram in which the behavior of each class is independently captured. Statecharts, in turn, extend finite state machine models with a hierarchical representation of states and 'and' composition to denote concurrency. In an Objectchart, the behavior of each class is brought out by the following components:

- State Diagram: This is a state transition model for the object showing the different states and the transitions among the states.

- Transition Specification: For each arc in the Statechart, an event name is specified. An event may be qualified with a condition. Thus $e[c]$ triggers a transition if and when e occurs and c is true at that time.

- Invariants: Each state may have an invariant relation. State transitions must respect specification invariants.

Figure 1 shows a refined alarmclock statechart.

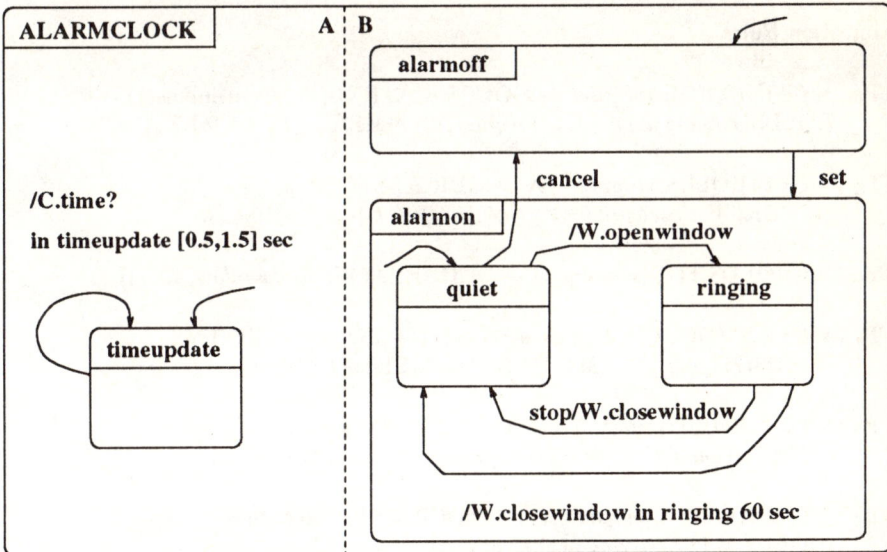

Figure 1: Refined alarm clock statechart.

Using the predicates introduced in the previous section, the formal specifications for the states and transitions are given below:

Initial Rules

IR_1 : $\text{OCCUR}(initial\_alarmclock, t) \rightarrow \text{OCCUR}(initial\_alarmclock.A, t') \wedge$
$\text{OCCUR}(initial\_alarmclock.B, t') \wedge \text{MEETS}(t, t')$

IR_2 : $\text{OCCUR}(initial\_alarmclock.A, t) \rightarrow \text{HOLDS}(timeupdate, t') \wedge \text{MEETS}(t', t)$

IR_3 : $\text{OCCUR}(initial\_alarmclock.B, t) \rightarrow \text{HOLDS}(alarmoff, t') \wedge \text{MEETS}(t', t)$

IR_4 : $\text{HOLDS}(alarmoff, t) \wedge \text{OCCUR\_ATEND}(set, t) \rightarrow$
$\text{OCCUR}(initial\_alarmon, t'') \wedge \text{MEETS}(t'', t)$

IR_5 : $\text{OCCUR}(initial\_alarmon, t) \rightarrow \text{HOLDS}(quiet, t') \wedge \text{MEETS}(t', t)$

Hierarchical Rules

HR_1 : $\text{HOLDS}(alarmclock, t) \leftrightarrow \text{HOLDS}(alarmclock.A, t) \wedge$
$\text{HOLDS}(alarmclock.B, t)$

HR_1 : $\text{HOLDS}(alarmclock.A, t) \leftrightarrow \text{HOLDS}(timeupdate, t)$

HR_1 : $\text{HOLDS}(alarmclock.B, t) \leftrightarrow \text{HOLDS}(alarmoff, t) \otimes \text{HOLDS}(alarmon, t)$

HR_1 : $\text{HOLDS}(alarmon, t) \leftrightarrow \text{HOLDS}(quiet, t) \otimes \text{HOLDS}(ringing, t)$

Transition Rules

TR_1 : $\forall\, t\, \exists\, t', t''(\text{HOLDS}(quiet, t) \wedge \text{OCCUR\_ATEND}(W.openwindow, t) \rightarrow$
$\text{HOLDS}(ringing, t') \wedge \text{HOLDS}(quiet, t'') \wedge \text{MEETS}(t', t) \wedge \text{MEETS}(t'', t'))$

TR_2 : $\forall\, t\, \exists\, t'(\text{HOLDS}(ringing, t) \wedge \text{OCCUR\_ATEND}(stop, t) \rightarrow$
$\text{OCCUR}(W.closewindow, t') \wedge \text{MEETS}(t', t))$

TR_3 : $\forall\, t(\text{HOLDS\_FOR}(ringing, t) \rightarrow \text{OCCUR\_IN}(W.closewindow, 60, t))$

TR_4 : $\forall\, t\, \exists\, t', t''(\text{OCCUR}(W.closewindow, t) \rightarrow \text{HOLDS}(quiet, t) \wedge$
$\text{HOLDS}(ringing, t'') \wedge \text{MEETS}(t, t') \wedge \text{MEETS}(t, t''))$

TR_5 : $\forall\, t\, \exists\, t'(\text{HOLDS}(quiet, t) \wedge \text{OCCUR\_ATEND}(cancel, t) \rightarrow$
$\sim \text{HOLDS}(quiet, t') \wedge \text{HOLDS}(alarmoff, t') \wedge \text{MEETS}(t', t))$

TR_6 : $\forall\, t, t'(\text{HOLDS}(timeupdate, t) \wedge \text{OCCUR\_DURING}(C.time, t', t) \rightarrow$
$(\text{HOLDS\_WITHIN}(timeupdate, 0.5, 1.5, t') \rightarrow$
$\text{OCCUR\_WITHIN}(C.time, 0.5, 1.5, t')))$

An analysis of the properties of a statechart based on potential behaviors (for a given initial state and a sequence of transitions), potential traces (for a given initial state and a specified behavior) and model checking cannot be done without a formal semantics. We are attempting to define a large number of supplementary predicates in Allen's logic to generate actions (updates, triggers and transactions) which will have the potential expressiveness for formally defining and reasoning about statecharts and objectcharts. The work on a formal verifier (model checker for objectcharts) and related complexity results are in progress.

4   Conclusion

The focus of research in this paper is on formal specification approaches to model time and reason on timing properties of information systems. There are a number of similarities between the functional formalism and Allen's temporal logic formalism that we discussed in this paper. Both methods represent events explicitly, model time as a continuum and relate events to intervals of times of their occurrences. Temporally and causally related events can be represented through predicates and are compared by their associated time intervals. Further, both formalisms enable the reasoning about time to be performed by means of explicit reference to time.

In both formalisms, past and future are treated symmetrically, in the sense that an event for any interval t can imply an information with respect to intervals preceding t (past) as well as information about intervals following t (future). For example, the assertion OCCUR($moved$(Mary,$\mathcal{P}$),t) implies that there is an interval of time s preceding t when Mary was working on a project different from $\mathcal{P}$. In order to know precisely the project Q in which she was engaged prior to being transferred to $\mathcal{P}$, we must look at the history of the event $employed$(Mary,x) and the predicate OCCUR($employed$(Mary,x),s), subject to the restriction (AFTER(t, s) $\vee$ MEETS(t, s)). The functional formalism has a number of primitive functions relating past and future with current time. For example,

$$\text{LAST}_1, \text{LAST}_2, \text{NEXT}_1, \text{NEXT}_2, : E \rightarrow (\overline{\mathbf{R}}) \rightarrow (\overline{\mathbf{R}})$$

have the following meaning:

- For every $e \in$ E, $\text{LAST}_1(e), \text{LAST}_2(e), \text{NEXT}_1(e), \text{NEXT}_2(e)$ are functions defined over $\overline{\mathbf{R}}$

- $\text{LAST}_1(e)(r) = t_1$, if the last initiated time of the event e strictly before t was t_1

- $\text{LAST}_2(e)(t) = t_2$, if the last completed time of the event e strictly before t was t_2

- $\text{NEXT}_1(e)(t) = t_3$, if t_3 is the first initiation time of e strictly after time t

- $\text{NEXT}_2(e)(t) = t_4$, if t_4 is the first completion time of e strictly after time t

For each project x for which the event $employed$(Mary,x) is defined, the interval [LAST_1 ($employed$(Mary, x))(t), LAST_2($employed$(Mary, x))(t)] associates the duration of Mary's employment on project x. Hence the project Q satisfying the property

$$\mathrm{LAST}_2(employed(\mathrm{Mary,Q}))(t)\mathrm{LAST}_2(employed(\mathrm{Mary,x}))(t), x \neq Q.$$

is the project from which Mary was transferred to $\mathcal{P}$.

Events, properties and processes are distinguished in Allen's formalisms; however, in the functional formalism there is no such distinction. Allen's logic lacks expressiveness of quantitative temporal requirements. The functional formalism supports the specification of qualitative (ordering in time), relative (metric notion), and relativistic (relating observations to moments of their occurrence) aspects of real-time systems. A system may be specified at different levels of abstraction, from a description of its highest level requirements to a detailed description of its (abstract) implementation, under both formalisms. However, nondeterminism cannot be expressed independently of time. Although both formalisms seem to promote modularity of system specification, the functional specification model is compositional and consequently the proof structure cannot be complex. There is no proof procedure given for Allen's logic [?]. As shown in [1], rigorous mathematical proofs based on function compositions and the property of reals can be developed for functional formalisms. It is the case that no formal verification procedure along the lines of mechanical theorem proving exists for both formalisms discussed in this paper.

Our current research is following the paths where the disadvantages of Allen's logic and the functional formalism can be remedied, their expressive power can be compared and sound proof systems can be developed. We are pursuing the application of Allen's logic to provide semantics for objectcharts and hence to conduct model checking. The significance of this approach is the synthesis of event-based logic formalism and the state transition-based objectchart formalism. Moreover, event descriptions in Allen's logic, viewed as describing updates to database, may lead to extensions for describing temporal database transactions.

Finally, Allen's logic does not incorporate any default reasoning. Incremental software development process start with incomplete knowledge and as the system progresses more and more facts and requirements are taken into account. Such systems are extremely difficult to specify and reason about. In [?], several categories of incompleteness have been enumerated. The most interesting category, called *partial specification* arises whenever the specification of system components admit more than one set of possible behaviors. We attribute this to three interesting situations: 1) the stated precondition for an action is 'loose' and the specification does not explicitly state what happens to the system when the precondition fails; 2) neglecting to mention what happens to objects that are not directly involved in an action; 3) failing to describe all the consequences of one execution of an action. Based on "the qualification and the prediction problem" [11] studied for commonsense reasoning and our intention to deal with systems involving concurrency and real-time, a nonmonotonic logic of time, knowledge and action which will serve as the basis of a formal specification language is being developed [7]. The goal of this logic formalism is to be able to specify and reason about system behavior that (i) may be incompletely specified; (ii) may involve concurrency at higher levels of problem description; (iii) deals with durational events and (iv) represents and reasons continuously changing phenomena under the passage of time.

Acknowledgements

I would like to thank Ramesh Achuthan, Fangqing Dong, Geetha Ramanathan and Dimitri Kourkopoulos for sharing several sessions of stimulating discussions of this work. Their ideas, suggestions and criticism were helpful in producing this paper.

References

[1] Alagar, V.S. and Ramanathan, G., "Functional Specification and Proof of Correctness for Time Dependent Behavior of Reactive Systems", *Formal Aspects of Computing*, 3, 1991, pp. 253–283.

[2] Alagar, V.S. and Kourkopoulos, D., "(In)completeness in Specifications", Technical Report, Department of Computer Science, Concordia University, Montreal, 1992.

[3] Alagar, V.S., Dong, F., and Achuthan, R., "Semantics and Model Checking of Objectcharts: An experience with Allen's logic", Technical Report, Concordia University, Montreal (in preparation).

[4] Allen, J.F., "Towards a General Theory of Action and Time," *Artificial Intelligence*, 23, 1984, pp. 123–154.

[5] Coleman, D., Hayes, F., and Bear, S., "Introducing Objectcharts or How to Use Statecharts in Object-Oriented Design", *IEEE Transactions on Software Engineering*, 18, 1992, pp. 9–18.

[6] Harel, D., "Statecharts: A Visual Formalism for Complex Systems", *Science of Computer Programming*, 8, 1987, pp. 231–274.

[7] Kourkopoulos, D., "Non-monotonic Logics of Time, Knowledge and Action", Master's Thesis (in preparation), Department of Computer Science, Concordia University, Montreal, Canada.

[8] Ramanathan, G., "A Functional Model for the Specification and Analysis of Distributed Real-Time Systems: Formalisms and Applications", Ph.D. Thesis, Concordia University, Montreal, Canada, 1988.

[9] Ramanathan, G. and Alagar, V.S., "Specification of Real-Time Distributed Database Systems", *Proceedings of Computer Systems and Software Engineering*, The Hague, May 1992, pp. 101–106. (Hague paper)

[10] Ramanathan, G., "Unified Framework for Database Specification: Functional Approach", (this volume)

[11] Shoham, Y., **Reasoning about change**, Massachusetts Institute of Technology, 1988.

A Unified Framework for Database Specification: Functional Approach*

Geetha Ramanathan

Department of Computer Science and Information Processing

Brock University

Ste. Catharines, Ontario, Canada L2S 3A1

Abstract

A formal functional model for describing data and reasoning about the events manipulating them in a dynamic distributed database system is presented. As opposed to some of the recent attempts that add time as an attribute to a model and then embed the augmented model in a logical framework for deductive reasoning, this paper introduces a uniform functional development methodology for treating time dependent aspects of both data and procedures in data modeling. The expressive power of this approach is illustrated by a formal specification and correctness proof of a concurrency control method.

1 Introduction

Databases constitute an important central component of computerized information systems, serving business and scientific endeavors. The traditional view of a database is that it is a collection of data capturing a certain state of objects being modeled; it is also supposed to contain either implicitly or explicitly the relationships among the modeled objects. The four aspects of data pertaining to an object are object name, object property, object attributes and time (of observation). Of these four aspects of data, time is the most difficult aspect to model. On the one hand, time affects object properties and hence must be captured in databases; however, most of the database operations can be studied with respect to a relativistic notion of time. The aspect of cause and effect can be brought out through a study of relations and functional dependencies between the events that change database state. In other words, absolute notion of time as understood in physical sciences is not necessary for modeling most of the databases. However, there are some databases that are predominantly dynamic in nature wherein relativistic and metric notion of time are essential to be modeled. Typical examples of this kind are databases supporting the software development of reactive systems such as hospital health monitoring, telephony and avionic systems. In these applications there is a frequent need for both current and historical data. Since traditional database models permit only snapshots containing the most recently recorded information, they are totally inadequate for modeling dynamic databases. In addition to maintaining past

*This research is supported by a grant from the Natural Sciences and Engineering Research Council of Canada.

history, dynamic databases should be endowed with some inference apparatus for predictive purposes. This capability is especially useful for knowledgebase systems whose corporate memory expands as the application domain is progressively explored through observation and logical inference. Recently there has been a great deal of interest in modeling time in information systems. One of the earliest papers addressing this issue and arguing in favour of including time explicitly in database modeling is Bubenko [3]. This point of view has been pursued in a more formal manner by Lundberg [8]. In this work, the concept of event is axiomatized within the framework of first-order predicate logic, the language used for modeling data. The inclusion of event in data model is significant in that the model can uniformly capture both active and passive events, the event relationships, the event orderings and consequently the various states of the system. First order predicate logic is a well studied formal system in which resolution theorem proving is perhaps the most commonly used method for performing deductions. It is also easy to implement due to the single inference rule which is used. The most difficult part, however, is that part which converts formulas into clausal form. The other limitations are the inherent undecidability issues and the fact that two valued logic cannot handle incomplete knowledge and consequent null values arising in databases. The approach taken by Clifford and Warren [4] uses the most powerful Montague's Intension Logic in formalizing historical databases. By providing one more dimension of time and treating null values in a semantically consistent manner they have enriched the relational model. One of the most important aspects of their work is the categorization of database constraint into extensional database constraint and intensional database constraint. In a similar fashion Tansel [13] has extended the relational model to support the temporal dimension of data. In [12], the approach taken is to model temporal semantics independent of any specific data model. This is achieved through time sequences defined on a class of objects.

In this paper, we discuss the concepts event, time and concurrency using a functional model. The functional approach for database has several advantages [9]. We have demonstrated the expressive power of functional approach to specification of complex systems in [1, 2]. The formal functional model consists of a small number of primitives and permits us to define application domain dependent functions based on them. The semantics is based on well known concepts of function compositions and the application of higher order functions. The deductive support is based on function comparison and two valued logic.

Section 2 formalizes the notion of event and time. The structure and semantics are briefly stated in this section; the reader is referred to our work [2] for a detailed discussion. We also skip discussing functional model of data. The reader is referred to the work of Orman [9]; our treatment is similar yet more expressive. In our work [10], we have provided constructs needed for the specification of real-time databases. Section 3 formalizes the database notion of concurrency, provides a formal description of a concurrency control algorithm and then prove its correctness; this part of our work distinguishes us from all the other previously reported work regarding time dependent databases. Section 4 contains a brief summary.

2   On Event and Time

Similar to the view adopted by Jackson [6] and Orman [9], a database is viewed as recording events as they are observed happening in the passage of time. Thus events are durational and time is continuous. In these respects we differ from Jackson and Orman who consider events as instantaneous. For us the database model being an abstraction of the real world should be faithful to the observations and should not unduly be constrained by implementation criteria. There are three types of events : (1) Environmental event (associated with an entity such as CUSTOMER in a banking application); (2) System event (such as OPENing and CLOSEing of accounts) and (3) Transaction event (denoting state changes). Events in the first two types are durational, may occur repeatedly and may demand minimum (maximum) delays between successive occurrences. The frequency and duration of event occurrences need not be a constant. By letting all durational events (instantaneous events have infinitesimally small durations) in the model, a uniform semantic structure is imposed on the modeled objects. Hence transactions submitted by users, updates on recorded information and system level events such as message passing can be treated uniformly within the model.

There is a very close association between entities and events. As observed by Orman [9], "The distinction between entities and events is not essential to and ignored by the data model, since all entities can be viewed as events corresponding to their entry in the system". The point is that event is a manifestation in the system of the real world entity and consequently its behavior governs and is governed by that of the event. The entity relationships introduce the associated event relationships within the model. For example, the events *customers* and *accounts* in the data model correspond to the entry of a customer and opening an account. These events continue to happen in the system until the departure of the customer in real life. Hence the event has an initiation time and a termination time. Since two different customers need not enter and depart at the same time, the event occurrences corresponding to the two customers have different durations of existence. Moreover, the k-th customer departing from the system need not necessarily be the k-th customer to enter the system. Hence event histories must be formalized with care.

The primitive objects that we wish to characterize are formalized as events. As mentioned earlier, there are three classes of events, and we let E denote all event names. That is, for a given database system, each name in E will uniquely identify a specific event in the system. For example, E may contain events *on-hook*, *dial-digits*, *off-hook*, *line-busy*, *line-free*, *connect*, *ring-back*, etc. in the context of modeling a telephone network; more general examples of events common to many database systems are *send*, *receive* and *assign*. It should be noted that event constants are different from event occurrences. The activities or the occurrence of events are subject to time constraints due to two important factors : there is an interaction with the environmental entities periodically; or, time is imposed by mutual exclusion, synchronization and ordering of the events. Thus "what is the effect of an event and when the event causing the effect occurs" are important to be considered together. Although the entire sequence of event occurrences may be nonterminating, the individual events may be ideally viewed as happening continuously over piecewise continuous intervals. Hence we identify time Π with $\Re$, the real line. To deal effectively with extreme cases, we let $\bar{\Pi} = \Re \cup \{\infty\} \cup \{-\infty\}$ and $\bar{\mathcal{N}} = \mathcal{N} \cup \{0\} \cup \{+\infty\}$.

2.1 Basic concepts of event and time

The set E of events is countable and its elements are names identifying the events that can happen in a system. In our model, an event $e \in E$ can occur any number of times; however, within a finite period of time, e can occur only finite number of times. Further, we do not restrict the durations of different occurrences of an event to be equal. This leads us to associate two sequences with each event—one indicating the chronological order of the starting time of its different occurrences and the other indicating the chronological order of the completion time of its different occurrences. Chronological completion time sequence need not correspond to the completion time of the occurrences denoted by starting time sequence. Hence, for each event e, we define a mapping P_e from $\mathcal{N}$ to $\bar{\mathcal{N}}$ to map the indices of the chronological completion time sequence onto the indices of the sequence of completion times corresponding to the starting time sequence. More formally, we have the following definitions:

Let INC $= \{f \mid f : \bar{\mathcal{N}} \rightarrow \bar{\Pi}$ and $f(n) \geq f(m), n \geq m\}$;
that is, INC is the set of all non-decreasing functions from $\bar{\mathcal{N}}$ to $\bar{\Pi}$.
Let R $\subseteq$ INC $\times$ INC, $R = \{ <f,g> \mid \forall n \in \bar{\mathcal{N}}, f(n) \leq g(n) \}$;
that is, $<f,g> \in$ R if $f \leq g$ where the function comparison "$\leq$" is done pointwise.
Define higher order functions $TIME_1$ and $TIME_2$, $TIME_j$: E $\rightarrow$ INC, $j = 1, 2$ such that
$TIME_j(e)(0) = -\infty$, $j = 1, 2$, $TIME_j(e)(\infty) = +\infty$, $j = 1, 2$, and
$< TIME_1(e)$, $TIME_2(e) > \in$ R, $e \in$ E.
The collection of triples $\{< e, TIME_1(e), TIME_2(e) > \mid e \in E \}$ restricted by the relation R satisfy the following axioms:
$\forall u, v \in \bar{\Pi}, 0 < u < v < \infty$, and $\forall e \in E$, $|X| < \infty$, $|Y| < \infty$, where
$X = \{ k \mid k \in N, u \leq TIME_1(e)(k) \leq v\}$
$Y = \{ k \mid k \in N, u \leq TIME_2(e)(k) \leq v\}$.
This ensures that in every finite interval of time, there can only be a finite number of initiations or completions for an event.

We define a function P_e : $\mathcal{N} \rightarrow \mathcal{N}$ with $P_e(0) = 0, P_e(\infty) = \infty$ such that the composite function $CTIME_2(e) = TIME_2(e) \circ P_e$ denotes the sequence of completion times corresponding to the sequence of initiation times in $TIME_1(e)$. Both the time functions $TIME_1$ and $TIME_2$ are infinitely supremum and infinitely infimum distributive functions, and it is shown in [11] that such functions admit inverses; the definitions of these inverse functions are given below:
$\bar{TIME}_1(e) \equiv COUNT_1(e)$: $\bar{\Pi} \rightarrow \bar{\mathcal{N}}$ where $COUNT_1(e)(t)$ is the number of initiations of e strictly before t.
$TIME_1(\bar{e}) \equiv LCOUNT_1(e)$: $\bar{\Pi} \rightarrow \bar{\mathcal{N}}$ where $LCOUNT_1(e)(t)$ is the number of initiations of e up to and including t.
$\bar{TIME}_2(e) \equiv COUNT_2(e)$: $\bar{\Pi} \rightarrow \bar{\mathcal{N}}$ where $COUNT_2(e)(t)$ is the number of completed occurrences of e strictly before t.
$TIME_2(\bar{e}) \equiv LCOUNT_2(e)$: $\bar{\Pi} \rightarrow \bar{\mathcal{N}}$ where $LCOUNT_2(e)(t)$ is the number of completed occurrences of e up to and including e.

2.2 An Algebraic Structure for E

We define a partial order relation "$\leq$" on E as follows: Two events e, f are related under the relation $\leq$ iff
$[TIME_1(e) \geq TIME_1(f)] \wedge [CTIME_1(e) \geq CTIME_1(f)]$. Relation $\leq$ characterize overlapping events. Strict precedence $\ll$ between any two events e and f is defined as follows:
$e \ll f$ if $CTIME_2(f) \leq TIME_1(e)$. (E, $\ll$) form an irreflexive poset.

The **sum** g of two events e and f has the property that g is initiated whenever e is initiated or whenever f is initiated and the observed termination times of g is the corresponding observed termination times of e or f. The $TIME_j$ sequence of g is the merge sequence of the $TIME_j$ sequences of e and f; that is, $g = e + f$ if

$$LCOUNT_1(g) = LCOUNT_1(e) + LCOUNT_1(f) \text{ and}$$
$$LCOUNT_2(g) = LCOUNT_2(e) + LCOUNT_2(f); \text{ or}$$
$$COUNT_1(g) = COUNT_1(e) + COUNT_1(f) \text{ and}$$
$$COUNT_2(g) = COUNT_2(e) + COUNT_2(f);$$

For any event e, we define **integer** events $f = e + i$ as follows:

$$[TIME_1(f)(n + i) = TIME_1(e)(n) \text{ and } CTIME_2(f)(n + i) = CTIME_2(e)(n),$$
$$n \in \mathrm{N}, \; TIME_1(f)(k) = CTIME_2(f)(k) = -\infty, \; k \leq i].$$

If the different occurrences of an event are nonoverlapping then the event is called single occurrent event. For those events, $[TIME_1(e+1) \geq CTIME_2(e)]$. An event f is called a **subevent** of e, $f \subseteq e$, if there exists an increasing function $r : \bar{N} \to \bar{N}$ such that $[TIME_1(f) = TIME_1(e) \circ r]$ and $[CTIME_2(f) = CTIME_2(e) \circ r]$.
An event f is called a **partial event** of e if $[TIME_1(f) \geq TIME_1(e)]$ and $[CTIME_2(f) \leq CTIME_2(e)]$.

3 Multiple Copy Update Problem in Distributed Databases

For our discussion in this section, the notion of a database is a set of data items without regard to the granularity of data items. At any instant, an item v_i can take a value $VALUE(v_i)$ from a domain $DOM(v_i)$. A transaction is a sequence of read/write operations enforced by admissible queries in the system. In a fully redundant distributed database system, each site has a complete copy of the database and $VALUE(v_i^s)$ denotes the value of i-th data item at the s-th site. At any instant, it may be insisted that an access to the database should see the same information regardless of which copy is accessed. This is a strong condition requiring complex and costly coordination mechanisms. A somewhat weaker condition is the notion of database consistency incorporating two aspects: *mutual consistency* of redundant copies and *internal consistency* of each copy.

Mutual consistency requires that at any time all database copies are identical. In practice, this is difficult to achieve. Hence a weaker version of mutual consistency is to require that when all transactions are completed, multiple copies must converge to the same final state.

Internal consistency brings out two issues : semantic integrity and serializability. The task of enforcing semantic integrity is not specific to distributed databases and so is not considered as an issue here. That is, we assume that each transaction preserves the integrity of the database. A concurrent transaction set preserves internal consistencies only if there is a sequential order for the atomic components of the transaction preserving the required integrity constraints; in this case, the transactions are said to be serializable. Towards axiomatizing mutual consistency and serializability, the events are defined next.

Assumptions

1. There are n sites and each site has a database copy and a controller for obtaining permission to schedule the processing of a transaction. The database copies have m variables v_1, v_2, ... v_m and the variable v_i at the s-th site is denoted v_i^s.

2. Each site has a storage processor and is responsible for manipulating data in that site.

3. Only those data items bound to a transaction can be changed by an execution of that transaction.

$submit_i$:   event that a transaction is submitted to the access controller C_i at the i-th site.

$execute_i$:   event that a transaction is being executed at the i-th site.

$update_j^i$:   event that a transaction submitted to the i-th site is taken up for updating the local copy of the database at the j-th site, $j \neq i$.

Specification of Mutual Consistency

Let $c_k^s : \bar{\Pi} \rightarrow \bar{\mathcal{N}}$ such that $c_k^s(t) = COUNT_2(ASSIGN(v_k^s))(t)$, $t \geq 0$, $k = 1$, ... m and $s = 1$, ... n. (The number of times a variable is updated need not be the same in all sites). At any time t, $1 \leq i \neq j \leq n$ and $\forall k$, $1 \leq k \leq m$

$$COUNT_2(\sum submit_i)(t) = COUNT_1(\sum execute_i)(t)$$

$$= COUNT_2(\sum execute_i)(t) = COUNT_1(\sum_{i \neq j} update_j^i + execute_j)(t)$$

$$= COUNT_2(\sum_{i \neq j} update_j^i + execute_j)(t)$$

$$\rightarrow VALUE(v_k^1)(c_k^1) = VALUE(v_k^2)(c_k^2) = \ldots = VALUE(v_k^n)(c_k^n).$$

Specification of Serializability

The distributed execution of transactions is serializable if there is a sequential schedule (consistent with integrity constraints) for the execution of transactions such that the sequence of values taken by a data item at any site during the original execution of the transactions is a subsequence of the values taken by the same data item in the serial execution of the transactions. Hence, $VALUE(v_i^k) = VALUE(v_i) \circ q_i^k$, where $q_i^k : \bar{\mathcal{N}} \to \bar{\mathcal{N}}$ is a nondecreasing function, $1 \leq i \leq m$, and $1 \leq k \leq n$. Here, if e denotes the serialized executions then v_i's are assumed to be modified due to e.

Specification of Starvation-free System

A transaction should be committed within a finite amount of time. That is,

$$[TIME_2(submit_i)(k) < \infty] \to [[TIME_1(update_j^i)(k) < \infty, \forall j \neq i] \text{ and}$$

$$[TIME_1(execute_i)(k) < \infty]], 1 \leq i \leq n, k \geq 1.$$

Next, we discuss a simple synchronous algorithm for solving this problem and provide a formal proof of its correctness. It is assumed that for a given set of transactions, the ordering can be deduced from a tag attached to each transaction. The algorithm enforces a voting procedure based on message exchanging between controllers so that agreements on global sequence of transactions can be reached.

An Informal Description of a Synchronous Voting Algorithm

At any time, the set of transactions in the system is assumed to be totally ordered. The ordering can be based on their time of arrival. That is, if a transaction T_1 is submitted earlier than T_2 then T_1 has higher priority than T_2. If T_1 and T_2 are submitted at two different sites C_i and C_j at the same time, then T_1 has higher submitted to a site, the controller broadcasts a vote for this transaction, if it has not already initiated a voting for a previous transaction. The receiving site compares the priority of T with the priority of each incomplete transaction at that site. If T has higher priority, then a vote is broadcast to all sites; otherwise, T is queued. Whenever every site receives $(n-1)$ votes for a transaction, the transaction is executed on that site. After completing the execution, end-signals are broadcast. After receiving $(n-1)$ end-signals, a site processes the transaction of next highest priority.

A Formal Specification of the Algorithm

Definition of Events

$send_{ij}$:	event that C_i sends a request for voting to C_j, $i \neq j$.
$next_{ij}$:	event that the request for voting goes from C_i to C_j, $i \neq j$.
get_{ij}:	event that C_j receives the request for voting from C_i, $i \neq j$.
ack_{jk}^i:	event that C_j sends an acknowledgement to C_k for a transaction submitted to C_i, $j \neq k$, $i \neq j$.
$back_{jk}^i$:	event that the acknowledgement goes from C_j to C_k for a transaction submitted to C_i, $i \neq j$, $j \neq k$.
$dens_{jk}^i$:	event that C_k receives the acknowledgement sent by C_j for a

transaction submitted to C_i, $i \neq j$, $j \neq k$.

$send\_end^i_{jk}$: event that C_j sends an end-signal to C_k for a transaction submitted to C_i, $j \neq k$.

$next\_end^i_{jk}$: event that the end signal goes from C_j to C_k for a transaction submitted to C_i, $j \neq k$.

$get\_end^i_{jk}$: event that C_k gets the end-signal from C_j for a transaction submitted to C_i, $j \neq k$.

Informal and Formal Descriptions of Steps

1. The controller C_i at the i-th site sends a request to every other controller for voting on a new transaction submitted to it if

   (a) it has completed issuing end-signals to all other controllers for the previous transaction submitted at C_i.

   (b) it has received end-signals from all other controllers for the last transaction submitted at C_i.

   (c) there are outstanding transactions at C_i for execution.

$$TIME_1(send_{ij}) = \max\{ TIME_2(submit_i),$$
$$\max_{k \neq i}\{ TIME_2(get\_end^i_{ki} + 1), \qquad\qquad (1)$$
$$TIME_2(send\_end^i_{ik} + 1)\}\}$$

2. The controller C_j at the j-th site issues an acknowledgement (vote) to C_k for a transaction T submitted to C_i if :

   (a) among the requests submitted to the j-th site, C_j does not have any outstanding (pending) transaction whose priority is greater than the priority of T.

   (b) among the incomplete transactions for which requests were received for voting by C_j from other sites, there is no transaction with priority greater than the priority of T.

Let f_j be the function which at any time t determines the number of completed transactions in the system from among those submitted to the j-th site: $f_j : \bar{\Pi} \to \bar{\mathcal{N}}$,

$$f_j = \min\{\min_{s \neq j}(COUNT_2(send\_end^j_{js})), \min_{s \neq j}(COUNT_2(get\_end^j_{sj}))\}.$$

and $(f_j + 1)(t) = f_j(t) + 1$.

Similarly, let g^r_j be the function which at any time t determines the number of transactions completed in the system from among those submitted to r-th site, $r \neq j$. $g^r_j : \bar{\Pi} \to \bar{\mathcal{N}}$,

$$g^r_j = \min\{\min_{s \neq j}(COUNT_2(send\_end^r_{js})), \min_{s \neq j}(COUNT_2(get\_end^r_{sj}))\},$$

and $(g^r_j + 1)(t) = g^r_j(t) + 1$.

Now we can formally state the conditions:

$$COND_1 = [COUNT_2(submit_j) = f_j] \vee [(COUNT_2(submit_j) > f_j) \wedge$$

$$((TIME_2(submit_j) \circ (f_j + 1) > TIME_2(submit_i) \circ LCOUNT_2(get_{ij})) \vee$$

$$((TIME_2(submit_j) \circ (f_j + 1 = TIME_2(submit_i) \circ LCOUNT_2(get_{ij})) \wedge$$

$$(i < j)))] \tag{2}$$

$$COND_2 = \wedge_{r \neq j} [(COUNT_2(get_{rj}) = g_j^r) \vee ((COUNT_2(get_{rj}) > g_j^r) \wedge$$

$$((TIME_2(submit_r) \circ (g_j^r + 1) > TIME_2(submit_i) \circ LCOUNT_2(get_{ij})) \vee$$

$$((TIME_2(submit_r) \circ (g_j^r + 1) = TIME_2(submit_r) \circ LCOUNT_2(get_{ij})) \wedge$$

$$(i < r))))] \tag{3}$$

Define events e_j and h_j^r, $r \neq j, r = 1, \dots, n$, as follows:

$$TIME_1(e_j)(n) = TIME_2(e_j)(n) = \min\{t \mid f_j(t) = n\}$$

$$TIME_1(h_j^r)(n) = TIME_2(h_j^r)(n) = \min\{t \mid g_j^r(t) = n\}$$

Then,

$$ack_{jk}^i = [get_{ij} \mid [COND_1 \wedge COND_2]] +$$

$$(e_j + \sum_{r \neq j} h_j^i) \mid [(COUNT_2(get_{ij}) > COUNT_1(ack_{ji}^i)) \wedge \tag{4}$$

$$COND_1 \wedge COND_2], \; k \neq j, \; i \neq j$$

3. The storage processor at site i executes a transaction when C_i has received the acknowledgement from all other controllers.

$$TIME_1(execute_i) = \max_{j \neq i}\{TIME_2(dens_{ji}^i)\} \tag{5}$$

4. Storage processor at site j updates a transaction submitted to C_i when it has received the acknowledgements from the rest of the controllers and it has acknowledged the transaction to other controllers.

$$TIME_1(update_j^i) = \max\{\max_{k \neq i,j}\{TIME_2(dens_{kj}^i)\}, \max_{k \neq j}\{TIME_2(ack_{jk}^i)\}\} \tag{6}$$

Relations Among the Events

[H1] $\quad get_{ij} \leq next_{ij} \leq send_{ij}, \; \forall j \neq i$

[H2] $\quad dens^i_{jk} \leq back^i_{jk} \leq ack^i_{jk}, \; \forall k \neq j, \; \forall j \neq i$

[H3] $\quad TIME_1(send\_end^i_{ij}) = TIME_2(execute_i), \; \forall i, \; i \neq j$

[H4] $\quad get\_end^i_{ij} \leq next\_end^i_{ij} \leq send\_end^i_{ij}, \; \forall i, \; i \neq j$

[H5] $\quad get\_end^i_{jk} \leq next\_end^i_{jk} \leq send\_end^i_{jk}, \; \forall i, \; \forall j \neq i, \; \forall k \neq j$

[H6] $\quad TIME_1(send\_end^i_{jk}) = TIME_2(update^i_j), \; \forall k \neq j, \; \forall j \neq i, \; \forall i$

Proof of Correctness

We prove two lemmas and then show that the proof of correctness follows from these lemmas.

Lemma 1 proves that the execution sequence corresponds to the total order imposed by the priority. Lemma 2 proves that the updates and execution of a transaction are completed before the update or execution of another transaction starts. Let $T_1, T_2, \ldots , T_n$ be the sequence of transaction defined by the total ordering. Consider the event u_i defined as follows:

$$TIME_1(u_i) = \min_{j \neq i}\{TIME_1(execute_i), \; TIME_1(update^i_j)\}$$

$$TIME_2(u_i) = \max_{j \neq i}\{TIME_2(execute_i), \; TIME_2(update^i_j)\}$$

<u>Lemma 1.</u> Let the k-th occurrence of $\sum u_i$ be the k_1-th occurrence of u_j for some j, and the $(k-1)$-st occurrence of $\sum u_i$ be the k_2-th occurrence of u_r for some r. Then

$$TIME_2(submit_r)(k_2) < TIME_2(submit_j)(k_1)$$

or

$$[TIME_2(submit_r)(k_2) = TIME_2(submit_j)(k_1)) \wedge (r < j)].$$

That is, the transactions are executed in the decreasing order of their priority.

<u>Proof.</u> If the result is not true, then

$$TIME_1(ack^r_{js})(k_2) \geq \max\{\max_{s \neq j}\{TIME_2(get\_end^j_{sj})(k_1)\},$$

$$\max_{s \neq j}\{TIME_2(send\_end^j_{js})(k_1)\}\}$$

$$\rightarrow [(TIME_1(ack^r_{js})(k_2) \geq TIME_2(execute_j)(k_1))$$

$$\wedge(TIME_1(ack^r_{js})(k_2) \geq TIME_2(update^j_s)(k_1))] \qquad (7)$$

$$\rightarrow TIME_1(ack^r_{js})(k_2) \geq TIME_2(u_j)(k_1),$$

$$TIME_1(execute_r)(k_2) \geq TIME_1(ack^r_{js})(k_2)$$

$$\rightarrow TIME_1(execute_r)(k_2) \geq TIME_2(u_j)(k_1),$$

But,

$$TIME_1(update_s^r)(k_2) \geq TIME_2(ack_{js}^r)(k_2), \; s \neq r, \; s \neq j$$

and

$$TIME_1(update_j^r)(k_2) \geq TIME_2(ack_{js}^r)(k_2).$$

This gives

$$TIME_1(u_r)(k_2) \geq TIME_2(ack_{js}^r)(k_2)$$

$$\geq TIME_2(u_j)(k_1).$$

$$\rightarrow \quad TIME_1\left(\sum u_i\right)(k-1) \geq TIME_2\left(\sum u_i\right)(k)$$

This contradicts the property that $TIME_1$ is an increasing function. Hence the lemma is proved.

<u>Lemma 2</u>. The storage processor for site i processes T_j iff processing of T_1, T_2, ..., T_{j-1} are completed. That is, both u_i and $\sum u_i$ are single-occurrent events.

<u>Proof</u>. From [H3],

$$\forall j \neq i, \; send\_end_{ij}^i \ll execute_i$$

$$\rightarrow \quad TIME_1(send\_end_{ij}^i) \geq TIME_2(execute_i)$$

$$\rightarrow \quad TIME_1(send\_end_{ij}^i + 1) \geq TIME_2(execute_i + 1)$$

$$\rightarrow \quad \max_{j \neq i}\{TIME_1(send\_end_{ij}^i + 1)\} \geq TIME_2(execute_i + 1).$$

From [H5] and [H6]

$$get\_end_{jk}^i \ll update_j^i, \; \forall k \neq j, \; \forall j \neq i.$$

$$\rightarrow \quad TIME_1(get\_end_{jk}^i + 1) \geq TIME_2(update_j^i + 1)$$

$$\rightarrow \quad TIME_1(get\_end_{ji}^i + 1) \geq TIME_2(update_j^i + 1), \; j \neq i$$

$$\rightarrow \quad \max_{j \neq i}\{TIME_1(get\_end_{ji}^i + 1)\} \geq \max_{j \neq i}\{TIME_2(update_j^i + 1)\}.$$

From (1),

$$\forall j \neq i,$$

$$TIME_1(send_{ij}) \geq \max_{j \neq i}\{TIME_2(get\_end_{ji}^i + 1), \; TIME_2(send\_end_{ij}^i + 1)\}$$

$$\geq max\{TIME_2(execute_i + 1), \max_{j \neq i}\{TIME_2(update_j^i + 1)\}\}$$

$$\geq TIME_2(u_i + 1)$$

$$\rightarrow send_{ij} \ll u_i + 1$$

But

$$execute_i \ll send_{ij}$$

and

$$update_j^i \ll send_{ij}, \ j \neq i$$

imply that

$$u_i \ll send_{ij}.$$

Hence,

$$u_i \ll u_i + 1$$

which proves that u_i is single-occurrent.

Next, we prove that $\sum u_i$ is a single-occurrent event; that is,

$$TIME_1(\sum u_i)(k) \geq TIME_2(\sum u_i)(k-1), \ k \geq 1.$$

Let the k-th occurrence of $\sum u_i$ be k_1-th occurrence of u_j for some j and $(k-1)$-st occurrence of $\sum u_i$ be the k_2-th occurrence of u_r for some r. It is known from Lemma 1 that the transactions are executed in the decreasing order of their priority. So, from (4),

$$\forall s, \ TIME_1(ack_{rs}^j)(k_1) \geq$$

$$\max\{\max_{s \neq r}\{TIME_2(get\_end_{sr}^r)(k_2)\}, \ \max_{s \neq r}\{TIME_2(send\_end_{rs}^r)(k_2)\}\}$$

$$\rightarrow \ TIME_1(ack_{rs}^j)(k_1) \geq TIME_2(execute_r)(k_2)$$

and

$$TIME_1(ack_{rs}^j)(k_1) \geq TIME_2(update_s^r)(k_2), \ r \neq s$$

$$\rightarrow \ TIME_1(ack_{rs}^j)(k_1) \geq TIME_2(u_r)(k_2)$$

Since

$$TIME_1(update_s^j)(k_1) \geq TIME_2(ack_{rs}^j)(k_1),$$

$$TIME_1(execute_j)(k_1) \geq TIME_2(ack_{rj}^j)(k_1)$$

and from (6),

$$TIME_1(update_r^j)(k_1) \geq TIME_2(ack_{rs}^j)(k_1),$$

it follows that

$$min\{TIME_1(execute_j)(k_1),\ TIME_1(update_r^j)(k_1)\}$$

$$\geq\ max\{TIME_2(ack_{rj}^j)(k_1),\ TIME_2(ack_{rs}^j)(k_1)\}.$$

Hence

$$TIME_1(u_j)(k_1)\ \geq\ TIME_2(u_r)(k_2).$$

That is, $\sum u_i$ is single occurrent.
Finally, we prove that the algorithm specification is correct; that is, it meets the problem specification.

Proof of Mutual Consistency

Lemma 1 and Lemma 2 imply that transactions are executed in the order of their priority. Moreover, they prove that the execution and update corresponding to one transaction is done before the execution and update of another one starts. So, if at time $t > 0$ we have

$$\begin{aligned}
COUNT_1(\sum execute_i)(t)\ &=\ COUNT_2(\sum execute_i)(t)\\
&=\ COUNT_1(\sum_{i\neq j} update_j^i\ +\ execute_j)(t)\\
&=\ COUNT_2(\sum_{i\neq j} update_j^i\ +\ execute_j)(t)\ =\ k
\end{aligned}$$

then $COUNT_1(\sum u_i)(t)\ =\ COUNT_2(\sum u_i)(t)\ =\ k$.

Hence by Lemma 2,

$$COUNT_1(\sum u_i)\ \circ\ LAST_1(ASSIGN(v_j^1))\ =$$

$$COUNT_1(\sum u_i)\ \circ\ LAST_1(ASSIGN(v_j^2))\ =$$

$$...\ =\ COUNT_1(\sum u_i)\ \circ\ LAST_1(ASSIGN(v_j^n))\ =$$

$$=\ k',\ k' \leq k.$$

Hence $COUNT_2(ASSIGN(v_j^s))(t)\ =\ k',\ \forall s.$
$\rightarrow\ VALUE(v_j^s)\ \circ\ COUNT_2(ASSIGN(v_j^s))(t)\ =\ VALUE(v_j^s)(k'),\ \forall s.$

That is, $T_{k'}$ is the last transaction that changed the value of v_j at all sites. This proves the claim that for every variable v_j,

$$VALUE(v_j^1)(k')\ =\ VALUE(v_j^2)(k')\ =\ VALUE(v_j^n)(k').$$

Proof of Serializability

Lemma 2 proves this.

Proof of Starvation Freeness

We prove that

$$\forall i, k, \ TIME_2(submit_i)(k) \ < \ \infty \ \rightarrow \ TIME_1(u_i)(k) \ < \ \infty$$

Let $TIME_2(submit_i)(k) \ = \ t$.

$$\rightarrow \ LCOUNT_2(\sum submit_i)(t) \ = \ s \ < \ \infty,$$

since only finite number of occurrences happen in a finite interval of time.

$$\rightarrow \ TIME_1(\sum u_i)(s') \ = \ TIME_1(u_i)(k), \ s' \ \leq \ s.$$

Since $\forall r > 0, \ dur(\sum u_i)(r)$ is finite,

$$TIME_1(\sum u_i)(s') \ \leq \ TIME_2(submit_i)(k) \ + \ \sum_{r=1}^{s-1} dur(\sum u_i)(r) \ + \ st',$$

where $t' = 2\times$ (maximum communication delay between sites).
Hence $TIME_1(u_i)(k) \ < \ \infty$.

4   Concluding Remarks

In [JcW83] Clifford and Warren have listed several problems for "future research" and two of them are: (1) incorporating temporal semantics in functional model of data and (2) conceiving time as not as *moments* but as *intervals*. This paper is a contribution to solving both these problems. Time sequence modeled as infinite sequences of intervals capture duration, continuity, periodicity, ordering, and if necessary non-termination. It is well known that state-oriented data models have difficulty in capturing integrity constraints based on the ordering of event sequences. This functional model can capture such constraints with both rigor and clarity.

Previous attempts for providing temporal semantics in databases have concentrated on the representational and implementation oriented operational details. In this paper, we have lifted the abstraction one level up where implementation details are not part of study. At the same time, the formalism has provided a small number of primitive functions and the ability to define application dependent functions based on these with function composition and conditionals as operators. The major advantage of this approach is the ease with which an implementation based on current functional programming software [5, 6, 7, 9] can be derived.

References

[1] V.S. Alagar and G.Ramanathan, "Formal Environment and Tools Description for the Analysis of Real-Time Concurrent Systems", *Workshop on the Specification and Verification of Concurrent Systems*, 1988. Also in BCS-FACS *Workshop Series*, 1, 1989.

[2] V.S. Alagar and G. Ramanathan, "Functional Specification and Proof of Correctness of Time Dependent Behavior of Reactive Systems", *Formal Aspects of Computing*, 3, 1991, 253-283.

[3] J.A. Bubenko, Jr., "Information Modeling in the Context of System Development", *IFIP Congress* Invited Paper, Tokyo, 1980, 395-411.

[4] J. Clifford and D.S. Warren, "Formal Semantics for Time in Databases", *ACM Transactions on Database Systems*, 8, 1983, 214-254.

[5] P. Henderson, "Functional Programming, Formal Specification and Rapid Prototyping", *IEEE Transactions on Software Engineering*, SE-12, 1986, 241-250.

[6] M. Jackson, **System Development**, Englewood Cliffs, NJ:Prentice Hall, 1983.

[7] C.B. Jones, **Software Development: A Rigorous Approach**, Englewood Cliffs, NJ:Prentice Hall, 1980.

[8] B. Lundberg, "An Axiomatization of Events", *BIT*, 22, 1982, 291-299.

[9] L. Orman, "Functional Development of Database Applications", *IEEE Transactions on Software Engineering*, 14, 1988, 1280-1292.

[10] G. Ramanathan and V.S. Alagar, "Specification of Real-Time Distributed Database Systems", *Proceedings of the Int.Conference on Computer Systems and Software Engineering*, 1992, 101-106.

[11] L.E. Sanchis, "Data Types as Lattices: Retractions, Closures and Projection", *RAIRO Theoretical Computer Science*, 11, 329-344, 1977.

[12] A. Segev and A. Shoshani, "Logical Modeling of Temporal Data", *ACM SIGMOD Conference Record*, 1987.

[13] A.U. Tansel, "Adding Time Dimension to Relational Model and Extending Relational Algebra", *Information Systems*, 13, 1986.

Using VDM within an Object-Oriented Framework

Lynn S. Marshall
Linda Simon
Bell-Northern Research Ltd.
P. O. Box 3511 Station C
Ottawa, Ontario, Canada K1Y 4H7
ph: (613) 765-4856
fax: (613) 763-4222
e-mail: lynnmar@bnr.ca

Abstract

The formal specification of OSI network management protocols presents a challenge as the structure and semantics of the information to be communicated across an interoperable interface is modelled as managed objects. It is necessary to integrate formal techniques into the specific object-oriented framework developed by the ISO management standards.

This paper examines the suitability of VDM as a candidate formal description method for use in specifying the behaviour of OSI managed objects. To investigate the suitability of incorporating object-oriented concepts such as inheritance within VDM, a case study of a simplified Log managed object class is examined.

1 Introduction

1.1 Background

The International Organization for Standardization (ISO) is developing a set of standards for managing Open Systems Interconnection (OSI)-based networks. These standards have adopted an object-oriented approach to the specification of management information as seen in protocol exchanges by open systems involved in management activities.

Within this approach, logical and physical resources (e.g. protocol state machines, modems, applications) to be managed by a remote system across a standardized interface are modelled as *managed objects*. Managed objects that share the same definition are instances of the same *managed object class*. A managed object class is defined in terms of: the *attributes* visible at the managed object boundary, the *operations* that may be applied to the managed object, the *notifications* which are emitted by the managed object when some event occurs, and the *behaviour* exhibited by the managed object.

Inheritance is an important concept of the OSI management object model. It provides a mechanism for incremental or relative specification, whereby a new managed object class (a subclass) may be derived from one or more existing managed object class(es) (referred to as its superclasses). The OSI management object model [7] defines a set of inheritance rules that ensure that every instance of a subclass is compatible with its superclass.

1.2   Motivation

The managed object class definitions specify the structure and semantics of the information which is conveyed in protocol exchanges between different systems, and hence represents standards which are the basis for the implementation of compatible OSI systems. It is therefore essential that these specifications be unambiguous, complete and concise.

A notation for describing the syntactical aspects of OSI managed objects has been developed [8], however, it does not provide a formal framework for defining the behaviour of managed objects.

The objective of this paper is to examine the suitability of VDM as a candidate specification technique for formally specifying the behaviour of managed objects. It is motivated, in part, by some earlier work reported in [12] which proposed defining managed object behaviour in terms of pre-conditions and post-conditions written in English. The VDM concepts of state and operations can be intuitively mapped onto the managed object concepts of attributes, and operations and notifications, respectively. Furthermore, work on interpreting the language Z in an object-oriented framework [3, 9] suggest that object-oriented concepts including inheritance can be readily accommodated. Bear [2] has done some work on structuring VDM specifications, but he has not looked at inheritance.

To investigate the suitability of VDM as a candidate specification technique we take as a case study the Log managed object class, which is based on a simplified version of the OSI managed object class described in natural language in [5].

The remainder of this paper is organized as follows. An informal description of the Log managed object is given in Section 2. In Section 3, we discuss our experiences in developing a VDM formal description of the Log and a subclass of the Log. Section 4 provides an overview of the VDM specification itself. A discussion of the analysis of the specification can be found in Section 5. Section 6 presents our conclusions.

2   An Informal Description of the Log Managed Object

Here we present a simplification of the ISO Log control function. The Log managed object class is a conceptual repository for storing information about various events that have occurred. It also provides the ability for an external system to control which information is selected for logging.

Notifications emitted by managed objects within the local system are received by the conceptual log pre-processing function (see Figure 1). This function forms a *potential log record*.

Conceptually, a potential log record is distributed to all Logs that are contained within the local system. Each Log contains a *discriminator construct* attribute which specifies the characteristics a potential log record must have in order to be selected for logging.

Interoperable
Interface

Managed System

Managing
System 1

Operations

Log
Rec

Log
Rec

Log
1

Man-
aged
Object

Notification

Managing
System 2

Operations

Potential
Log
Record

Log
Pre-
Processing
Function

Log
Rec

Log
Rec

Log
n

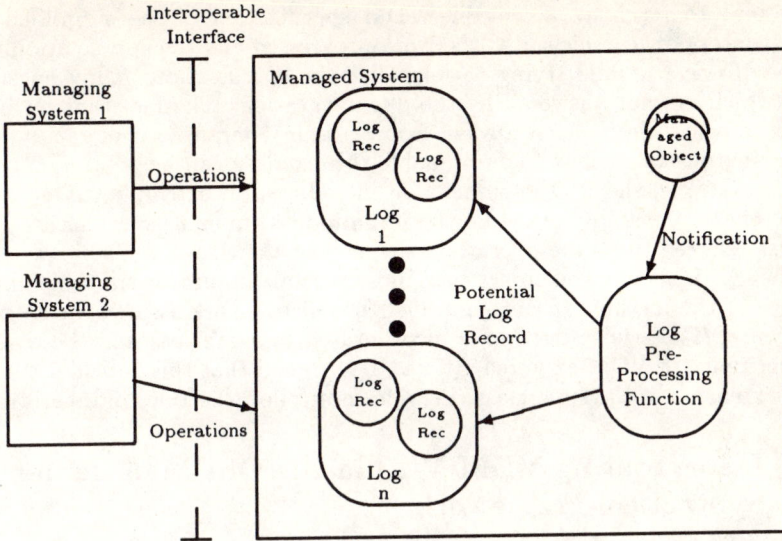

Figure 1: Log Conceptual Model

If the discriminator construct evaluates to true for a potential log record and the Log is in the *unlocked* administrative state and in the *enabled* operational state, then a new log record will be created. Here we assume that the log has infinite capacity. This new log record will contain all of the information contained in the potential log record supplemented with additional information generated as part of the logging process (e.g. log record identifiers and logging time).

With the exception of the operational state (which represents the operational capability of a Log to perform its function), all attributes of a Log may be modified by a managing system by sending a *set* operation to that Log. The values of all attributes of a Log may be retrieved by sending a *get* operation to that Log.

A *create* operation may be sent by a managing system to request that the managed system create a Log managed object, thereby requesting new or additional logs be defined. A *delete* operation may be sent by a managing system to request the deletion of a Log (and its contained log records).

A Log generates an *attribute change* notification whenever one of its attributes is changed. An *object creation* notification and an *object deletion* notification are emitted by a Log when that Log is created and deleted, respectively.

3 Developing the VDM Specification

3.1 Issues Arising from the Informal Specification

Writing the formal description starting from an informal specification [5] turned out to be more difficult than originally expected. It required several iterations through reading the documentation, writing a formal description, and discussion, to reach an acceptable VDM specification of the simplified log. Many concepts became clear as the work progressed and the specification took shape. However, while trying to formalize the specification, many questions arose which are not answered by the documentation. The fact that formalizing an informal description always requires many iterations and raises many interesting questions shows how valuable this exercise can be.

For example, the ISO document [5] introduces an attribute, usage state, which reflects the ability of the Log to accommodate more *users*. This attribute is never referred to by the operations defined for the class.

The ISO Log managed object class includes a maximum log size which limits the size of the log file. In our simplified specification we assume the Log can be infinite. The size restriction is incorporated in a subclass and the concept of inheritance in VDM explored. It was determined that this subclass is not a strict extension of the superclass (i.e. does not follow the rules of inheritance).

3.2 Incorporating VDM Within the OSI Management Syntactical Framework

A primary objective was to use VDM within the syntactical framework provided by the standardized OSI Management *template* notation [8]. The *managed object class* (MOC) template specified in [8] forms the basis of the formal definition of a managed object. This template consists of a number of elements, one of which is the behaviour definition.

The behaviour definition may be documented by use of natural language text or by the use of formal description techniques; although, in practice only natural language has so far been used. Here, we propose that VDM be used for formally describing the behaviour of managed objects.

Data types referred to in the other elements of the MOC template are specified using Abstract Syntax Notation One (ASN.1) [6].[1] Since VDM specifications include both a data typing and a behavioural component, an issue concerns how to tie the ASN.1 data typing descriptions to formal VDM behaviour specifications. The specifications presented in this paper are given entirely in VDM. The approach taken was to manually translate the ASN.1 specifications to VDM types. Potential areas of future study include the automatic translation of ASN.1 to VDM and the ability to reference directly ASN.1 data descriptions within a VDM behavioural specification.

Syntactically, inheritance is achieved by including the names of the superclass(es) in the *derived from* element of the MOC template. This element is presumed to automatically import all characteristics from the superclass definition(s). Therefore, only the extended characteristics introduced by the subclass are documented in the other elements of the MOC template. A set of rules is specified in [8] for combining the inherited characteristics with those characteristics explicitly declared in the other elements of the MOC template.

Our objective is to specify only the extended behaviour in the MOC template and to enhance [8] to specify the rules for combining this VDM specification with the VDM specifications documented in the superclass(es) template.

---

[1]ASN.1 is a notation for the description of data structures which was developed by ISO for the abstract specification of data types and values in OSI application protocols. ASN.1 is used to express the abstract syntax of the data types and values associated with managed object characteristics that are conveyed in OSI management protocols.

The rules for providing extensible behavioural specifications are discussed in the following subsection.

3.3 The VDM Style Appropriate for Inheritance

One of the key features of the ISO Standards for OSI Managed Objects is the notion of inheritance. While VDM is not an object-oriented formal method, it is possible to adopt a VDM style appropriate for Managed Objects.

VDM provides the notion of *satisfaction* [10]. It provides a framework for showing that a concrete formal description is a valid implementation of (i.e. *satisfies*) a more abstract description. The *implementation* (concrete description) must meet the *specification* (abstract description) but may be defined on a larger domain and may be more determined (i.e. less non-deterministic). Thus for each operation the concrete pre-condition may be weaker and the post-condition may be stronger.

This is exactly the concept necessary for inheritance in managed object terminology. A subclass must exhibit all the behaviour of the superclass, but may introduce additional (consistent) behaviour.

Thus a subclass specification of a managed object is derived from a superclass description by weakening the pre-condition and strengthening the post-condition of the applicable operations.

When expressing a subclass specification, only the additional information need be given. This will avoid repetition, aid in understandability, and tie in with the current OSI management template format. Thus a subclass is assumed to inherit the operations exactly as stated in the superclass unless an extension is given. If an extension is given, the new pre-condition is "or"ed ($\vee$) with the superclass pre-condition, and the new post-condition is "and"ed ($\wedge$) with the superclass post-condition. This will guarantee that the inheritance rules are met.

Taking the original log specification and attempting to derive a subclass for it, again required several iterations. To extend the behaviour of an operation by only weakening the pre-condition and strengthening the post-condition requires that the superclass operation be in an appropriate form. While this research has not yet disclosed exactly what this appropriate form might be, some conclusions can be drawn.

The split between the pre- and the post-condition is very important. Generally it seems to be best to put as much information in the pre-condition as possible. This seems to make extension go more smoothly. If the operation has a pre-condition of **true** (e.g. returns a flag indicating whether or not the operation was successful), it may be necessary to introduce a new operation which does have a pre-condition. The original operation may *quote* (VDM's equivalent to subroutine call) this new operation and the new operation will be extensible. It is also important that the post-condition be extensible. The **others** clause of the **case** construct and the **else** clause of the **if** construct should be avoided.

A further consideration is necessary when extending a managed object. The OSI management standard [7] allows subclasses to define new attributes as needed. This capability could be provided in VDM by leaving part of the top level state undefined and adding the necessary definitions in the subclasses.

This is not very elegant and we have adopted the RAISE [4] approach[2], which allows extra fields to be added later with no mention of them in the original description.

In addition to adding new data types to a subclass, we may also add additional parameters to an operation. ISO management standards allow "holes" to be left in operation and notification signature definitions which can be filled in by the subclasses. An extendable definition is indicated in ASN.1 by providing a parameter of the "ANY DEFINED BY" type. To avoid the need for signature changes in the VDM specification it is best to structure the signature of such operations in such a way that the parameters are a set of parameter type and value pairs, instead of a list of parameter values whose type is determined by the signature. The function describing the valid types of the parameter set can be extended in the subclass definition.

3.4 Notifications and Triggers

In VDM we model both managed object operations and managed object notifications by VDM operations. An operation occurs if it is requested and the pre-condition is true (i.e. the pre-condition is a guard). A notification occurs whenever the pre-condition becomes true (i.e. the pre-condition is a trigger). To indicate a notification in the VDM specification we call the pre-condition a trigger. Whenever necessary this special operation will fire and issue a notification.

4 Overview of the VDM Specification

Only excerpts from the specification will be presented here. The authors will be pleased to provide copies of the complete specification upon request. Mario Wolczko's VDM LaTeX Macros [14] and the SpecBox Tool [1] were used to prepare the VDM specification.

4.1 Architecture

Since the *create* and *delete* operations have cross-object constraints, it is not possible to model a single Log in isolation. The specification is presented in two levels, or modules. The upper *Coordinator* level takes care of the creations and deletions, while most of the functionality is in the lower *Log* level.

The Coordinator level receives a request from outside the system, performs various checks, and then invokes (or, in VDM terminology, *quotes*) the corresponding Log level operation for the chosen Log(s).

4.2 Type and State Definitions

The Coordinator level state is:

---

[2]RAISE stands for Rigorous Approach to Industrial Software Engineering. The RAISE Specification Language (RSL) supports model-oriented, algebraic, explicit, axiomatic, applicative, imperative, and concurrent styles. The RAISE Method is based on the stepwise refinement paradigm.

```
compose Logs of
      loginfo : Loginfo
end
```

Log information is a map from Log id to Log.

$Loginfo = $ map $Log\text{-}id$ to Log

Log is defined in the Log module. The Log state contains the log information, the log records, and possibly an outgoing notification message.

```
compose Log of
          info : Log-info
        logrecs : Log-records
         notif : [Not-msg]
end
```

Log information consists of: the log id, the construct describing the conditions that must be met for a message to be passed on, the administrative state (controlled by a manager), and the operational state (controlled by the local system). Other fields may be added later, as indicated by the keywords at least. This idea is inspired by RAISE (see section 3.3). We could express this concept in standard VDM, but this notation is more elegant and concise.

```
compose Log-info of at least
           log-id : Log-id
        disc-const : Discriminator-construct
       admin-state : Administrative-state
          op-state : Operational-state
end
```

The subclass definition then expands the Log information to include the maximum log size as follows:

```
extend Log-info with
      maxrecs : Maxnum
end
```

4.3   Coordinator Behaviour

CREATE-LOGS creates a new log and invokes CREATE-LOG to trigger the OBJECTCREATION notification. The attributes given can include log id, discriminator construct, and administrative state. Those not supplied are given default values. Since *newlog* may have extra fields added in the future, we avoid the use of the *mk-* function.

$CREATE\text{-}LOGS$ $(attrs: Attr\text{-}info)$

ext wr $loginfo$: $Loginfo$

pre dom $attrs \subseteq \{LOGIDTYPE, DISCCONSTTYPE,$
        $\overline{ADMINSTATE}TYPE\} \land$
    $(LOGIDTYPE \in$ dom $attrs \Rightarrow$
        $attrs(LOGIDTYPE) \notin$ dom $loginfo)$

post let $newlog \in Log\text{-}info$ in
$\quad newlog.log\text{-}id =$ if $LOGIDTYPE \in$ dom $attrs$
$\qquad\qquad\qquad$ then $attrs(LOGIDTYPE)$
$\qquad\qquad\qquad$ else $picklogid()$
$\wedge\, newlog.disc\text{-}const =$ if $DISCCONSTTYPE \in$ dom $attrs$
$\qquad\qquad\qquad$ then $attrs(DISCCONSTTYPE)$
$\qquad\qquad\qquad$ else $EMPTY$
$\wedge\, newlog.admin\text{-}state =$ if $ADMINSTATETYPE \in$ dom $attrs$
$\qquad\qquad\qquad$ then $attrs(ADMINSTATETYPE)$
$\qquad\qquad\qquad$ else $UNLOCKED$
$\wedge\, newlog.op\text{-}state = getopstate()\, \wedge$
$\exists log \in Log \cdot post\text{-}CREATE\text{-}LOG(mk\text{-}Log(newlog, \{\,\}, nil), log)\, \wedge$
$\qquad loginfo = \overline{loginfo} \dagger \{newlog.log\text{-}id \mapsto log\}$

When extending this operation in the subclass we omit the signature since it is unchanged. orpre indicates the additional pre-condition which is "or"ed with the original, and andpost indicates the additional post-condition to be "and"ed with the original. Now we can also refer to the maxrecs field of *Log-info*. CREATE-LOGS now possibly has a new attribute: the maximum size information.

CREATE-LOGS
orpre dom $attrs \subseteq \{LOGIDTYPE, DISCCONSTTYPE,$
$\qquad ADMINSTATETYPE, MAXSIZE\}\, \wedge$
$\quad (LOGIDTYPE \in$ dom $attrs$
$\qquad\qquad \Rightarrow\ attrs(LOGIDTYPE) \notin$ dom $loginfo)$
andpost $newlog.maxrecs =$ if $MAXSIZE \in$ dom $attrs$
$\qquad\qquad\qquad$ then $attrs(MAXSIZE)$
$\qquad\qquad\qquad$ else 0

Whenever a Log needs to produce a notification, NOTIFICATION-LOGS will fire.

NOTIFICATION-LOGS $\quad n: Not\text{-}msg$
ext wr $loginfo\ :\ Loginfo$
trigger $\exists lid \in$ dom $loginfo \cdot pre\text{-}NOTIFICATION\text{-}LOG(loginfo(lid))$

post let $lid \in$ dom $\overline{loginfo} \cdot$
$\qquad pre\text{-}NOTIFICATION\text{-}LOG(\overline{loginfo}(lid))$ in
$\quad \exists lid \in Log \cdot post\text{-}NOTIFICATION\text{-}LOG(\overline{loginfo}(lid), log, n)\, \wedge$
$\qquad loginfo = \overline{loginfo} \dagger \{lid \mapsto log\}$

4.4 Log Behaviour

We run into a problem when extending ADD-RECORD which adds a potential log record to the log if the necessary conditions are met. Now that there is a maximum size, the behaviour actually changes and cannot be extended within the inheritance framework. The original operation is:

ORIG-ADD-RECORD $\quad (plr: Pot\text{-}log\text{-}record)$
ext wr $logrecs\ :\ Log\text{-}records$
$\quad$ rd $info\quad\ :\ Log\text{-}info$

post if $shouldlog(plr, info)$
    then $\exists t \in Time \cdot gettime(t) \wedge$
                $\exists rid \in Log\text{-}record\text{-}id \cdot pickrecid(info.log\text{-}id, rid) \wedge$
$$logrecs = \overleftarrow{logrecs} \dagger \{rid \mapsto mk\text{-}Log\text{-}record(t, plr)\}$$
    else $logrecs = \overleftarrow{logrecs}$

A new operation must be added to describe the subclass: FINITE-ADD-RECORD now must check that the maximum size has not been reached.

$FINITE\text{-}ADD\text{-}RECORD$ $(plr: Pot\text{-}log\text{-}record)$

ext wr $logrecs$: $Log\text{-}records$
    rd $info$: $Log\text{-}info$

post if $info.maxrecs = 0 \vee info.maxrecs > \text{card dom } \overleftarrow{logrecs}$
    then $post\text{-}ORIG\text{-}ADD\text{-}RECORD(plr, \overleftarrow{logrecs}, info, logrecs)$
    else $logrecs = \overleftarrow{logrecs}$

5 Analysis

Having completed the specification we can use the formal description to determine if certain properties hold. For example:

1. Will a locked Log always respond to an unlock request?

2. Is it true that a Log can only log records it receives (i.e. it cannot invent records itself)?

The answer to these two questions (based on our model of the system) is yes. Examining the appropriate VDM operations allows us to easily answer questions such as these.

6 Conclusions

The perspective of our work differs from [2, 3] in that our primary goal was not to propose extensions to an existing specification language (in our case VDM), to accommodate *object-orientation*. Rather, our main objective was to investigate whether an existing formal specification language could be used within a specific object-oriented framework developed for OSI management.

Based on the work presented in this paper and that in a similar paper examining the ISO Discriminator managed object [13], we conclude that VDM is well-suited for specifying the behaviour of OSI managed objects and can be used within the existing OSI management syntactical framework with minimal extensions. The proposed extensions to VDM are:

1. the use of the trigger keyword in VDM operation pre-conditions for describing the behaviour of OSI managed object *notifications*.

2. the use of special keywords and notation for explicitly identifying extensions to VDM operation and type definitions to accommodate the OSI management concept of inheritance.

Areas for future study identified in this paper include:

1. a formal treatment of the relationship between ASN.1 and VDM,

2. the development of general guidelines for structuring pre- and post-conditions to facilitate extensibility,

3. formalizing the relationships among managed objects [11].

Our experiences reinforce the benefits of using formal specification techniques in standards development. In producing a formal description of the ISO Log managed object from an existing informal one, a number of ambiguities in the latter were identified and proposed changes to clarify these ambiguities were submitted to the appropriate ISO standards committee. Furthermore, given the formal specification we were able to prove a number of properties of the Log managed object, thus providing increased confidence in the correctness of the standard.

References

[1] Adelard. *SpecBox User Manual*. Coborn House Business Centre, London, UK, 1991.

[2] Bear, S. *Structuring for the VDM Specification Language*. Proceedings VDM'88: VDM—The Way Ahead. Eds. R. Bloomfield, L. Marshall, R. Jones. Lecture Notes in Computer Science 328, September 1988, pp. 2–25.

[3] Duke, R., Rose., G. and Lee, A. *Object-Oriented Protocol Specification*. Proceedings of the Tenth International IFIP WG6.1 Symposium on Protocol Specification, Testing and Verification, 12–15 June 1990, Ottawa, Canada, pp. 323–339.

[4] Eriksen, Kirsten E., and Prehn, Søren. RAISE Overview. Computer Resources International A/S, 1991.

[5] ISO. Systems Management—Part 6: Log Control Function. (ISO/IEC JTC1/SC21 N-4862), Output of the editing meeting held in Kyoto, Japan, May 1990.

[6] ISO. Final Text of IS 8824, Information Technology—Open Systems Interconnection—Specification of Abstract Syntax Notation One (ASN.1). (ISO/IEC JTC1/SC21 N-4720), April 1990.

[7] ISO. Structure of Management Information Part 1—Management Information Model. (ISO/IEC JTC1/SC21 N-5252), Output of the editing meeting held in Paris, France, January 1990.

[8] ISO. Structure of Management Information Part 4—Guidelines for the Definition of Managed Objects. (ISO/IEC JTC1/SC21 N-4852), Output of the May 1990, Editing Meeting held in Kyoto, Japan.

[9] ISO. Architectural Semantics, Specification Techniques and Formalisms, Working Document. (ISO/IEC JTC1/SC21 N-4887), 1990.

[10] Jones, C. B. Systematic Software Development Using VDM. Prentice-Hall International, Second Edition, 1990.

[11] Marshall, L. S. and Simon, L. *Using VDM to Specify Managed Object Relationships*. To appear in: Proceedings of the IFIP TC6/WG6.1 Fifth International Conference on Formal Description Techniques (FORTE'92), Perros-Guirec, France, 13–16 October 1992, Eds. M. Diaz and R. Groz, Elsevier.

[12] OSI/Network Management Forum. *J-Team Technical Report on Modelling Principles for Managed Objects*. Issue 1, Draft 8, December 17, 1990.

[13] Simon, L. and Marshall, L. S. *Using VDM to Specify Managed Objects*. Proceedings of the IFIP TC6/WG6.1 Fourth International Conference on Formal Description Techniques (FORTE'91), Sydney, Australia, 19–22 November 1991, Eds. G. A. Rose and K. R. Parker, Elsevier.

[14] Wolczko, Mario. *Typesetting VDM with LaTeX*. Department of Computer Science, University of Manchester, UK, March 1988.

Software Engineering Environments – what do we want?

Pankaj Goyal

U S WEST Advanced Technologies, Inc.,

Boulder, Colorado, U.S.A.

Abstract

Computer Aided Software Engineering (CASE) caught the imagination of the software industry by suggesting that the automation – so successfully performed by software to various tasks – can be applied to the software development tasks themselves. This is nothing new. From the inception of the software industry, tools have been designed to help automate software development tasks. Over the past decade, the importance of CASE has been recognized and tools have been developed that help in many software development tasks. Inspite of these developments, the so called "software crisis" gets on becoming worse, and the penetration of CASE has been abysmally low.

1 Current Situation

This section presents a brief overview of the Computer-Aided Software Engineering (CASE) and Software Development Environments (SDE). Software development may be characterized in terms of the:

- process used in the development; these include the different software development life cycle (SDLC) models, such as the "waterfall" [1], "spiral" [2], "evolutionary" [3,4], etc.

- methodology used; these include the traditional structured analysis and design, Information Engineering, etc.

- tools used to support both the process and the methodology.

A number of researchers have measured the effort expended in various efforts; [5] contains details of many such results. It is clear that there is a large variation in the distribution of effort between large-, medium- and small- scale software development. For example, [5] shows that the effort expended in the coding phase ranges from over 65% for small scale software development to less than 12% for large scale development. The cost of defect removal, as expected, is significantly higher for large scale development than for small scale development.

The "waterfall" model of software development is a sequential set of activities and, ideally, requires the completion of the preceding phase before proceeding to the next. In the evolutionary development approach, on the other hand, it is not necessary that the requirements be complete. It is possible to start implementation of the first version of the product without the need to fully specify the requirements for the succeeding versions of the product. In addition to the development process, user requirements for extendibility, flexibility and openness (for connectivity to other systems/applications) impose constraints on the choice of application architectures.

In a typical organization the effort needed to maintain existing code consumes about 60% or more of the total software development and maintenance budget/effort. The continued enhancement of systems over time destroys any structure that might have been designed into the original applications. The process for maintenance and enhancement (M&E), typically, is different from new development processes: after the initial definition of the requirements for the change, the design and code changes are identified and their impact assessed, and then the code is modified. The existing design and other documents need to be reconciled with the coding changes made.

It is therefore apparent that there is a wide variability in the needs of the software development community. This variety of development needs defines certain requirements for the development tools and environments. The ideal environment should be flexible and extensible, allowing users to add, replace or remove tools in the environment. The tools in the environment would support the different aspects of work performed and, ideally, be independent of the methodology used during development. The tasks supported by the environment are related to the development process and is not just a set of tools supporting a set of discrete individual tasks.

Let us now examine the nature and characteristics of two different approaches to CASE:

- Integrated CASE (I-CASE): consists of a collection of tools that support the various phases of the life cycle, such as, analysis and design. The tools are integrated via a shared repository that allows the already developed models to be shared by the different tools (Figure 1).

- "Mix-n-Match" (also called the Open tool box approach): consists of various tools. These tools may have been integrated via some tool integration framework [6,7] (Figure 3).

1.1 The Evolution of Software Development and Software Development Environments

Currently we are nearing the completion of a cycle in the evolution of software development. The original software development life cycle (more accurately a sequence of steps rather than a cycle) concentrated on the upper level activities of analysis and design. A lot of stress was placed on understanding the business models and how the new software application would fit in the existing business environment. In the 1960's the emphasis shifted to programming and was followed by an explosion in programming languages. By the late 1960's, coding completely dominated the software development life cycle. This period also marked the acceptance o programming as a profession. The emergence of ever complex software applications in the 70's resulted in increasing emphasis on testing activities. Maintenance also became a fact of life. It actually became a major activity by the late 70's, with bug fixing being only a minor part of its activity, and yet the development life cycle did not change to accommodate this fact. The life of software, by then, had begun to exceed the life of the machines on which they were developed and the programmers who originally developed it – software had a life of its own, it entered an organization but never left. Large teams of programmers became increasingly assigned to maintenance activities. It was soon realized that a lack of proper analysis and design documentation hampered maintenance.

Every stage of the evolution in software development has been accompanied by a spurt in tool support. In the 60's and 70's a large number of Programming languages were developed, followed by various structured development methodologies. CASE followed with its emphasis on up stream activities and tool support. The shift away from coding as a major activity had begun. Table 1, gives data from some typical software development projects [5] and it is immediately apparent why coding is not the important activity, even in new development; high levels of software quality and productivity improvements can only result from some of the other activities and these also impact upon the maintenance costs. The implications of the data given in Table 1 are very important. Any attempt to improve productivity by a degree of magnitude, by the adoption of a single tool, methodology, technology or process, across the spectrum of applications is bound to fail. It is necessary to select tools, methods, technologies and processes suitable for the particular application size and type. For example, coding tools and technologies (such as object technology) will have the maximum impact on small sized projects, unless they also address the issues related to the other activities.

Size (Function Points)	Management	Defect Removal	Paper Work	Coding
10	11	17	7	65
1280	14	30	26	30
40,960	18	37	33	12

Table 1: Percentage effort expended on different activities [5]

By the 1980's all major business functions in organizations had been reduced to code. Large programmer teams were busy keeping these systems running. There was very little activity that could support changes in the business environment. In the 60's and 70's rush to automate, the business processes and models had taken a back seat, making the 1980's an era of turmoil for the MIS organizations. MIS could not keep pace with the demand for changes which were being driven by the rapid changes taking place in the business environment. It dawned upon the user and development communities that the business processes and models, rather than the functional or data model of applications, should flow through and encompass the application systems, their development and life cycle. In this scheme maintenance would be the adoption of the business processes and models to the changing business needs.

This new reality will drive the next evolution of the software development cycle. We are now completing a cycle and returning back to modeling the business processes and models. The following sub-sections survey the two different approaches to software development environments.

1.2 Integrated CASE (I-CASE)

A number of vendors provide ICASE environments. In the past the tool sets in these environments have concentrated on supporting the "upper" half (analysis and design) of the development activities; this is one reason why some of these tool sets are referred to as Upper CASE.

Figure 1 shows a typical configuration. The repository allows for the sharing of already developed information and this permits a continuous work-flow between the different life-cycle phases. Some of the ICASE environments provide support for a particular methodology and limited code generation. Recently, there has been a move to integrate re-engineering tools, albeit very primitive ones.

In most I-CASE environments to-date, the tool set has been developed by a single vendor and it is very difficult, if not impossible, to add a new tool or to replace an existing tool with a more appropriate tool. So, if the environment does not include, say, a testing tool then the testing is done outside the environment, thereby loosing some of the benefits of an integrated environment. This limitation also impacts technology evolution and the ability of an organization to exploit new developments.

An organization that has a variety of development efforts may need different I-CASE solutions. This imposes additional expense for training and in some cases the need for additional different variety of hardware.

Recent research in this area has concentrated on developing Knowledge based support for the CASE environment [8]. Over the next couple of years we should expect to see some intelligent support in the CASE arena.

1.3 Mix-n-Match Approach

In this approach an independently developed collection of tools is brought together to support the development effort. Recently tool integration frameworks, an open infrastructure that enables the creation of a customizable software development environment (SDE), have become available. These SDE support a set of integrated user-defined tools. The integration framework may provide:

- a common user-interface for all tools,

- a tool invocation or message passing mechanism,

- a process integration mechanism, and

- a data and model sharing facility between tools.

There has been a growing realization for the importance of tool integration, and many vendors have begun to cooperate in an effort to develop an industry-wide integration framework. Hewlett-Packard has proposed the "toaster model" (Figure 2) and this has been adapted by a number of industry consortia as well as individual vendors, both in the US. and Europe (e.g., European Computer Manufacturer's Association).

on user interface (or presentation) aims to provide a common model
~~ ~~~~~~tion across all the tools. This aims to reduce the mental burden of
the user. As users switch between the use of tools, they continue to interact
with the tools in a similar way. Two presentation standards have emerged in
the workstation arena: OSF/Motif and OPEN LOOK (trademarks of the Open
Systems Foundation and AT&T, respectively).

1.3.2   Control (or tool invocation) Integration

This facilitates the automatic invocation of tools to support user tasks. For
example, when the user completes the editing of program code the appropriate
language compiler is invoked. Control integration is provided by such systems
as the Broadcast Message Server from Hewlett-Packard, and ToolTalk from
SunSoft.

1.3.3   Process Integration

Process integration allows the SDE to support, monitor, control and manage
a coherent development methodology. Thus, the environment can be used to
ensure compliance with some defined process and corporate defined standards.
Ideally, the environment would consist of tools to define and/or model processes and assist users in performing the tasks associated with various process
activities and roles. Process management enables subsequent task owners to
be informed whenever a task is completed. It also allows certain background
activities to be performed. For example, when a developer "checks-in" a piece
of code into the configuration management system, automatic code complexity
analysis can be performed and if and only if the complexity is less than the
defined upper limit would the code be checked-in. The same piece of code may
be checked-in after review by the manager. Similarly, the code reviewers could
be automatically handed the code for review whenever it has been marked as
being "final".

1.3.4   Data Integration

Data and/or model integration aims at sharing the data/information produced
by one tool to be made available to the other tools. This facilitates the avail-
ability of information whenever and from wherever they need it. This information has to be in the "right" form to be of use at that given instance. This
means that data produced by one tool should be manipulatable by another
tool. For example, a developer may want access to the associated functional
requirements, and when making changes to the code be able to see the affected
requirements and vice versa.

1.3.5   Current Capability

Figure 3 shows a typical "mix-n-match" environment. In this scheme the tools
from different vendors are integrated together. Ideally, the aim is to integrate the "best-in-class" tools for each development activity. New tools can be

brought into this environment fairly easily as can old tools be replaced by new ones.

When an old tool is replaced, however, most of the work already done is "lost", viz., is unavailable in the new set-up. On the positive side it is possible to evolve the environment to support special projects and new technology usage.

Sometimes "best-of-class" tools are not available on the development hardware being used. With the emergence of frameworks that allow tools to be invoked from any machine on a network, it is now possible to build an environment that consists of heterogeneous hardware. These frameworks also permit cross-development, thereby, mitigating the need for keystroke and mental retooling; the developer can continue to use the hardware of choice and be able to compile and link on any other machine on the network.

The problem of multiple user interfaces and interaction mechanisms is being addressed by some vendors defining a set of standards in these areas, for example, HP's SoftBench and IBM's SAA. Our experience suggests that these are not sufficient. Further standardization needs to take place so that users do not have to perform mental retooling whenever they move from using one tool to the other.

The "mix-n-match" approach suffers from a lack of a common repository. Many efforts have been underway to define common data models. These include PCTE [9, 10] and AD/Cycle [11], to name a couple. While there has been a lot of work and cooperation among various vendors and organizations, the adoption of these models has not taken place. Many existing tools contain local repositories. However, the lack of a common repository prevents data sharing between the tools, except for some activities (such as, edit, compile, link) and prevents a continuous work-flow.

A common shared repository needs to be supported by a "tools data integration layer" (Figure 4). The "tools data integration layer" (TDIL) provides the tool specific interface, including any needed data transformation, for tools that do not support the public interface for the shared repository; many existing tools would fall in this category.

1.4   Summary of differences

Table 2 summarizes the differences between the I-CASE and "mix-n-match" approaches. Currently both environments, typically, also suffer from a lack of good tools for planning, project management, tracking and control.

One of the key defects in both approaches is the lack of tools for process management support. The development process to be used is tailored according to project needs and available resources. The development process then needs to be managed, monitored and controlled. Process management plays a key role in effective resource management, delivery of quality to the customer on time and budget.

It is instructive to examine why software development environments have not lived up to their promise of improving productivity of software development multiple folds.

- "one shoe size fits all": As mentioned before there is a considerable diversity in the nature of applications, development process and methodologies.

	Advantages	Disadvantages
I-CASE	• Continuous work-flow • single vendor • methodology support • data integration • process support	• Non extensible • Cannot adopt to process • Different environments for different methodologies • No process support
Mix-n-Match	• Extensible • Best-of-class • Can evolve with technology changes	• No methodology support • Multiple vendor • Dis-continuous work-flow • No process support

Table 2: Summary of differences between ICASE and Mix-n-Match

The environments need to support different processes, methodologies, application architectures, as well as, a variety of tools and technologies.

- "focus": The focus of many of the tools and environments is to facilitate some of the "up stream" activities. These up stream activities do not include the initial business planning and decision making, one of the key areas in need of productivity improvement (see below). The other area is the lack of M&E tools to support the bulk of the activity in a software development shop. Testing, which is both labor intensive and critical to the quality of delivered software, is another major area lacking in tool support. The automatic tracability for the source of the defect introduction, automatic test case generation, and an analysis of the test results in terms of expected reliability and defects likely remaining are some of the useful features that a test tool must provide.

- "disregard for the end-to-end process": The end-to-end process can be thought to consist of the following four areas: front-end, pre-software development activities (problem formulation, planning, business impact analysis, infra-structure impact analysis, etc.), software development (from requirements to testing), post-delivery activities (installation, training, migration, operation, etc.) and M&E.

In this context the software development activities are a small portion of the end-to-end process.

2 Requirements for a Next Generation Software Development Environment

The business process driven development environment requires support for:

- Business Process Modeling: to capture business processes and to evaluate how changes in the process affects the business. This impact analysis would also point to the changes required in the supporting software systems.

- Business Planning: driven by the identified changes this will analyze, given the available resources and priorities, a plan for making the changes happen. The business planning system with its complete knowledge of existing systems and models would also help develop the transitioning plans. These plans would take into account all possible impacts.

- Software development: will take the identified changes and transform these into the supporting software systems. The software systems would need to be extremely extensible and be driven by transformations of the business models, thus keeping them consistent with business processes.

- Enabling methodologies and frameworks: will provide support for the analysis, design and evolution of business processes and models, and their transformation into supporting systems.

These are some very high level generic requirements. In the next section we will discuss what role can formal systems play in this scheme.

Figure 5 shows a high level metamodel that can be used to model processes. In this model a process is assumed to be some sequence of tasks, each task is composed of a set of sub-tasks and is related to other tasks by a Temporal relationship. Tasks consume and produce resources; to allow resources to be acquired and released during task execution, certain atomic sub-tasks may only be performing the task of acquiring and/or releasing resources. A resource may be data, hardware and/or software; software can be modeled as an application, tool or utility. An action, or an atomic task, is a type of task and, therefore, also consumes and produces resources. External and/or some internal entities trigger or invoke tasks.

How can we use the process model? Let us consider a trivial example. We want to capture the process of sending a "bill" for some services rendered to customers. The customer, an external entity, utilizes some service(s). The utilizes process will consist of tasks that render the service and record the cost. At given intervals, an external event will invoke the billing process.

The billing process consists of the tasks {Produce bill, Print bill, Mail bill}. The produce bill task consists of sub-tasks for getting and collating all charges incurred and outstanding for a customer. It would also update accounting records. The print bill process will take this data and print the bill according to some customer defined preferences.

Let us now capture some of the dynamic properties of the model. This can be done in a number of ways. Here we shall use the state transition approach to capture some of the dynamic behavior of the model. Figure 6 shows one state transition model defining the different transitions.

This model is not complete. It needs to be extended to capture versions and configurations. Thus, an applications would be modeled in terms of its constituent modules and/or object classes. Also many of the linkages need to be further specified. Formal systems can play an important role in the modeling of the processes and all associated information including process activations.

3 Where can Formal Systems help?

The investigation into formal systems has mainly been restricted, so far, for their use in specification of programs and their verification [12]. As has been pointed out before the problem of software development has to be looked from a broader perspective. In this section we will consider some of the areas in which formal systems can help. Further research in theses areas and in the applicability of already developed techniques is needed.

3.1 Use of Formalisms in Business Planning and Modeling

The first question to consider is what are the formal models for processes? One could take a very narrow definition of what a process is:

- Process: a set of inputs which are acted upon by a set of actions to produce a set of outputs. The set of actions are related to each other by some sequencing or dependency relationship, and may also be constrained by temporal relationships.

So what can be specified? Using the available formalisms the above notion of a process can easily be captured. Using these formalisms can we capture the inter-process relationships, viz., develop a process model.

- What questions can be addressed by this model?

- What information can it provide about the business?

- Can we test and/or validate our models? It is important to consider test case generation for formal systems as it may reduce the need for fool-proof automatic validation techniques.

- Can we make incremental or Δ changes to the business process model and discern their impact?

These are just some of the many questions that need to be addressed by this process model. The last question requires that we understand how to specify and capture incremental changes to our formal models.

The type of business process models will have to cover the entire spectrum of a business's activities. For example, marketing, purchasing, resource allocation, hiring, etc. It is only then that the enterprise can be modeled.

From the tool perspective, what kind of tool would support the creation, management and maintenance of these models? A graphics based process design tool based on the underlying formal process models should not be difficult to construct; some recent tool development in other areas has been based on existing formal languages such as SDL.

3.2 Relationship of the Business Process Models to the Supporting Systems

Given a business process model, we need to relate the business processes to supporting application systems. Each system should perform a cohesive set of business related tasks/actions. These systems should be "atomic" with respect to the business processes, thereby, minimizing the impact of business model changes on the set of supporting systems. Transformations supported by the framework would allow the systems to be "dynamically wired" together to support the business model. This dynamic wiring can be figured from the business process models and the application system models. The systems and infrastructure need to be extremely flexible to accomplish this task. So the fundamental question is:

- How can we map and/or transform the business process models onto system representation models?

This may require the development of some form of canonical representation for application functionality/data. The representation would have to be programming language independent and should be able to provide transformation from and to the canonical representation and the program code. How do we compose these representations to create composite representations.

Given such an environment, what are the issues that need to be addressed:

- When a business model changes by Δ, can we limit the change in the supporting systems to a similar incremental amount?

- Given what changes need to be made, can we identify all areas of impacts, thereby, allowing the development of a plan?

From the users perspectives we also need to specify usability and reliability requirements amongst others.

3.3 Modeling of Existing Applications

Over the decades organizations have developed application support systems for every facet of their activity. These systems and their supporting data are a strategic asset, albeit a very expensive one to maintain. The research into formalisms should consider the development of tools to reverse create application system models with respect to the business process models. This mapping of existing systems against business processes would identify both gaps and duplication of activities.

From the identified map, we would then take individual existing systems and model them in terms of our "atomic" representations. These can then be extracted, and related to the various models, if there is such a need to do so. This will surely be required in the transitioning phases.

4 Conclusions

In this paper we have surveyed the current situation with respect to software development environments. There is a widely held belief that integrated software development environments will lead to dramatic improvements in productivity and software quality. Software productivity and quality have become critical for the success of most products (e.g., the cost of automated test equipment is typically 75% software and 25% hardware).

Formal systems can be useful in ameliorating some of the problems currently faced in the development of ideal software development environments. This area of work has, however, been mostly ignored by researchers in the field.

References

[1] W.W. Royce, "Managing the Development of Large Software Systems: Concepts and Techniques", *Proceedings WESCON*, 1970.

[2] B. Boehm, "A Spiral Model of Development and Enhancement", *ACM SIGSOFT Notes*, 11(4):14-24, 1986.

[3] M. Dyer, "Software Development Processes", *IBM Systems Journal*, 19(4):451-465, 1980.

[4] T. Gilb, "Evolutionary Development Versus Waterfall Model", *ACM SIG-SOFT Software Engineering Notes*, 10(3):49-62, 1985.

[5] T. Capers Jones, **Applied Software Measurement**, McGraw Hill, 1991.

[6] M. Chen, R.J. Norman, "A Framework for Integrated CASE", *IEEE Software*, 9(2):18-22.

[7] I. Thomas, B.A. Nejmeh, "Definitions of Tool Integration for Environments", *IEEE Software*, 9(2):29-35, 1992.

[8] G.M. Clemm, "The Workshop System - A Practical Knowledge-based Software Environment", *ACM SIGSOFT*, 13(5):55-64, 1988.

[9] PCTE, Technical Report ECMA-149, European Computer Manufacturer's Association, Geneva, Dec. 1990.

[10] I. Thomas, "PCTE Interfaces: Supporting Tools in Software Engineering Environments", *IEEE Software*, 6(6):15-23, 1989.

[11] V.J. Marcurio et al., "AD/Cycle Strategy and Architecture", *IBM Systems Journal*, 29(2):170-188, 1990.

[12] D. Bjoerner, C. Jones, **Formal Specifications and Software Development**, Prentice-Hall, London, 1982.

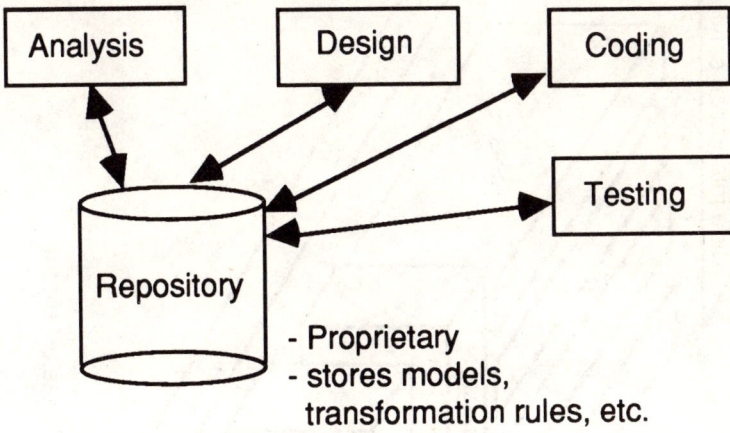

Figure 1. A typical ICASE

134

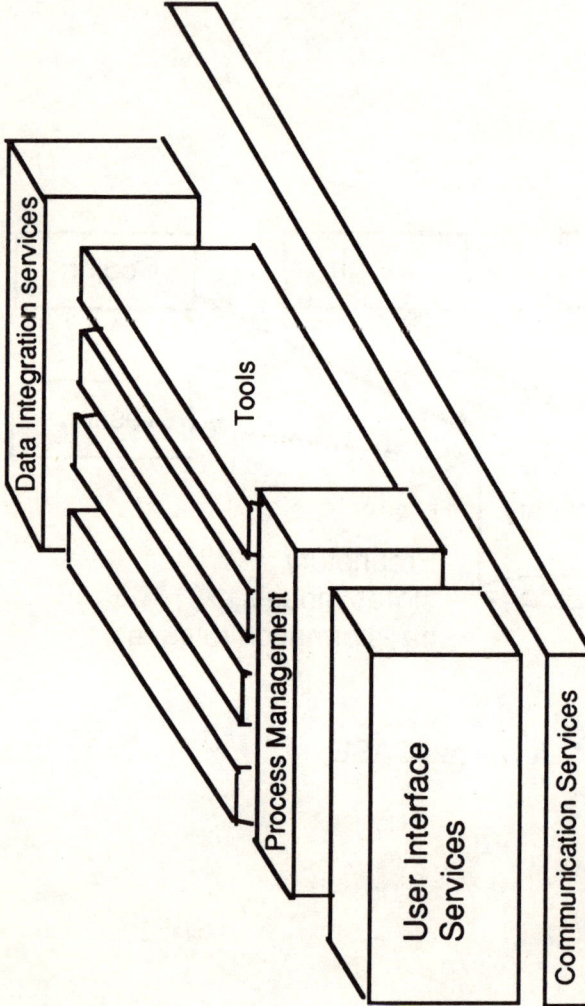

Figure 2. The "Toaster" Model

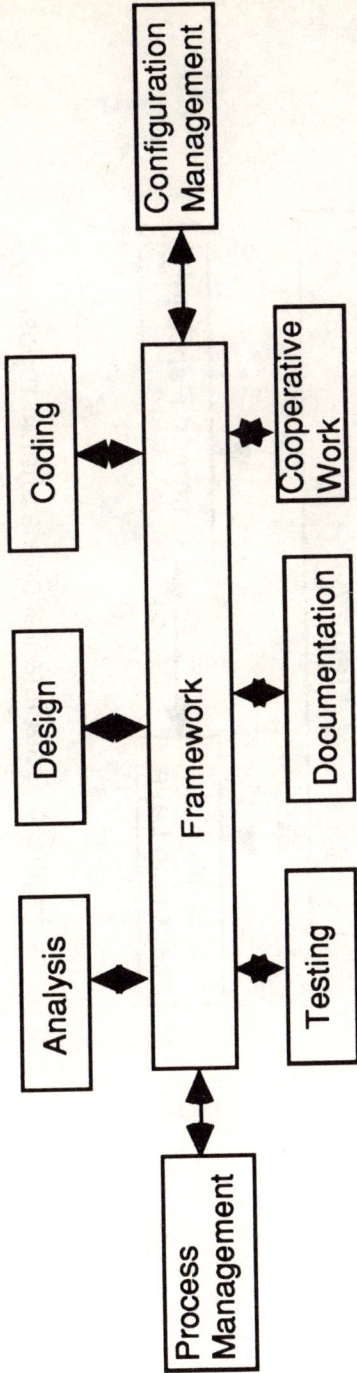

Figure 3. "Mix-n-Match" Approach

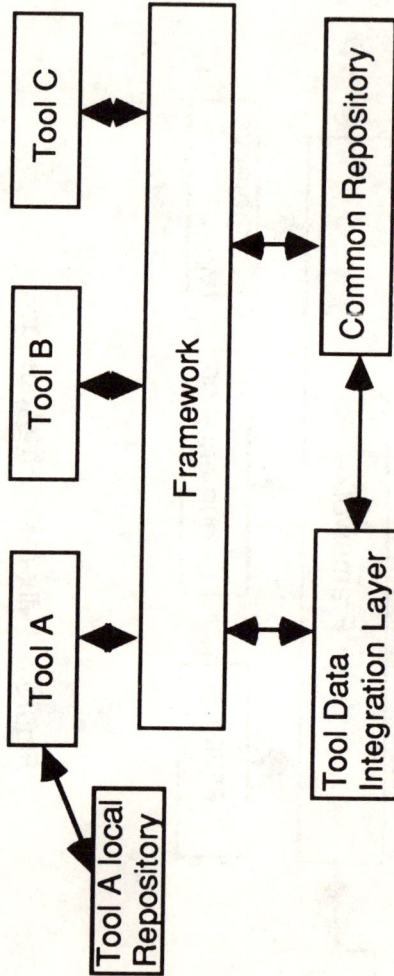

Figure 4. Data Integration via shared repository

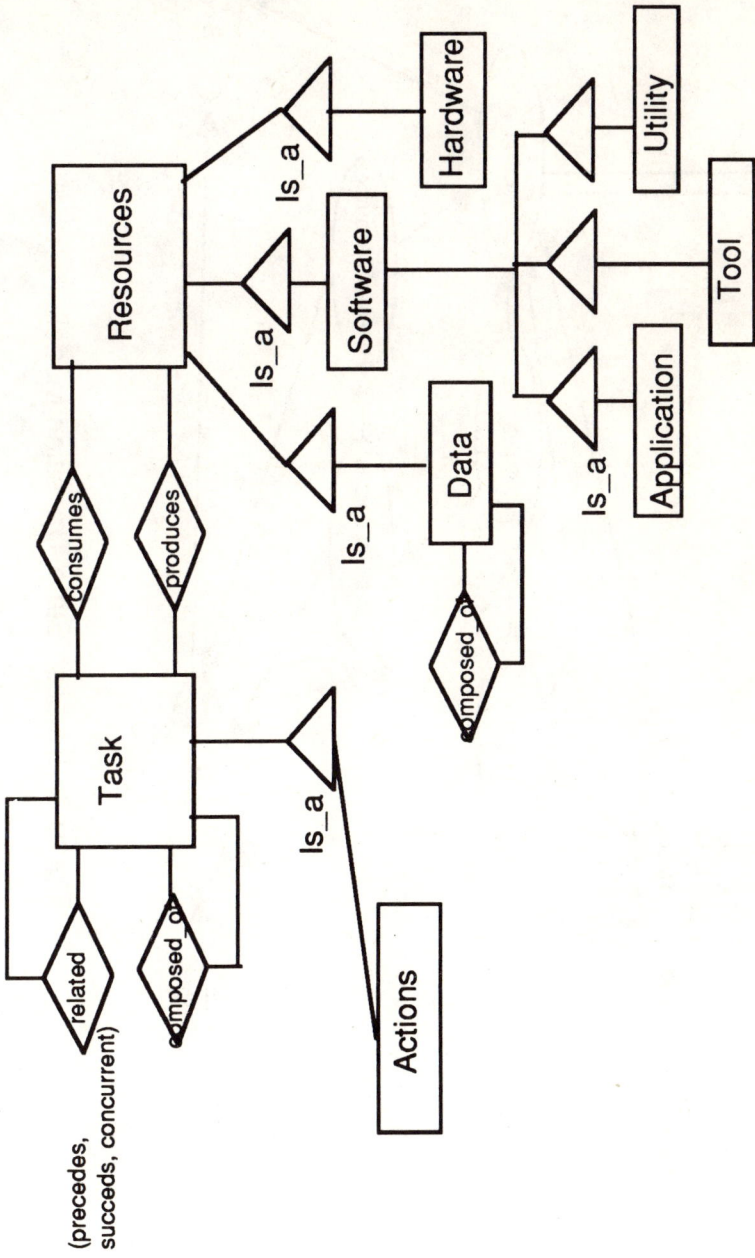

Figure 5. A High level Process Model

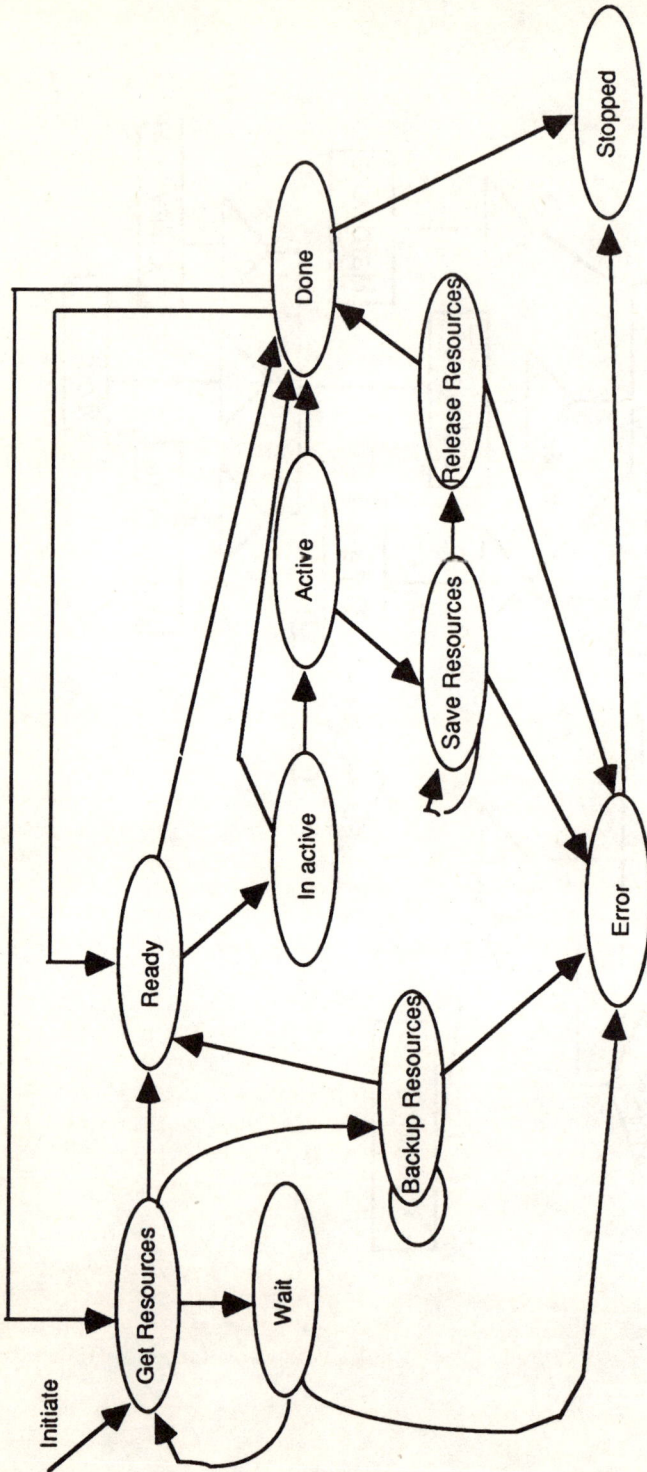

Figure 6. Process State Transition Model

Efficient Deduction and Induction: Key to the Success of Data-Intensive Knowledge-Base Systems

Jiawei Han

School of Computing Science

Simon Fraser University

Burnaby, B.C., Canada V5A 1S6

Abstract

The development of powerful and efficient deduction and induction mechanisms is the key to the success of Very Large Knowledge-Base systems (VLKBs). Based on our study, we propose (1) an efficient deduction method which applies query-independent compilation and set-oriented, chain-based evaluation in deductive databases, and (2) an efficient attribute-oriented induction method for knowledge discovery in databases. A large knowledge-base system should support both mechanisms and their integration.

1   Introduction

The startling achievements of the researches and developments of database systems in the past two decades have set a solid foundation for the development of the next generation information management systems, which, according to many people's views [24, 26], are very large knowledge-base systems (VLKBs). The research on deductive database systems and knowledge discovery in databases are two important directions towards this goal [24, 23]. An influential architecture of high-performance VLKB systems is *tight coupling of knowledge system with database system* [22, 26, 24], that is, construction of an *integrated* data-intensive knowledge-base system. There are many research issues on the development of such a system, such as semantic data modeling [15], compilation and query evaluation [13, 2, 1], integration of deductive and object-oriented databases [16, 5, 28], negation, disjunction and updates [8], parallelism, data- and knowledge- distribution and heterogeneity [24], application software developments [25], etc. However, we feel that the key to the success of such a system is the support of powerful and efficient deduction and induction techniques. A powerful deduction mechanism should provide users with capabilities to query about data and knowledge stored in the knowledge-base and perform reasoning based on data and knowledge rules. A powerful induction mechanism should be able to extract knowledge from data and discover important relationships among data and knowledge. Clearly, a sophisticated knowledge-base system should support both deduction and induction mechanisms.

This paper presents our view points and some research results on the efficient implementation of deduction and induction mechanisms in knowledge-base systems. The presentation is organized as follows. In Section 2, we discuss the realization of efficient deduction by query-independent compilation and set-oriented, chain-based query evaluation. In Section 3, we discuss the implementation of efficient induction by an attribute-oriented approach. In Section 4, we argue that a powerful system should have an elegant integration of both mechanisms and propose some ideas on such an integration. We summarize our discussion in Section 5.

2   Efficient Deduction in Databases

As an important extension to relational database technology, deductive database systems represent a promising direction towards declarative query processing, high-level database programming, and the development of expert database systems. Deductive database technology has wide applications in business management, engineering design, spatial databases, and knowledge-base systems.

Although many deductive database systems adopt the syntax of logic programming languages, the interfaces for deductive database systems can be SQL-like, icon-based, etc. It can be constructed based on an extended deductive entity-relationship model [12] and supported by an object-oriented back-end [27]. A database system is deductive if it supports high-level views by sophisticated deduction rules and a declarative query interface.

Many techniques have been proposed and studied for efficient deduction and query evaluation in databases [2, 26, 17]. The compilation and evaluation methods can be classified into three approaches: (i) *interpretation* (e.g., Prolog evaluation and the query/subquery approach [2]), (ii) *query-dependent compilation and magic sets evaluation* (e.g., the magic rule rewriting and semi-naive evaluation [2]), and (iii) *query-independent compilation and chain-based evaluation* (e.g., [14]). Query-independent compilation transforms a set of deduction rules into highly regular compiled formulas and facilitates the quantitative analysis of deductive queries, constraint-based reasoning, and efficient query evaluation.

2.1   Query-independent compilation of recursions

Although recursions can be in complex and irregular forms, most recursions in practical applications can be compiled into *chain* or *pseudo-chain* forms to which efficient query analysis and evaluation techniques can be applied [14, 13]. By compiling complex recursions into highly regular chain forms, the selection-pushing technique can capture more bindings in sophisticated recursions than the traditional rule rewriting techniques.

We compare binding propagation between query-independent compilation and traditional binding propagation approaches.

Binding propagation in traditional approaches, such as the rule/goal graph and magic rule rewriting [1, 26, 2], rewrites a recursion into an equivalent, but more efficiently evaluable one for a specific query form based on the analysis of binding propagation in a rule/goal graph [26]. A query is evaluated by first computing *magic set*, the portion of the database relevant to the query, and then performing semi-naive evaluation on the derived magic sets. By this approach, bindings are propagated in the *backward direction* in the sense that the bindings are propagated from the head to the body in a rule and from the

IDB subgoal in the body of a rule to the head of its unifying rule (the rule which unifies it). However, for some recursions, binding information should be propagated in both forward and backward directions. That is, bindings should also be propagated *forward* from the body to the head in a rule and from the rule unifying the IDB subgoal to the corresponding IDB subgoal in the body of the original rule. Such propagation cannot be caught by the traditional approaches, such as the rule/goal graph analysis. As a result, a rule/goal graph-based rule rewriting technique, such as magic rule rewriting, is unable to capture such kind of bindings and thus generates unnecessarily large magic sets for such recursions.

The query-independent compilation technique overcomes this difficulty by compiling a linear recursion into a compiled form which captures the bindings propagated in both forward and backward directions among different expansions. Efficient query evaluation plans can be generated based on the analysis of such compiled forms. This can be illustrated by an example.

Example 1. We analyze the binding propagation of a query "$?-r(c, c_1, c_2, Y)$" on a linear recursion defined below, where c's are constants, X's and Y's are variables, and r is a recursive predicate defined by EDB predicates a, b and e.

$$r(X, X_1, X_2, Y) \leftarrow a(X, Y), r(X_1, X_2, X_3, Y_1), b(X_3, Y_1). \tag{1}$$
$$r(X, X_1, X_2, Y) \leftarrow e(X, X_1, X_2, Y). \tag{2}$$

Following the binding propagation rules, the bindings in the adorned goal, r^{bbbf}, are propagated to the subgoal r in the body of the recursive rule, resulting in an adorned subgoal, r^{bbff}, which are in turn propagated to the next expansion, resulting in an adorned subgoal, r^{bfff}, etc. Finally, the subgoal r^{ffff} cannot propagate any bindings to subsequent expansions, and the binding propagation terminates. The process is presented below.

$$r^{bbbf}(X, X_1, X_2, Y) \leftarrow$$
$$a^{bf}(X, Y), r^{bbff}(X_1, X_2, X_3, Y_1), b^{bb}(X_3, Y_1). \tag{3}$$

$$r^{bbff}(X_1, X_1, X_2, Y_1) \leftarrow$$
$$a^{bf}(X_1, Y_1), r^{bfff}(X_2, X_3, X_4, Y_2), b^{bb}(X_4, Y_2). \tag{4}$$

$$r^{bfff}(X_2, X_2, X_3, Y_2) \leftarrow$$
$$a^{bf}(X_2, Y_2), r^{ffff}(X_3, X_4, X_5, Y_3), b^{bb}(X_5, Y_3). \tag{5}$$

The above rule/goal graph-directed binding propagation cannot reduce the set of data to be examined in the semi-naive evaluation, and the magic set involves the entire data relations. Moreover, it is easy to verify that reordering of the subgoals cannot improve the evaluation efficiency. However, if bindings are allowed to be propagated in the forward direction as well, the binding of X_1 and Y_1 in (5) can be propagated to Y_1 in (4), which makes X_3 bound in both (4) and (5). Similarly, X_4 will be bound in (5) and (6) via the binding of X_2. Such bindings can be propagated to any future expansions. This kind of binding propagation can be captured by query-independent compilation of linear recursions [14]. The normalized, equivalent rule set is presented below.

$$r(X, X_1, X_2, Y) \quad \leftarrow \quad a(X, Y), t(X_1, X_2). \tag{6}$$
$$t(X_1, X_2) \quad \leftarrow \quad ab(X_1, X_3), ab(X_2, X_4), t(X_3, X_4). \tag{7}$$
$$t(X_1, X_2) \quad \leftarrow \quad e(X_1, X_2, X_3, Y_1), b(X_3, Y_1). \tag{8}$$
$$t(X_1, X_2) \quad \leftarrow \quad ab(X_1, X_3), e(X_2, X_3, X_4, Y_2), b(X_4, Y_2). \tag{9}$$
$$ab(X_1 X_3) \quad \leftarrow \quad a(X_1, U), b(X_3, U). \tag{10}$$

Obviously, the available bindings can be easily propagated in the normalized recursion as shown below.

$$r^{bbbf}(X, X_1, X_2, Y) \quad \leftarrow \quad a^{bf}(X, Y), t^{bb}(X_1, X_2).$$
$$t^{bb}(X_1, X_2) \quad \leftarrow \quad ab^{bf}(X_1, X_3), ab^{bf}(X_2, X_4), t^{bb}(X_3, X_4).$$
$$t^{bb}(X_1, X_2) \quad \leftarrow \quad e^{bbff}(X_1, X_2, X_3, Y_1), b^{bb}(X_3, Y_1).$$
$$t^{bb}(X_1, X_2) \quad \leftarrow \quad ab^{fb}(X_1, X_3), e^{bfff}(X_2, X_3, X_4, Y_2), b^{bb}(X_4, Y_2).$$

The detailed compilation technique is presented in [14], which shows that a *single linear recursion* (with one linear recursive rule and one or more nonrecursive rules) can be compiled, independent of query forms, into either a *bounded recursion* (a set of nonrecursive rules) or a *chain recursion* (a formula with a single chain or a set of synchronous chains). Moreover, many application-oriented recursions can be compiled into *asynchronous chain recursions* and be evaluated by partial transitive closure algorithms [13]. Some other recursions can be compiled into *synchronous chain* forms (e.g., the *same generation* recursion) [2] and be evaluated by *counting* or *magic sets* methods [1, 2]. Furthermore, optimization can be performed on the compiled expressions, and quantitative analysis can be performed by incorporation of query instantiation, integrity constraints and database statistics.

2.2 Chain-based evaluation of compiled recursion

Since most recursions in deductive databases can be compiled into chain or pseudo-chain forms, *chain-based evaluation* can be explored on the compiled recursions, which can be viewed as an extension of relational database query analysis and optimization techniques because a compiled chain consists of a set of highly regular relational expressions. In contrast to magic sets method which treats a recursion like a black box, the compilation makes explicit the regularity of the operation sequences within a recursion, on which quantitative analysis and optimization can be explored systematically.

Flexible evaluation strategies can be applied to deductive queries in complex forms. The evaluation algorithms can be classified into four classes: *nonrecursive, total closure, query closure* and *existence checking*. Different query instantiations and inquiries may require different strategies in the evaluation of specific compiled chains. A *quad-state variable binding analysis* method [9] is developed, which distinguished four states for each variable in a predicate, (i) *instantiated but not inquired* (query constant), (ii) *instantiated and inquired* (partially bound), (iii) *uninstantiated but inquired* (unbound), and (iv) *uninstantiated and not inquired* (irrelevant to the query). Quantitative information can be incorporated in the quad-state variable binding analysis for the selection of appropriate query processing strategies. Such a quantitative analysis, similar to the access path selection and query plan generation for relational queries, can be performed based on the characteristics of the compiled chains, query instantiations, inquiries, integrity constraints, and database statistics of extensional relations [10].

Although function-free recursions cover an interesting class of recursions in deductive databases, many recursions in practical applications contain function symbols, such as structured data objects, arithmetic functions, and recursive data structures (lists, trees, sets, etc.). By transforming functions into functional predicates, the compilation and evaluation techniques developed for function-free recursions can be extended to functional ones [10]. Furthermore, the method can be generalized to many logical rules containing stratified negation and even with higher-order syntax and first-order semantics [5]. Therefore, query-independent compilation represents a powerful technique which transforms deduction rules into simple, easily-analyzable forms and facilitates the application of efficient evaluation methods.

In general, the chain-based query evaluation method consists of chain-following, chain-splitting, existence checking, and constraint-based evaluation techniques. The following subsections illustrate the ideas of these techniques using some application-oriented examples.

2.2.1 Chain-following and chain-split evaluation

The simplest chain-based evaluation is to select a more restrictive *starting end* of a chain and follow the compiled chains in the evaluation, which is called *chain-following evaluation*.

Example 2. The recursion *length* defined by (11) and (12) can be compiled into a double-chain recursion. For the query "$? - length([a, b, c], N)$", the adorned compiled rule set is (13) and (14).

$$length([\,], 0). \tag{11}$$
$$length([X|L_1], succ(N_1)) \leftarrow length(L_1, N_1). \tag{12}$$

$$length^{bf}(L, N) \leftarrow L =^{bb} [\,], N =^{fb} 0. \tag{13}$$
$$length^{bf}(L, N) \leftarrow cons^{ffb}(X, L_1, L),$$
$$length^{bf}(L_1, N_1), succ^{bf}(N_1, N). \tag{14}$$

The query can be evaluated by *counting* [1]. Starting at $L = [a, b, c]$, the *cons*-predicate is evaluated, that derives $L_1 = [b, c]$, and *count* (a variable in the *counting* implementation) is incremented by 1. The evaluation of the *cons*-chain terminates when $L_1 = [\,]$ and *count* $= 3$. Then $N_1 = 0$ initiates the *succ*-chain, which is evaluated *count* times and derives the length of the chain, $N = 3$. □

Depending on the available query bindings, *some* functional predicates in a chain generating path may not be immediately evaluable. In this case, a chain generating path should be partitioned into two portions: *immediately evaluable portion* and *buffered portion*. The former is evaluated but the latter is buffered until the *exit portion* (the expression which corresponds to the body of the exit rule) is evaluated. Then the buffered portion obtains sufficient binding information for evaluation (otherwise, the query is not finitely evaluable), and the evaluation proceeds in a way similar to the evaluation of multi-chain recursions, except that the corresponding buffered values should be patched in the evaluation. Such an evaluation technique is called chain-split evaluation [10].

Example 3. The recursion *append* defined by (15) and (16) can be compiled into a single-chain recursion. For the query "$? - append(U, V, [a, b])$" with the adorned predicate $append^{ffb}$, the adorned rule set is (17) and (18).

$$append([\,], L, L). \tag{15}$$
$$append([X|L_1], L_2, X|L_3]) \quad \leftarrow \quad append(L_1, L_2, L_3). \tag{16}$$

$$append^{ffb}(U, V, W) \quad \leftarrow \quad U =^{fb} [\,], V =^{fb} W. \tag{17}$$
$$append^{ffb}(U, V, W) \quad \leftarrow \quad cons^{ffb}(X_1, W_1, W), append^{ffb}(U_1, V, W_1), \\ cons^{bbf}(X_1, U_1, U). \tag{18}$$

A chain-split evaluation technique should be applied in the evaluation. That is, the chain "$cons(X_1, U_1, U), cons(X_1, W_1, W)$" is split into two portions: the U-predicate "$cons(X_1, U_1, U)$" and the W-predicate "$cons(X_1, W_1, W)$". Applying the exit rule derives the first set of answers: $U = [\,]$ and $V = [a, b]$. At the first evaluation of the recursive rule, the U-predicate is not immediately evaluable. The evaluation proceeds along the W-predicate only, which derives $W_1 = [b]$ and $X_1 = a$ from $W = [a, b]$. X_1 is buffered, and W_1 is passed to the exit expression, making $V = [b]$ and $U_1 = [\,]$. Then the U-predicate is evaluable since X_1 and U_1 are available. It derives $U = [a]$. Thus, the second set of answer is $U = [a]$, $V = [b]$. Similarly, the evaluation may proceed on the W-predicate further, which derives the third set of answer: $\{U = [a, b]$, $V = [\,]\}$. □

2.2.2 Existence checking evaluation

Query evaluation of a compiled chain should start at a more selective end of the chain (called the start end) and proceed towards the other end of the chain (called the finish end). An existence checking evaluation, which terminates before the complete evaluation of a chain, can be applied when the variables at the finish end are not inquired.

Example 4. The recursion $member(X, L)$, defined by (19) and (20), can be normalized into a single-chain recursion. The rule set with the adornment bb is (21) and (22).

$$member(X, [X|L_1]). \tag{19}$$
$$member(X, [Y|L_1]) \quad \leftarrow \quad member(X, L_1). \tag{20}$$

$$member^{bb}(X, L) \quad \leftarrow \quad cons^{bfb}(X, L_1, L). \tag{21}$$
$$member^{bb}(X, L) \quad \leftarrow \quad cons^{ffb}(Y, L_1, L), member^{bb}(X, L_1). \tag{22}$$

A query, "$? - member([a], [b, a, c, d])$", can be evaluated by an existence checking evaluation algorithm because the variables at both ends of the chain are instantiated but not inquired. Notice that $L = [b, a, c, d]$ must be the start end, otherwise the *cons*-predicate is not immediately evaluable. The evaluation proceeds as follows. The first evaluation of exit rule derives no answer since $L_1 = [a, c, d]$, but $b \neq X$. The second evaluation (after evaluating the recursive rule) derives $L_1 = [c, d]$, and $a = X$, which is *true*. The evaluation terminates because one *true* answer is adequate to the query. The evaluation has to proceed until $L_1 = [\ ]$ *only if* L contains no element a. In this case, the answer to the query is *false*. $\Box$

2.2.3 Constraint-based evaluation

Query constraints (instantiations) can be applied to a compiled recursion to reduce search space during iterative evaluation. Take single-chain recursion as an example, query constraints can be enforced at both ends of a compiled chain. Usually, the processing starts at a more restrictive end and proceeds to a less restrictive end (*finish end*). It is straightforward to push query constraints at the start end of the chain. However, care should be taken when pushing query constraints at the finish end.

Example 5. An IDB predicate *tour*(*FnoList, Dep, Arr, Fare*), defined by (23) and (25), represents a sequence of connected flights with the initial departure city *Dep*, the final arrival city *Arr* and the total fare *Fare*, where *flight* is an EDB predicate representing the stored flight information.

$$tour([Fno], Dep, Arr, Fare) \leftarrow flight(Fno, Dep, Arr, Fare). \tag{23}$$

$$tour([Fno|FnoList], Dep, Arr, Fare) \leftarrow$$
$$flight(Fno, Dep, Int, F_1), tour(FnoList, Int, Arr, F_2), \tag{24}$$
$$Fare = F_1 + F_2. \tag{25}$$

The recursion can be compiled into a single-chain recursion (26) and (27).

$$tour(L, D, A, F) \leftarrow$$
$$flight(Fno, D, A, F), cons(Fno, [\ ], L), sum(F, 0, F). \tag{26}$$
$$tour(L, D, A, F) \leftarrow$$
$$flight(Fno, D, I, F_1), sum(F_1, S_1, F),$$
$$cons(Fno, L_1, L), tour(L_1, I, A, S_1). \tag{27}$$

Suppose a query is to *find a set of (connecting) flights from Vancouver to Zurich (Switzerland), with at most 4 hops and with the total fare between $500 to $800*, that is,

$$? - tour(FnoList, vancouver, zurich, F),$$
$$F \geq 500, F \leq 800, length(FnoList, N), N \leq 4.$$

According to the compiled form, D, L and F are located at one end of the chain (called the *departure end*); while A, L_1 and S_1 are at the other end of the chain (called the *arrival end*). The information at the departure end is, (i) $D =$ "*vancouver*", (ii) $500 \leq F \leq 800$, and (iii) $FnoList = L, length(FnoList, N)$, $N \leq 4$; while the information at the arrival end is, (i) $A =$ "*zurich*", (ii) $L_1 = [\ ]$, and (iii) $S_1 = 0$.

Since the information at the arrival end is more selective than that at the departure end, the arrival end is taken as the *start end*. Thus, all the query constraints at this end are pushed into the chain for efficient processing.

The query constraints at the finish end cannot be pushed into the chain in iterative evaluation without further information. For example, pushing the constraint, $Fare \geq 500$, into the chain will cut off a promising connection whose first hop costs less than 500. On the other hand, it is clearly beneficial to push the constraint, $Fare \leq 800$, into the chain to cut off any hopeless connections when the accumulative fare is already beyond 800. However, a constraint like $Fare = 800$ cannot be pushed into the chain directly, but a transformed constraint, $Fare \leq 800$, can be pushed in for iterative evaluation.

A systematic way to pushing query constraints at the finish end can be derived from the interactions between query constraints and monotonicity constraints [10]. If the value (or the mapped value) of an argument in the recursive predicate monotonically increases during the evaluation, a query constraint which blocks such an increase is useful at reducing the search space in iterative evaluation.

Based on the monotonicity constraint of the argument $Fare$, a *termination restraint template*, $Fare \not> C$, is set up, where C is a variable which can be instantiated by a *consistent* query constraint. For example, a constraint, $Fare \leq 800$, or $Fare = 800$, instantiates the template to a *concrete termination restraint*, $Fare \not> 800$. However, the constraint, $Fare \geq 500$, is not consistent with the termination restraint template. Thus, it cannot instantiate a termination restraint. An instantiated termination restraint can be pushed into the chain for efficient processing.

Similarly, a constraint, $Dep = "vancouver"$, can be used for constraint pushing if we have the airport location information and a constraint, *same flight direction*, (a monotonic constraint on flight direction). A concrete termination restraint, $longitude(Dep) \not> longitude (vancouver)$, can be derived, and the tuples generated at any iteration with the departure airports located to the west of Vancouver is pruned in the chain processing. Also, the constraint, $"length(FnoList, N), N \leq 4"$, can be pushed into the chain for iterative evaluation. $\square$

3 Techniques for Knowledge Discovery in Databases

Although many rules in a knowledge-base system are explicitly provided by experts, a substantial body of valuable knowledge could be implicitly stored in the database. It is crucial to extract knowledge from the information stored in databases using powerful and efficient knowledge discovery techniques.

A major challenge of learning in databases is computational efficiency. We developed an attribute-oriented induction method [3, 11] which strives for efficiency in two aspects: (i) knowledge-directed learning, and (ii) attribute-oriented induction. The former is achieved by providing knowledge about the learning task, data relevance, expected rule forms and concept hierarchies. The latter is achieved by an attribute-oriented concept tree ascending technique, which performs generalization attribute by attribute until the relevant data is generalized to a certain level and the size of the generalized relation is reasonably small. Then, more flexible induction methods can be applied to the relatively small set of (generalized) data according to different criteria, such as quantitative measurement, expert knowledge, user-preference, and others.

Both techniques substantially reduce the search space and improve the efficiency of a database learning process.

Attribute-oriented induction integrates database operations with the learning process and provides a simple, efficient mechanism for learning various kinds of knowledge rules from large databases. The method learns both characteristic rules and classification rules. By registering in each generalized tuple the number of original tuples from which it is generalized, the method learns both qualitative and quantitative rules [11]. Quantitative information facilitates quantitative reasoning, incremental learning and learning in the presence of noise and exceptions.

Moreover, the attribute-oriented induction can be applied to the discovery of data evolution regularities in databases. Data evolution regularity characterizes the general trend of changes of data over time in a database. It can be further classified into characteristic rules and classification rules. In many applications, users are often interested in finding such regularities or trends of data evolution rather than examining the large volumes of data over time. The discovery of such knowledge includes the extraction of evolving data from corresponding database instances (with different timestamps) and attribute-oriented induction on the extracted data. Similarly, attribute-oriented induction can also be applied to knowledge discovery in extended-relational, deductive, and object-oriented databases.

Here we briefly present the method for discovery of characteristic rules from relational databases and refer more detailed study to [11].

3.1 Primitives for attribute-oriented induction

Three primitives are provided for the specification of a learning task: *task-relevant data, background knowledge,* and *expected representation of learning results.*

Data relevant to the discovery process: A database usually stores a large amount of data, of which only a portion may be relevant to a particular learning task. Relevant data may extend over several relations. A query can be used to collect task-relevant data from the database.

Task-relevant data can be viewed as examples for learning processes. Undoubtedly, *learning-from-examples* [19] should be an important strategy for knowledge discovery in databases. Most *learning-from-examples* algorithms partition the set of examples into *positive* and *negative* sets and perform *generalization* using the positive data and *specialization* using the negative ones [19]. Unfortunately, a relational database does not explicitly store negative data, and thus no explicitly specified negative examples can be used for specialization. Therefore, a database induction process relies mainly on generalization, which should be performed cautiously to avoid over-generalization.

Background knowledge: Concept hierarchies represent necessary background knowledge which directs the generalization process. Different levels of concepts are often organized into a taxonomy of concepts. The concept taxonomy can be partially ordered according to a general-to-specific ordering. The most general concept is the null description (described by a reserved word "*ANY*"), and the most specific concepts correspond to the specific values of attributes in the database. Using a concept hierarchy, the rules learned can be represented in terms of generalized concepts and stated in a simple and explicit form, which is desirable to most users.

Concept hierarchies can be provided by knowledge engineers or domain experts. This is reasonable for even large databases since a concept tree registers only the *distinct* discrete attribute values or ranges of numerical values for an attribute which are, in general, not very large and can be input by domain experts. Many concept hierarchies, such as *Birthplace*, are actually stored in the database implicitly. Also, concept hierarchies can be discovered automatically or refined dynamically based on the statistics of data distribution and the relationships between attributes [7, 11].

Different concept hierarchies can be constructed on the same attribute based on different viewpoints or preferences. For example, the birthplace could be organized according to administrative regions, geographic regions, sizes of cities, etc. Usually, a commonly referenced concept hierarchy is associated with an attribute as the default one. Other hierarchies can be chosen explicitly by preferred users in the learning process.

Representation of learning results: Many kinds of rules, such as *characteristic rules, discrimination rules, statistical rules*, etc. can be discovered by induction processes. A characteristic rule is an assertion which characterizes a concept satisfied by all or most of the examples in the class undergoing learning (called the **target class**). For example, the symptoms of a specific disease can be summarized by a characteristic rule. A discrimination rule is an assertion which discriminates a concept of the class being learned (the **target class**) from other classes (called **contrasting classes**). For example, to distinguish one disease from others, a discrimination rule should summarize the symptoms that discriminate this disease from others.

From a logical point of view, each tuple in a relation is a logic formula in conjunctive normal form, and a data relation is characterized by a large set of disjunctions of such conjunctive forms. Thus, both the data for learning and the rules discovered can be represented in either relational form or first-order predicate calculus.

A relation which represents *intermediate* (or *final*) learning results is called an *intermediate* (or a *final*) **generalized relation**. In a generalized relation, some or all of its attribute values are generalized data, that is, nonleaf nodes in the concept hierarchies. An attribute in a (generalized) relation is at a **desirable level** if it contains only a small number of distinct values in the relation. A user or an expert may like to specify a small integer for an attribute as a *desirable* attribute threshold. In this case, an attribute is at the *desirable* level if it contains no more distinct values than its *attribute threshold.* Moreover, the attribute is at the **minimum desirable level** if it would contain more distinct values than the threshold when generalized or specialized to a level lower than the current one. A special intermediate generalized relation R' of an original relation R is the **prime relation** of R if every attribute in R' is at the minimum desirable level.

Some learning-from-examples algorithms require the final learned rule to be in conjunctive normal form [19]. This requirement is unreasonable for large databases since the generalized data often contain different cases. However, a rule containing a large number of disjuncts indicates that it is in a complex form and further generalization should be performed. Therefore, the final generalized relation should be represented by either one tuple (a conjunctive rule) or a small number (usually 2 to 8) of tuples corresponding to a disjunctive rule with a small number of disjuncts. A system may allow a user to specify the preferred **generalization threshold** (or *generalized relation threshold*), a maximum number of disjuncts of the resulting formula. For example, if the threshold value is set to three, the final generalized rule will consist of *at most* three disjuncts.

Exceptional data often occur in a large relation. It is important to consider exceptional cases when learning in databases. Statistical information helps learning algorithms handle exceptions and/or noisy data [20]. A special attribute, *vote*, can be added to each generalized relation to register the number of tuples in the original relation which are generalized to the current tuple in the generalized relation. The attribute *vote* carries database statistics and supports the pruning of scattered data and the generalization of the concepts which take a majority of votes. The final generalized rule will be the rule which represents the characteristics of a *majority* number of facts in the database (called an **approximate rule**) or indicates *statistical* measurement of each conjunct or disjunct in the rule (called a **statistical rule**).

3.2 Basic principles of attribute-Oriented induction

A set of basic principles for attribute-oriented induction in relational databases are summarized as follows [11]).

1. Generalization on the smallest decomposable components: *Generalization should be performed on the smallest decomposable components (or attributes) of a data relation.*

2. Attribute removal: *If there is a large set of distinct values for an attribute but (1) there is no higher level concept provided for the attribute, or (2) its higher-level concepts are expressed in another attribute of the same tuple, the attribute should be removed in the generalization process.*

3. Concept tree ascension: *If there exists a higher level concept in the concept tree for an attribute value of a tuple, the substitution of the value by its higher level concept generalizes the tuple.*

4. Vote propagation: *The value of the vote of a tuple should be carried to its generalized tuple and the votes should be accumulated when merging identical tuples in generalization.*

5. Attribute threshold control: *If the number of distinct values of an attribute in the target class is larger than its attribute threshold, further generalization on this attribute should be performed.*

Principle 1 is based on the *least commitment principle* (commitment to minimally generalized concepts) which avoids over-generalization. Principle 2 corresponds to the generalization rule, *dropping conditions*, in *learning-from-examples* [19]. Principle 3 corresponds to the generalization rule, *climbing generalization trees*, in *learning-from-examples* [19]. Principle 4 is based on the merging of identical tuples. Principle 5 is based on the desirability of representation of each attribute at its desirable level. Thus, the above strategies are correct and necessary for the extraction of generalized rules from databases.

A basic attribute-oriented induction algorithm [11] has been derived based on the above principles, which extracts a prime relation from a large relevant data set. However, the prime relation may still contain more tuples than the generalization threshold because only *attribute* thresholds are utilized in the induction. Two approaches have been developed for the extraction of generalized rules from the prime relation: (1) further generalization to a *final generalized relation* confined by the generalization threshold and extraction of the inquired rule(s), and (2) direct extraction of generalized features and presentation of feature-based multiple rules.

We have the following two additional principles for further generalization.

1. Generalization threshold control: *If the number of tuples of a generalized relation in the target class is larger than the generalization threshold, further generalization on the relation should be performed.*

2. Rule formation: *A tuple in a final generalized relation is transformed to conjunctive normal form, and multiple tuples are transformed to disjunctive normal form.*

Based upon the definition of the generalization threshold, further generalization should be performed if the number of tuples in a generalized relation is larger than the threshold value. By further generalization on selected attribute(s) and merging of identical tuples, the size of the generalized relation will be reduced. Generalization should continue until the number of remaining tuples is no greater than the threshold value.

At this stage, there are usually alternative choices for selecting a candidate attribute for further generalization. Criteria, such as the preference of a larger reduction ratio on the number of tuples or the number of distinct attribute values, the simplicity of the final learned rules, etc., can be used for selection. Interesting rules can often be discovered by following different paths leading to several generalized relations for examination, comparison and selection. Following different paths corresponds to the way in which different people may learn differently from the same set of examples. The generalized relations can be examined by users or experts *interactively* to filter out trivial rules and preserve interesting ones [29].

3.3 Experiments on the NSERC grant information database

Based upon the attribute-oriented induction technique, a prototyped experimental database learning system, DBLEARN, has been constructed. The system, DBLEARN, takes learning requests as inputs, applies the knowledge discovery algorithm(s) on the data stored in a database, with the assistance of the concept hierarchy information stored in a concept hierarchy base. The outputs of the system are knowledge rules extracted from the database. The system is implemented in C with the assistance of UNIX software packages LEX and YACC (for compiling the DBLEARN language interface) and operates in conjunction with the SyBase DBMS software. A database learning language for DBLEARN is specified in an extended BNF grammar.

Experimentation using DBLEARN has been conducted on a real database, *the Grants Information database*, which contains the information about the

{ British Columbia } ⊂ B.C.
{ Alberta, Saskatchewan, Manitoba } ⊂ Prairies
{ Ontario } ⊂ Ontario
{ Quebec } ⊂ Quebec
{ New Brunswick, Nova Scotia, Newfoundland, Prince_Edward_Island} ⊂ Maritime
{ B.C., Prairies, Ontario, Quebec, Maritime, Others} ⊂ ANY(province)

Figure 1: A concept hierarchy for attribute *province*.

research grants awarded by NSERC (*the Natural Sciences and Engineering Research Council of Canada*) in the year of 1990-1991. The database consists of 6 large data relations. The central relation table, *award*, contains 10,087 tuples with 11 attributes.

The background knowledge in **DBLEARN** is represented by a set of concept hierarchies. In each hierarchy, the most general concept is the null description (described by a reserved word "ANY"), and the most specific concepts correspond to the specific values of attributes in the database. Figure 1 shows the concept hierarchy for provinces in Canada, where $A \subset B$ indicates that B is a generalization of A, and "⊂" is coded as "<" in the system. Notice that the superordinate concepts for 3 provinces *B.C.*, *Ontario*, and *Quebec* remain ungeneralized since these 3 provinces take most of research grants and it is our intention to distinguish these 3 from other provinces. Other concept hierarchies, such as $\{1 \ldots 19,999\} \subset 1\_20K$, $\{20,000 \ldots 39,999\} \subset 20\_40K$, ..., $\{26000 \ldots 26499\} \subset AI$ (where 26000, ... and 26499 represent NSERC discipline codes), are also stored in the concept hierarchy table. Many learning requests have be posed to this database during our experimentation. Interesting knowledge rules/relationships about NSERC research grant awards in relevance to geographic location, research areas, etc. have been discovered by our experimentation. One such experimental example is illustrated as follows.

Example 6. Let the query be to discover a characteristic rule for NSERC support of operating grants for AI (Artificial Intelligence) researchers in relevance to the geographical locations, the number of grants and the amount distribution of the grants in 1990 to 1991. The learning task is presented in DBLEARN as follows.

> learn characteristic rule for disc_code = "AI"
> from award
> where grant_code = "Operating_Grants"
> in relevance to amount, province, prop(vote), prop(amount)

Notice that *prop(attribute)* is a built-in function which returns the percentage of the summation of the *attribute* value in the generalized tuple divided by the summation of the same *attribute* value in the whole generalized relation. When the query is posed to the system, relevant data are collected by data retrieval from the Grant Information Database. Then attribute-oriented induction is performed on the collected data. The learning result of the query is presented in Table 1. The row "*Amount = 20_40K, Geo_Area = B.C., prop(num_of_grants)*

Amount	Geo_Area	prop(num_of_grants)	prop(amount)
1_20K	B.C.	5.6%	4.1%
1_20K	Prairies	15.5%	10.3%
1_20K	Quebec	14.1%	9%
1_20K	Ontario	25.3%	17.8%
1_20K	Maritime	2.8%	1%
20_40K	B.C.	12.7%	16.3%
20_40K	Prairies	5.6%	6.2%
20_40K	Ontario	9.8%	13%
20_40K	Maritime	1.4%	1.7%
40_60K	B.C.	1.4%	4%
40_60K	Ontario	4.2%	11.3%
> 60K	Quebec	1.4%	4.2%
$1,464,250	Canada	99.8%	98.9%

Table 1: Generalized relation for AI Operating Grants

= 12.7%, and prop(amount) = 16.3%" indicates that for the Operating Grants in AI in the amount between $20,000 and $39,999, B.C. researchers take 12.7% of the total number of grants and 16.3% of the total amount of grants. The last row contains the summary information of the entire generalized relation. Some negligible proportion (less than 1%) of the AI operating grants scattered across Canada are ignored in the table. Thus, the total number of grants in the table takes 99.8% of the total available AI operating grants.

The relationships between amount_category, geo_area, number_of_grants, amount_of_grants, etc. can be also presented in the pairwise form, when necessary, using the extracted prime relation. The system interacts with users for explicit instructions on the necessity of such a presentation.

The performance of the DBLEARN system is satisfactory. The response time of the above query (including the SyBase data retrieval time) is 20 seconds on an IPX SPARC workstation.

3.4 Discussion

Attribute-oriented induction provides a simple and efficient way to learn different kinds of knowledge rules in relational and extended relational databases. The major difference of our approach from previous developed *learning-from-examples* approach is attribute-oriented vs. tuple-oriented induction. It is essential to compare these two approaches.

Both tuple-oriented and attribute-oriented induction take attribute removal and concept tree ascension as their major generalization techniques. However, the former technique performs generalization tuple by tuple, while the latter, attribute by attribute.

The tuple-oriented approach examines the training examples one at a time to induce generalized concepts. In order to discover the most specific concept that is satisfied by all of the training examples, the algorithm must search every node in the search space which represents the possible concepts derived from the generalization on this training example. Since different attributes of a tuple may be generalized to different levels, the number of nodes to be searched for a training example may involve a huge number of possible combinations.

On the other hand, an attribute-oriented algorithm performs generalization on each attribute uniformly for all the tuples in the data relation at the *early* generalization stages. It essentially considers only the factored version space. An algorithm which explores different possible combinations for a large number of tuples during such a generalization process will not be productive since such combinations will be merged in further generalizations. Different possible combinations should be explored only when the relation has been generalized to a relatively small prime relation.

Another obvious advantage of our approach over many other learning algorithms is our integration of the learning process with database operations. In contrast to most existing learning algorithms which do not take full advantages of these database facilities [6, 20], our approach primarily adopts relational operations, such as selection, join, projection (extracting relevant data and removing attributes), tuple substitution (ascending concept trees), and intersection (discovering common tuples among classes). Since relational operations are set-oriented and have been implemented efficiently in many existing systems, our approach is not only efficient but easily exported to many relational systems.

Our approach has absorbed many advanced features of recently developed learning algorithms [20, 23]. As shown in our study, attribute-oriented induction can learn disjunctive rules and handle exceptional cases elegantly by incorporating statistical techniques in the learning process. Moreover, when a new tuple is inserted into a data relation, rather than restarting the learning process from the beginning, it is preferable to amend and fortify what was learned from the previous data. Our algorithms can be easily extended to facilitate such *incremental learning* [20]. Let the generalized relation be stored in the database. When a new tuple is inserted into a database, the concepts of the new tuple are first generalized to the level of the concepts in the generalized relation. Then the generalized tuple can be naturally merged into the generalized relation.

Furthermore, data sampling and parallelism can be explored in knowledge discovery. Attribute-oriented induction can be performed by *sampling* a subset of data from a huge set of relevant data or by first performing induction *in parallel* on several partitions of the relevant data set and then merging the generalized results.

Knowledge discovery methods can be utilized for querying database knowledge, cooperative query answering and semantic query optimization. General data characteristics for any specific set of data can be inquired directly in databases by high-level knowledge queries. Queries can also be answered intelligently using high level concepts and associated with general data statistics. Moreover, semantic query optimization can be further explored using the available knowledge of generalized rules and concept hierarchies.

4 An Integration of Deduction and Induction Mechanisms in Knowledge-Base Systems

A powerful knowledge-base system should integrate deduction and induction mechanisms because the deduction rules stored in a knowledge-base help the discovery of knowledge from data, while the induced rules help the organization of the knowledge-base and facilitate deductive reasoning and query evaluation. Here we present some interesting ideas on their possible integration.

First, attribute-oriented induction, which was originally developed for learning from relational databases, can be extended to learning in a data-intensive knowledge-base system which consists of both data and rules. Some data in a knowledge-base can be deduced by other data and deduction rules. Such data, if involved in a knowledge discovery process, can be first extracted by a deduction process using the techniques developed in deductive database research before induction. On the other hand, some knowledge in a knowledge-base may be defined jointly by rules and extensional facts. If a rule is defined by generalized data, it can be viewed as a portion of an intermediately generalized relation and be merged with other intermediately generalized relations in the learning process.

Secondly, in order to reduce the number of rules to be stored in such a system and simplify the organization of a knowledge-base, induction should be performed up to some halfly-generalized relations, which should be treated as the core of a set of generalized relation. The storage of such a *core* instead of a large number of minorly different generalized rules saves the storage space of a knowledge-base and speeds up further generalization processes.

Thirdly, knowledge rules can often be refined by both deduction and induction processes. Some deduction rules or induced rules may represent imprecise information, coarse descriptions of certain knowledge, or some old knowledge which has been modified substantially. Such rules should be refined by both deduction and induction processes. In the deduction process, rules are taken as useful knowledge in the guidance of explanation-based generalization [21], and such generalization refines the original rules. In the induction process, a rule is taken as a primitive model for learning. Following the model provided by the rule, induction can be performed on the data stored in the database in a model-constrained manner, which can be viewed as an integration of a model-driven approach and a data-driven approach [20]. The rule so induced from the database data is a refinement of the original rule. Efficient database-oriented rule refinement algorithms should be explored in depth.

Finally, the induced rules and meta-data may enhance the power and improve the performance of the system for deductive reasoning and query processing. Clearly, by learning from data and knowledge-base, a knowledge-base is enriched by the induced rules and meta-data. Thus, the system should be able to answer queries about the induced rules, general characteristics of the data and generalization hierarchies. Moreover, some queries can be processed by examining rules and meta-data or reasoning on them without accessing or with less accessing of databases. This can be viewed as a kind of semantic query optimization [18, 4], which applies not only deduction rules but also induced rules and generalization hierarchies.

5 Conclusions

An important consideration in the design and development of a knowledge-base management system is to efficiently support powerful deduction and induction mechanisms in large knowledge-base systems. We believe that a high-performance knowledge-base management system should be a tightly-coupled database system and knowledge system, which supports efficient deduction, induction and their integration. This paper outlines the deduction and induction mechanisms studied in our previous research and proposes their integration in the construction of data-intensive knowledge-base systems. There are many unsolved problems in this direction. Nevertheless, we feel that it represents a promising direction in the development of powerful and efficient data-intensive knowledge-base systems.

Acknowledgements

The work was supported in part by the Natural Sciences and Engineering Research Council of Canada under the grant OPG-3723 and a research grant from the Centre for Systems Science of Simon Fraser University.

References

[1] F. Bancilhon, D. Maier, Y. Sagiv, and J.D. Ullman. Magic sets and other strange ways to implement logic programs. In *Proc. 5th ACM Symp. Principles of Database Systems*, pp. 1–15, Cambridge, MA, March 1986.

[2] F. Bancilhon and R. Ramakrishnan. An amateur's introduction to recursive query processing strategies. In *Proc. 1986 ACM-SIGMOD Conf. Management of Data*, pp. 16–52, Washington, DC, May 1986.

[3] Y. Cai, N. Cercone, and J. Han. Attribute-oriented induction in relational databases. In G. Piatetsky-Shapiro and W. J. Frawley, editors, *Knowledge Discovery in Databases*, pp. 213–228. AAAI/MIT Press, 1991.

[4] U.S. Chakravarthy, J. Grant, and J. Minker. Logic-based approach to semantic query optimization. *ACM Trans. Database Syst.*, 15:162–207, 1990.

[5] W. Chen, M. Kifer, and D.S. Warren. Hilog as a platform for a database language. In *Proc. 2nd Int. Workshop on Database Programming Languages*, pp. 315–329, Gleneden Beach, OR, June 1989.

[6] T.G. Dietterich and R.S. Michalski. A comparative review of selected methods for learning from examples. In R. Michalski et. al., editor, *Machine Learning: An Artificial Intelligence Approach, Vol. 1*, pp. 41–82. Morgan Kaufmann, 1983.

[7] D. Fisher. Improving inference through conceptual clustering. In *Proc. 1987 AAAI Conf.*, pp. 461–465, Seattle, Washington, July 1987.

[8] A. Van Gelder, K.A. Ross, and J.S. Schlipf. The well-founded semantics for general logic programs. *J. ACM*, 38:620–650, 1991.

[9] J. Han. Multi-way counting method. *Information Systems*, 14:219–229, 1989.

[10] J. Han. Compilation-based list processing in deductive databases. In A. Pirotte, C. Delobel and G. Gottlob, editors, *Extending Database Technology - EDBT'92 [Lecture Notes in Computer Science 580]*, pp. 104–119. Springer-Verlag, 1992.

[11] J. Han, Y. Cai, and N. Cercone. Knowledge discovery in databases: An attribute-oriented approach. In *Proc. of 18th Int'l Conf. on Very Large Data Bases*, pp. 547–559, Vancouver, Canada, August 1992.

[12] J. Han and Z.N. Li. Deductive-ER: Deductive entity-relationship model and its data language. *Information and Software Technology*, 34:192–204, 1992.

[13] J. Han and W. Lu. Asynchronous chain recursions. *IEEE Trans. Knowledge and Data Engineering*, 1:185–195, 1989.

[14] J. Han and K. Zeng. Automatic generation of compiled forms for linear recursions. *Information Systems*, 17:299–322, 1992.

[15] R. Hull and R. King. Semantic database modeling: Survey, applications, and research issues. *ACM Comput. Surv.*, 19:201–260, 1987.

[16] M. Kifer and G. Lausen. F-logic: A higher order language for reasoning about objects, inheritance, and scheme. In *Proc. 1989 ACM-SIGMOD Conf. Management of Data*, pp. 134–146, Portland, Oregon, June 1989.

[17] R. Krishnamurthy and C. Zaniolo. Optimization in a logic based language for knowledge and data intensive applications. In Extending Database Technology, editor, *8) [Lecture Notes in Computer Science 303]*, pp. 16–33. Springer-Verlag, 1988.

[18] L.V.S. Lakshmanan and R. Missaoui. On semantic query optimization in deductive databases. In *Proc. 8th Int. Conf. Data Engineering*, pp. 368–375, Phoenix, AZ, Feb. 1992.

[19] R.S. Michalski. A theory and methodology of inductive learning. In Michalski et.al., editor, *Machine Learning: An Artificial Intelligence Approach, Vol. 1*, pp. 83–134. Morgan Kaufmann, 1983.

[20] R.S. Michalski, J.G. Carbonell, and T.M. Mitchell. **Machine Learning, An Artificial Intelligence Approach, Vol. 2**. Morgan Kaufmann, 1986.

[21] T.M. Mitchell, R.M. Keller, and S.T. Kedar-Cabelli. Explanation-based generalization: A unifying view. *Machine Learning*, 1:47–80, 1986.

[22] S. Naqvi and S. Tsur. **A Logical Data Language for Data and Knowledge Bases**. Computer Science Press, 1989.

[23] G. Piatetsky-Shapiro and W.J. Frawley. **Knowledge Discovery in Databases**. AAAI/MIT Press, 1991.

[24] A. Silberschatz, M. Stonebraker, and J.D. Ullman. Database systems: Achievements and opportunities. *Comm. ACM*, 34:94–109, 1991.

[25] S. Tsur. Deductive databases in action. In *Proc. 10th ACM Symp. Principles of Database Systems*, pp. 142–153, Denver, CO, May 1991.

[26] J.D. Ullman. **Principles of Database and Knowledge-Base Systems, Vol. 2**. Computer Science Press, 1989.

[27] J.D. Ullman. A comparison of deductive and object-oriented database systems. In obel et. al., editor, *Deductive and Object-Oriented Databases (DOOD'91) [Lecture Notes in Computer Science 566]*, pp. 263–277. Springer Verlag, 1991.

[28] C. Zaniolo. Object identity and inheritance in deductive databases: an evolutionary approach. In J.-M. Nicolas Kim and S. Nishio, editors, *Deductive and Object-Oriented Databases*, pp. 7–24. Elsevier Science, 1990.

[29] J. Zytkow and J. Baker. Interactive mining of regularities in databases. In G. Piatetsky-Shapiro and W.J. Frawley, editors, *Knowledge Discovery in Databases*, pp. 31–54. AAAI/MIT Press, 1991.

On Querying Temporal Deductive Databases[*]

Laks V.S. Lakshmanan and Daniel A. Nonen
Department of Computer Science
Concordia University
Montreal, Quebec

1 Introduction

Information about the objects modeled by databases changes in real-world applications. However, time is not managed in a uniform manner in most databases. Temporal databases have been introduced to fill this gap [15]. A survey of works on historical and temporal databases can be found in [16]. In this paper, we consider primarily temporal databases which associate a valid interval with each piece of temporal data. This can be done by adding a *From* and a *To* attribute to the data. For example, if t is a tuple in a temporal relation R, then $t.From$ is the first time that t is valid and $t.To$ is the final time t is valid. (If t is currently valid, the value of $t.To$ is the special system defined variable NOW which evaluates to the current system time.) The following problems arise in the context of temporal databases:

1. Writing queries is more difficult because even 'simple' queries may require many temporal comparisons;

2. Maintaining database consistency is problematic: for example, since data is not deleted when updates are made, many tuples will have the same 'key';

3. Query evaluation may be inefficient unless the properties of temporal attributes are recognized and exploited.[1]

Temporal database languages usually have special features to adapt them for use with temporal data. Two such languages are TQuel [15], a superset of Quel, and HSQL [14], a superset of SQL. They offer useful operators such as *precedes*, *contains*, and *overlaps* for comparing temporal intervals as well as DBMS support for maintaining database consistency. TQuel extends Quel's aggregate functions to the temporal domain. However, since HSQL and TQuel are based on relational algebra, they lack the expressive power of a deductive database language supporting recursion.

[*]This research was supported in part by a grant from the Natural Sciences and Engineering Research Council of Canada and in part by a grant from the Fonds Pour Formation De Chercheurs Et L'Aide À La Recherche of Quebec.
[1]Efficient temporal query processing techniques are not discussed in this paper; see *e.g.*, [7].

Temporal logic is the formalism used for the logic programming language TEMPLOG [1]. This formalism gives the language a great deal of elegance and expressive power. However, the user is limited to using the abstract temporal operators *next, always, eventually, until,* and *precedes* which may be unfamiliar and difficult for the uninitiated to use as a query language. Also, in the context of (temporal) databases, the expressiveness offered by these primitives is severely limited.

TEMPLOG has a Prolog-style execution model, and therefore, it is not truly declarative.

STATELOG [6] is based on Datalog[2] extended by the successor function to handle temporal queries. Its great strength is the capability to determine a finite representation for infinite query answers when the data is periodic in nature. Unfortunately, due to the high computational complexity of the problem, a finite representation can be determined for only certain periodic programs. Also, temporal database programming using only the successor function can be cumbersome.

In this paper, we introduce a language called TKL (*Temporal Knowledge-base Language*). TKL offers a uniform medium for queries, updates, and schema definition in temporal deductive databases. It has a graphic user interface in which, we believe, the expression of a query suggests its meaning (Section 2). We propose user-defined temporal data-types, in addition to a predefined temporal data-type, including a mechanism for handling temporal null values in stored relations and in queries, as well as a mechanism for modeling imprecise temporal data (Section 3). TKL has much of the expressive power of a Horn clause language with bottom-up evaluation and stratified negation. The semantics of TKL is defined with reference to this Horn clause language. However, with this expressive power come challenging theoretical issues: because we extend a deductive database language to allow function symbols, we must deal with the problem of detecting when a query has a finite number of answers (Section 4). Our conclusions are presented in Section 5.

2 TKL

The basic features of TKL are introduced in this section. For the basic concepts of deductive databases and datalog, the reader is referred to [17]. TKL supports recursive queries similar to a full-fledged deductive database language such as datalog and also supports features for the temporal domain. TKL has much of the power of Horn clause languages with bottom-up evaluation and stratified negation (see, *e.g.,* [2]). It has the built-in temporal predicates *precedes, contains, overlaps, etc.,* that are usually included in temporal database query languages as well as support for valid intervals and valid events for tuples. In this section, we introduce TKL informally using examples. In section 4, we develop the semantics of TKL and also address the implementation issues of TKL and the query finiteness problem.

In TKL, the *temporal attribute* names **From, To,** and **At** are reserved for *temporal* relations. There are two types of temporal relations: (i) *interval* relations, which have a closed valid interval in the form of the **From** and the

---

[2]Datalog, the language of function-free Horn clauses, is a vehicle query language for deductive databases.

To attribute associated with them; and (ii) *event* relations, which have the `At` attribute indicating the time an event occurs associated with them. Relations which do not have temporal attributes associated with them are called *non-temporal* relations.

Toward the goal of making the expression of a query suggest its meaning, TKL provides a graphic form-based interface in the spirit of QBE [18]. We informally introduce TKL by means of the next two examples.

Example 2.1 A company stores information about its employees using the relation scheme

```
emp(Name, Manager, Salary, Commissions, From, To)
```

to record the name of each employee, the name of the employee's manager, and the employee's earnings from salary and from commissions. The `From` and `To` attribute values give the valid interval of each tuple in this relation.

A query program to determine all the bosses of each employee can be written in TKL as follows. A menu allows the selection of rules, queries, or integrity constraints to be written, edited, browsed, or run. We select the action of writing a rule. Then we select the head of the rule from a list of IDB predicates in the database, or define a new IDB predicate interactively, if necessary. In this case, we define a new IDB predicate by supplying the predicate name `boss` and its attribute names and types: *i.e.,* `Emp_Name`(*string*), `Manager`(*string*), `From`(*DATE yy:mm:dd*)[3], and `To`(*DATE yy:mm:dd*). Then the first rule for the query program is written by requesting a `boss` form and a `emp` form using a menu. The system will then display on the screen empty forms similar to the following figure.

boss	Emp_Name	Manager	From	To		emp	Name	Manager	Salary	Commissions	From	To
bos1:					If emp1:							

Conditions:

TKL variables are unquoted strings beginning with an uppercase character or an underscore. Constants are (i) strings which are either quoted or begin with a lowercase character, (ii) numbers, (iii) the boolean constants *true* and *false*, or (iv) temporal constants (see Section 3). The strings `bos1` and `emp1` are called *form identifiers*. Unique form identifiers are automatically generated by the system for every displayed form. They can be used with an attribute name in the `Conditions` section, which appears after the last form, to refer to the corresponding field value. *E.g.,* `emp1.Name` refers to the field below `Name` in the form to the right of `emp1`. When a form identifier is used by itself, it refers to the valid interval or the valid event of the corresponding form. The empty forms are completed as follows to create the base rule for the query program.

boss	Emp_Name	Manager	From	To		emp	Name	Manager	Salary	Commissions	From	To
bos1:	Willy	Howard	F	T	If emp1:		Willy	Howard			F	T

Conditions:

This rule is equivalent to the SQL query Select *Name, Manager, From, To* From *emp*. Note that empty attribute value fields are interpreted as 'don't care' variables in TKL. The recursive rule is created by requesting a `boss` form, an

---

[3]Note the use of temporal data types for (temporal) attributes. More details on these data types can be found in Section 3.

emp form, and another **boss** form which are then completed as shown below. Notice that an employee's valid interval should be concurrent with the valid interval of each of his/her bosses.

bos1:

boss	Emp_Name	Manager	From	To
	Willy	Mr_Grim	F	T

if

emp1:

emp	Name	Manager	Salary	Commissions	From	To
	Willy	Howard			F1	T1

bos2:

boss	Emp_Name	Manager	From	To
	Howard	Mr_Grim	P2	T2

Conditions:
emp1 ~ bos2;
emp1 intersection bos2 = bos1

This rule cannot be expressed in a conventional relational query language. Notice that the first condition uses the form identifiers **emp1** and **bos2** and the built-in TKL predicate $\sim$ to specify that the corresponding valid intervals are concurrent, that is, they have some time instant in common. The second condition is used to extract the interval they have in common. (See section 3 for the precise definition of the temporal operators and built-in predicates.)

In the following example, we illustrate how a query is written using TKL. Note that a **P.** in an attribute value field of a form indicates that the value of that field is part of the query answer. If **P.** is entered in the first value field of a form, that is, the field under the form name, all attribute values of the form are part of the query answer.

Example 2.2 *Query*: Using the relations in Example 2.1, give the details of each employee whose earnings are more than 10% greater than his/her boss at some time since 1987, where an employee's earnings are his/her salary plus commissions.

Two **emp** forms and one **boss** form are needed to write this query. After displaying them on the screen, they can be completed as follows.

emp1:

emp	Name	Manager	Salary	Commissions	From	To
	Willy	Howard	Sw	Cw		

emp2:

emp	Name	Manager	Salary	Commissions	From	To
	Howard		Sh	Ch		

bos1:

boss	Emp_Name	Manager	From	To
P.	Willy	Howard		T

Conditions:
(Sw + Cw) > (Sh + Ch) * 1.1;
emp1 ~ emp2;
emp1 intersection emp2 = bos1;
T >= 87:01:01;

3   The Temporal Data Type

The temporal data type is used to represent the time of an event or to indicate the end points of a temporal interval. Temporal information may be stored using other data types such as string or integer, but it would not take advantage of the interpretations, optimizations, and integrity checks that have been developed for the temporal data type [7, 14]. Multiple temporal data types are allowed in TKL, unlike other temporal systems which allow only one temporal data type in a database.

In this section, we describe the built-in *DATE* temporal data type which is useful for many common applications. However, there are some applications that do not naturally fit into the 'date and time of day' format of the DATE data type: *e.g.,* it is difficult and unnatural to capture the idea that something occurs every Monday in the DATE format. Also, the time-frames needed for scientific databases are frequently specialized: *e.g.,* different units for measuring time may be required for particle physics and for astronomy. We allow user-defined temporal data types to handle cases like these. An important feature of the temporal data type is that imprecise temporal data is accommodated implicitly by using temporal units that represent a time interval (*flexible granularity*). We provide a simple method for interpreting these intervals which is similar in spirit to the treatment of null values in relational databases [3]. Finally, as is usual in temporal database systems, we provide a number of temporal comparison predicates for common temporal relationships in order to simplify queries.

The temporal data type may have one or more subfields. The built-in DATE data type, in the format yy:mm:dd:hh:MM:ss, is predefined with subfields for years, months, and days following the Gregorian calendar and for hours, minutes and seconds as usual on a 24-hour clock. Similarly, a user-defined temporal data type may be separated into subfields by one or more formatting characters such as the colon. In the sequel, we use the following conventions: let U be a temporal data type with n subfields separated by colons, denoted $<$ *subfield* n $>$:$<$ *subfield* $n-1$ $>$: ... :$<$ *subfield* 1 $>$; we say that G is a *valid temporal subtype* of U with m subfields, $m \leq n$, numbered from n down to $n - m + 1$, if G has m subfields and it is a prefix of U. Notice that each type G implicitly induces a set of constants of this type. We refer to them as temporal constants of type G.

We define a *temporal term* of type G as follows: (i) all temporal constants of type G are temporal terms of type G; (ii) all variables representing temporal constants of type G are temporal terms of type G; (iii) all strings of the form $sf_n : \ldots : sf_{n-m+1}$, where each sf_i, $n - m + 1 \leq i \leq n$ is either a constant which is allowed in the ith field of G or a variable symbol, is a temporal term of type G. For example, the DATE subtype term *92:M:D* may appear in a query about which month and day, denoted by the variables M and D, in 1992 something happened.

Two important properties of a temporal data (sub)type are its *tick* size and *granularity*. The selection of U determines the tick size, which is the shortest time period that can be represented by constants of type U (*i.e.,* a tick is the interval represented by one unit of the rightmost subfield of U). It is the atomic time unit for the data type. For example, the tick determined by the DATE data type is a second, but it may be more suitable to have a tick size of a minute for a business application; a tick of 100,000 years may be suitable for a database of geological samples; a tick of 10^{-12} seconds may be suitable for a database of elementary particles for a physics application. We define the *granularity* of a subtype G to be the number of ticks in its rightmost subfield. Let p be a temporal relation having temporal attribute(s) of type G. We define the *granularity of p*, denoted *gran(p)*, to be the granularity of the type associated with the temporal attribute(s) of *p*. Although multiple temporal data types are allowed, only one subtype (of one of them) may be used in *p*.

The granularity of a temporal relation reflects the imprecision of the valid interval or event of the data modeled by the relation. This imprecision may be a matter of convenience or due to a lack of information because of theoretical and/or practical limitations on the accuracy of time measurements. Later in this section, we propose methods for reasoning using imprecise temporal information.

The cardinality of the set of ticks is the largest integer that can be naturally represented on the target machine of the implementation, *viz.*, MAXINT. MAXINT is typically 2^{32} for an unsigned integer on a machine with a 32-bit word-size. The product of the tick size of the temporal data type and MAXINT determines the maximum time interval that can be represented using that data type. For example, if the tick size is one day and MAXINT is 2^{32}, the maximum time interval that can be represented is approximately 11,759,301 years.

The user must supply the *start-up* time for each temporal data type when a new database is defined. Temporal constants are mapped to integers internally. The start-up time maps to 0, represented as a signed integer if time is counted both forward and backward from the start-up time. If time is counted forward (backward) only, then the start-up time maps to 0 (MAXINT, resp.) represented as an unsigned integer.

3.1   User-Defined Temporal Data Types

User-defined temporal data types, just like the predefined DATE data type, have a fixed format. Associated with all data types, there is an interpretation function, which maps constants of that type to the integers. It is convenient to distinguish between the *base* of a numbering system, such as octal, decimal, hexadecimal, *etc.*, and the base of a temporal subfield which we call the *radix* of the subfield. For example, the radix of the hour subfield in the DATE data type is 24 while its base is decimal.

For user-defined temporal data types, the following specifications must be supplied by the user:

1. the radix and base for subfields $n - 1$ to 1 and the base for the nth subfield[4];

2. whether the subfield represents an ordinal integer as it does in the year, month and day subfield of DATE or a cardinal as in the hour, minute, and second subfields of DATE;

3. if the subfield represents a subrange of values then each string that may be a member of the subrange must be given in order beginning with the least member (*e.g.*, "January", ... , "December"); in this case, there is an ordinal number associated with each member of the subrange.

---

[4] The radix of the nth subfield may be considered MAXINT, MAXINT/2 − 1 OR MAXINT/2, depending on the how time is counted, however, incrementing this value may be considered an overflow error.

Example 3.1 Designers of a database for school schedules might want to tailor the temporal data type S to fit their needs as follows:

subfield 1: $1, \ldots, 8$; /* the number of periods in a school day */
subfield 2: mon, tues, wed, thurs, fri; /* school days */
subfield 3: winter, summer, fall; /* school terms */
subfield 4: base = 10, ordinal = yes; /* any integer representing a year */
start-up time: 92:winter:mon:1;
sense in which time is counted: Forward;

Thus, 92:fall:mon:1 refers to the first period on Monday during the fall term, 1992 and [92:fall:mon:1, 92:fall:fri:8] is the interval that includes all periods in a school week during the fall term of 1992. □

Some definitions are necessary before presenting the temporal interpretation function for user-defined temporal data types. Let t be a constant of type U. We define $SF(t, k)$ to be the value of the kth subfield of t. We define $Ord(U, k)$ to be 1 if the kth subfield of U is defined to have ordinal numbering, otherwise it is defined to be 0. Then the function $t\_to\_i(U, t)$, which maps a constant t of type U to an integer, is described as follows. Let $t_{start-up_U}$ be the start-up time given for U.

Let $j_o = \sum_{j=1}^{n} [SF(t_{start-up_U}, j) - Ord(U, j)] * rf(j)$;
Then $t\_to\_i(U, t_{start-up_U}) = 0$

$$t\_to\_i(U, t) = \begin{cases} (\sum_{j=1}^{n} [SF(t, j) - Ord(U, j)] * rf(j)) - j_o & \textit{if sign of } t \textit{ is } + \\ -(\sum_{j=1}^{n} [SF(t, j) - Ord(U, j)] * rf(j)) - j_o & \textit{if sign of } t \textit{ is } - \end{cases}$$

where $rf(1) = 1$,
$rf(j + 1) = rf(j) * radix(j + 1)$, $j = 1, \ldots, n - 1$, and
$j_o = t\_to\_i(U, t_{start-up_U})$.

The sign of t will be negative when the nth subfield is less than zero (*e.g.*, Aristotle was born in the year -384 (*i.e.*, 384 B.C.), in the DATE data type.). It is possible to support arithmetic functions on temporal data (sub)types by transforming them to corresponding functions on integers. It is also possible to construct the inverse mappings which can convert integers back to the corresponding temporal constants. The same inverse mapping is used to interpret variables in temporal terms. Temporal terms can be thought of as templates to be matched to integers. We say that field j of temporal term t *matches* an integer i if the following relation holds:

$$SF(t, j) = [((i + j_o) \bmod rf(j + 1)) \operatorname{div} rf(j)] + Ord(j), 1 \leq j \leq n,$$

where $rf(j)$ and j_o are as defined above and we define $rf(n + 1)$ to be the maximum value allowed in the nth subfield. If $SF(t, j)$ is the variable X_j, then X_j is assigned a value equal to the RHS of the above equation. We illustrate the use of the temporal interpretation function with the following example.

Example 3.2 With reference to Example 3.1, $rf(1) = 1$, $rf(2) = 8$, $rf(3) = 40$, $rf(4) = 120$, and $rf(4 + 1) = $MAXINT. The start-up time for temporal data type S is 92:winter:mon:1. Thus, the value of j_o is $t\_to\_i(S, 92\text{:winter:mon:1})$

= 11040. It follows that $t\_to\_i(S, 92{:}\text{fall:mon:}1) = 11120 - 11040 = 80$. To determine the value for the variable T such that the temporal term $92{:}T{:}\text{mon:}1$ will match 80, we evaluate the expression $(((80 + 11040)\text{mod}120) \text{ div } 40) + 1$ and get the value 3 for T, the ordinal corresponding to fall in the third subfield of S. □

3.2 Interpretation of Imprecision in Intervals and Events

Temporal relations must be assigned a temporal data type and a granularity when they are defined. We allow temporal relations to have different granularities, as appropriate for the precision of the available temporal information. Indeed, real-world temporal information is inherently imprecise. However, allowing flexible granularities introduces a complication in interpreting intervals which is illustrated in the following example.

Example 3.3 The relation *hours_worked(Name, From, To)* is used by a company to record the interval employees work each day with granularity of hour. A tuple s in this relation, <*Bob, 92:10:15:8, 92:10:15:17*>, can be interpreted as meaning Bob worked anywhere from 8 hours and 1 second to 9 hours, 59 minutes, and 59 seconds on October 15, 1992. □

To resolve the above problem, we make precise what exactly is meant by a valid interval or a valid event by specifying an *interpretation policy*. We provide two simple and useful interpretation policies called *narrow*, denoted by □, and *broad*, denoted by ◇. Applying the narrow interpretation to tuple s in Example 3.3 gives [92:10:15:8:59:59, 92:10:15:17:00:00], meaning that s holds for all times t in this closed interval. Likewise, the broad interpretation is [92:10:15:8:00:00, 92:10:15:17:59:59] meaning that there is a non-zero probability that s holds for all times t in this closed interval. The interpretation policies *broad* and *narrow* have interesting connections to the modalities *possibly* and *necessarily* arising in modal logic [4] as well as the concepts of *maybe answers* and *sure answers* studied in the context of relational databases with null values [3, 9]. Within the context of the temporal data type, it is convenient to think of *necessity* as a narrow interpretation and *possibility* as a broad interpretation.

We introduce the temporal *null* character '/' to indicate an unknown value when it appears in a temporal term. Referring once again to Example 3.3, the valid interval of tuple s could be represented using nulls as [92:10:15:8:/:/, 92:10:15:17:/:/]. A broad interpretation of an interval will include every tick that could possibly be in the interval. This is obtained by replacing every null in the *From* term with the minimum value for the field in which it appears and by replacing every null in the *To* term by the maximum value for the field in which it appears. Similarly, in a narrow interpretation, every null in the *From* field is replaced by the maximum value for that field and every null value in the *To* field is replaced by the minimum value for that field. It is now a simple matter to allow null values in stored relations: all that is needed is to extend the definition of temporal terms to allow '/' to be the value of a subfield. Nulls appearing in terms that are arguments of the built-in temporal predicates, which are defined formally below, are interpreted according to the interpretation policy associated with the temporal predicate.

The temporal attributes of interval relations can be represented internally by expanding each of the *To* and *From* attribute values into two integers, one for narrow interpretation and the other for broad interpretation. More formally, let R be a temporal interval relation with temporal data type U and $r \in R$ be a tuple where $r = < \bar{x}, f, t >$. Then the internal representation of r is $r_I = < \bar{x}, f^-, f^+, t^-, t^+ >$, where

$$f^- = t\_to\_i(U, f);$$
$$t^- = t\_to\_i(U, t);$$
$$f^+ = f^- + gran(R) - 1;$$
$$t^+ = t^- + gran(R) - 1.$$

Event attribute values are treated much like intervals by setting the single event temporal attribute value to both f and t and then proceeding in the same way as for interval relations.[5] Thus, the internal representation for events is the same as for intervals. This allows a uniform semantics for the built-in temporal predicates with either event or interval operands. More formally, let E be a temporal event relation with temporal data type U and $e \in E$ be a tuple, where $e = < \bar{x}, a >$. Then $e_I = < \bar{x}, a^-, a^+, a^-, a^+ >$ is the internal representation of e, where $a^- = t\_to\_i(U, a)$ and $a^+ = a^- + gran(E) - 1$.

We now define the built-in temporal predicates in terms of the internal representation of their operands. Let r_1 and r_2 be tuples from any interval or event relation in the database and let the internal representation of their temporal intervals be $I_1 = < f_1^-, f_1^+, t_1^-, t_1^+ >$ and $I_2 = < f_2^-, f_2^+, t_2^-, t_2^+ >$ respectively. In the following, by $\tau \in [f, t]$ we mean τ is a member of the set of ticks corresponding to the interval $[f, t]$.

- (*congruent*) Intuition: $I_1 \equiv I_2$ iff
  $(\forall \tau_1 \in [f_1^+, t_1^-] \; \exists \tau_2 \in [f_2^+, t_2^-] \; \tau_1 = \tau_2) \; \wedge \; (\forall \tau_2 \in [f_2^+, t_2^-] \; \exists \tau_1 \in [f_1^+, t_1^-] \; \tau_1 = \tau_2) \; \wedge \; (\forall \tau_1 \in [f_1^-, t_1^+] \; \exists \tau_2 \in [f_2^-, t_2^+] \; \tau_1 = \tau_2) \; \wedge \; (\forall \tau_2 \in [f_2^-, t_2^+] \; \exists \tau_1 \in [f_1^-, t_1^+] \; \tau_1 = \tau_2)$, i.e. I_1 is identical to I_2;
  Formal Definition:
  $I_1 \equiv I_2$ iff $(f_1^- = f_2^-) \; \wedge \; (f_1^+ = f_2^+) \; \wedge \; (t_1^- = t_2^-) \; \wedge (t_1^+ = t_2^+)$.

- (*equivalent*$_\Box$) Intuition: $I_1 =_\Box I_2$ iff $(\forall \tau_1 \in [f_1^+, t_1^-] \; \exists \tau_2 \in [f_2^+, t_2^-] \; \tau_1 = \tau_2)$ $\wedge \; (\forall \tau_2 \in [f_2^+, t_2^-] \; \exists \tau_1 \in [f_1^+, t_1^-] \; \tau_1 = \tau_2)$, i.e. every tick that must necessarily be in I_1 must necessarily also be in I_2, and vice versa;
  Formal Definition: $I_1 =_\Box I_2$ iff $(f_1^+ = f_2^+) \wedge (t_1^- = t_2^-)$.

- (*equivalent*$_\Diamond$) Intuition: $I_1 =_\Diamond I_2$ iff $(\forall \tau_1 \in [f_1^+, t_1^-] \; \exists \tau_2 \in [f_2^-, t_2^+] \; \tau_1 = \tau_2)$ $\wedge \; (\forall \tau_2 \in [f_2^+, t_1^-] \; \exists \tau_2 \in [f_2^-, t_2^+] \; \tau_1 = \tau_2)$, i.e. every tick that must necessarily be in I_1 might possibly also be in I_2;
  Formal Definition:
  $I_1 =_\Diamond I_2$ iff $(f_1^- \leq f_2^+) \wedge (f_2^- \leq f_1^+) \; \wedge \; (t_1^- \leq t_2^+) \wedge (t_2^- \leq t_1^+)$.

- (*precedes*$_\Box$) Intuition: $I_1 <_\Box I_2$ iff I_1 must necessarily end before I_2 might possibly begin;
  Formal Definition: $I_1 <_\Box I_2$ iff $t_1^+ < f_2^-$.

---

[5] Our use of the word *event* does not refer to a single tick in general, but to a sequence of ticks.

- (*precedes*$_\diamond$) Intuition: $I_1 <_\diamond I_2$ iff I_1 might possibly end before I_2 must begin;
  Formal Definition: $I_1 <_\diamond I_2$ iff $t_1^- < f_2^+$.

- (*contains*$_\square$) Intuition: $I_1\ in_\square\ I_2$ iff $\forall \tau_1 \in [f_1^-, t_1^+]\ \tau_1 \in [f_2^+, t_2^-]$, *i.e.*, every tick that might possibly be in I_1 must necessarily be in I_2;
  Formal Definition: $I_1\ in_\square\ I_2$ iff $(f_2^+ \le f_1^-) \wedge (t_1^+ \le t_2^-)$.

- (*contains*$_\diamond$) Intuition: $I_1\ in_\diamond\ I_2$ iff $\forall \tau_1 \in [f_1^+, t_1^-]\ \tau_1 \in [f_2^-, t_2^+]$, *i.e.*, every tick that must necessarily be in I_1 might possibly be in I_2;
  Formal Definition: $I_1\ in_\diamond\ I_2$ iff $(f_2^- \le f_1^+) \wedge (t_1^- \le t_2^+)$.

- (*overlaps* − *before*$_\square$) Intuition: $I_1 <|_\square I_2$ iff I_1 must necessarily begin before I_2 might possibly begin, I_1 must necessarily end before I_2 might possibly end, and I_1 and I_2 must necessarily have some tick in common;
  Formal Definition: $I_1 <|_\square I_2$ iff $(f_1^+ < f_2^-) \wedge (t_1^+ < t_2^-) \wedge (f_2^+ \le t_1^-)$.

- (*overlaps* − *before*$_\diamond$) Intuition: $I_1 <|_\diamond I_2$ iff I_1 might possibly begin before I_2 must necessarily begin, I_1 might possibly end before I_2 must necessarily end, and I_1 and I_2 might possibly have some tick in common;
  Formal Definition: $I_1 <|_\diamond I_2$ iff $(f_1^- < f_2^+) \wedge (t_1^- < t_2^+) \wedge (f_2^- \le t_1^+)$.

- (*consecutive* − *before*$_\square$) Intuition: $I_1 <||_\square I_2$ iff $\forall \tau_1 \in [t_1^-, t_1^+]\ \exists \tau_2 \in [f_2^-, f_2^+]\ \tau_1 + 1 = \tau_2$, *i.e.*, one tick after I_1 must necessarily end, I_2 must necessarily begin;
  Formal Definition: $(t_1^- + 1 = f_2^-) \wedge (t_1^+ + 1 = f_2^+)$.

- (*consecutive* − *before*$_\diamond$) Intuition: $I_1 <||_\diamond I_2$ iff $(\exists \tau_1 \in [t_1^-, t_1^+]\ \exists \tau_2 \in [f_2^-, f_2^+]\ \tau_1 + 1 = \tau_2$; *i.e.*, one tick after I_1 might possibly end, I_2 might possibly begin; Formal Definition: $I_1 <||_\diamond I_2$ iff
  $(t_1^- + 1 \le f_2^- \wedge f_2^- \le t_1^+ + 1) \vee (t_1^- + 1 \le f_2^+ \wedge f_2^+ \le t_1^+ + 1) \vee$
  $(f_2^- \le t_1^- + 1 \wedge t_1^- \le f_2^+) \vee (f_2^- \le t_1^+ + 1 \wedge t_1^+ \le f_2^+)$.

In a similar fashion, we define $>_\square$, $>_\diamond$, $|>_\square$, $|>_\diamond$, *etc.* We define the following derived predicates. Note that $\circ$ is one of $\square$ or $\diamond$.

- (*overlap*$_\circ$) $I_1 |_\circ I_2$ iff either $I_1 <|_\circ I_2$ or $I_1 |_\circ> I_2$ holds;

- (*concurrent*$_\circ$) $I_1 \sim_\circ I_2$ iff either $I_1 |_\circ I_2$ or $I_1\ in_\circ\ I_2$ or $I_2\ in_\circ\ I_1$ holds.

Let t_1 and t_2 be temporal terms. We define the value of $max(t_1, t_2)$ to be the maximum of t_1 and t_2 and the value of $min(t_1, t_2)$ to be the minimum of t_1 and t_2. When I_1 and I_2 are concurrent, we define the value of $I_1 \cap I_2$ to be the interval $[max(I_1.From, I_2.From), min(I_1.To, I_2.To)]$ and the value of $I_1 \cup I_2$ to be the interval $[min(I_1.From, I_2.From), max(I_1.To, I_2.To)]$. When I_1 and I_2 are not concurrent, we leave $I_1 \cap I_2$ and $I_1 \cup I_2$ undefined.

We end this section with an example using the temporal data type in a Horn clause program. In the remainder of this paper, we use $*$ instead of $\square$ and $+$ instead of $\diamond$.

Example 3.4 This example shows the differences in philosophy implied by the choice of temporal interpretation policy.

The tick-size of a company's database is a day for the DATE temporal data type. The following schemes are used to store accounts receivable and accounts payable information.

```
receivable(Client, Amount, At)
payable(Creditor, Amount, At)
```

Both of these schemes have a granularity of month and the value of their `At` attribute indicates when payment should be received or made. The times when payments are actually received and payments are actually made by the company are stored using the `receipts` scheme and the `payments` scheme respectively, each of which have a granularity of a day.

```
receipts(Name, Amount, At)
payments(Name, Amount, At)
```

The following rules are used a find clients who are late in making their payments and to find creditors to which the company is late in making its payments at some time T.

```
late_receipt(C,T,T1):-receivable(C,A,T),not receipts(A,C,T1),T1<*T.
late_paying(C,T,T1):-payable(C,A,T),not payments(C,A,T1),T1<+T.
```

The only essential difference between these queries is in their temporal interpretation policies. As a result of this difference, it appears to be company policy to consider a client to be in arrears if he/she has not paid by the first day of the month payment is due. On the other hand, the company considers itself to be in arrears only if it has not paid a creditor by the last day of the due month.

□

4 Semantics, Query Finiteness, and Implementation

In this section, we give semantics of TKL in terms of datalog extended with function symbols and stratified negation. Then, we discuss the integrity constraints (ICs) needed to maintain data consistency in a temporal (deductive) database. This is followed by a discussion of our proposal for detecting certain classes of *superfinite* programs, a sufficient condition for finiteness, to identify query programs that have a finite number of answers. Finally, we discuss some aspects of the TKL implementation.

4.1 Semantics of TKL

The meaning of TKL queries, rules and ICs can be given by (i) translating them into datalog extended with stratified negation and function symbols and (ii) applying the semantic interpretation for this extended datalog [17] to the translated rules. We show how to translate a TKL query into its corresponding Horn clause r and then we illustrate the procedure using the query from Example 2.2. A TKL query is translated into the corresponding Horn clause by performing the following steps. (Rules and ICs are handled in much the same way.)

1. Replace the reserved word NOW with the current system time and date using the appropriate granularity; uniformly replace TKL variables with new variable symbols; replace each empty field with a new variable symbol;

2. Replace form identifiers in the **Conditions** section with

   (i) the corresponding attribute value when they appear in the *dot* field accessor notation,

   (ii) the corresponding valid event or valid interval when they are used with built-in temporal predicates;

3. Map constant temporal terms to the corresponding integers;

4. Create the head predicate of r, $query(X_1, \ldots X_k)$, where $query$ is a reserved predicate symbol, as follows. Let $A_1, \ldots, A_k$ be the distinct attribute value fields which either contain 'P.' or the first field of whose form contains 'P.'. Then we assign to each X_i the value appearing in A_i, $1 \leq i \leq k$. This value can be a variable or a constant.

5. For each form in the query, append a subgoal p to r where p is the predicate symbol corresponding to the form and the arguments of p are taken from the corresponding attribute values of the form;

6. For each arithmetic or temporal expression x *op* y in the **Conditions** section, where x and y are integers, reals, strings, or temporal terms, create a subgoal using a built-in predicate as follows. Let p_{op} be the built-in predicate symbol corresponding to *op*. Then $p_{op}(x, y, z)$ is the corresponding subgoal where z corresponds to the value of the arithmetic expression. Nested arithmetic expressions are handled by replacing x *op* y by z in the parse tree for the expression and repeating the above procedure. Finally, append the resulting subgoals to the body of r;

7. For each condition $x \, \tau \, y$ in the Conditions section, where x and y are integers, reals, strings, or temporal terms and τ is $<, <=, =, >=, ! =$ (*not equal*) or a built-in temporal predicate, create a subgoal as follows: let p_τ be the built-in predicate symbol corresponding to τ; append $p_\tau(x, y)$ to r;

8. If any form or condition is negated, negate the corresponding subgoal.

Next, we illustrate the above procedure by applying it to the query from Example 2.2.

Example 4.1 We transform the TKL query from Example 2.2 into the corresponding Horn clause by first performing variable replacements and insertions, substituting intervals for form identifiers, and mapping temporal terms to constants. For simplicity, we assume *87:01:01* maps to 0. This yields the following equivalent TKL query.

emp1:

emp	Name	Manager	Salary	Commissions	From	To
	V01	V02	V03	V04	T01	T02

emp2:

emp	Name	Manager	Salary	Commissions	From	To
	V02	V05	V06	V07	T03	T04

bos1:

boss	Emp_Name	Manager	From	To
P.	V01	V02	T05	T06

Conditions:

(V03 + V04) > (V06 + V07) * 1.1;

[T01, T02] ~ [T03, T04];

[T01, T02] intersection [T03, T04] = [T05, T06];

T06 >= 0;

Since **P.** appears only in the first value field of the **bos1** form, the only output values are **V01, V02, T05,** and **T06.** Thus, the head predicate is $query(V01, V02, T05, T06)$. The predicate symbols corresponding to the form names **boss** and **emp** are *boss* and *emp*, respectively. Subgoals corresponding to the forms are created using these predicate symbols, where their arguments are taken from the corresponding field values. The tree corresponding to the first line in the **Conditions** section is shown below.

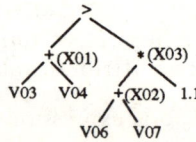

The built-in predicates corresponding to $+$, $*$, and $>$ are *plus, times,* and *gt.* The subgoals corresponding to the subexpressions with atomic operands are $plus(V03, V04, X01)$ and $plus(V06, V07, X02)$. According to Step 6, the subtrees that these subgoals represent are replaced in the expression tree by $X01$ and $X02$. These replacement values are shown in parentheses in the diagram above. We continue in this way to the root of the tree. The remaining conditions are handled similarly. The built-in predicates corresponding to $\sim$, **intersection,** and $>=$ are *concurrent, intersection,* and *gte.* Finally, the corresponding Horn clause is

$query(V01, V02, T05, T06)$:-
 $emp(V01, V02, V03, V04, T01, T02)$, $emp(V02, V05, V06, V07, T03, T04)$,
 $boss(V01, V02, T05, T06)$, $plus(V03, V04, X01)$, $plus(V06, V7, X02)$,
 $times(X02, 1.1, X03)$, $gt(X01, X03)$, $concurrent(T01, T02, T03, T04)$,
 $intersection(T01, T02, T03, T04, T05, T06)$, $gte(T06, 0)$. □

Integrity constraints can be expressed in TKL in much the same manner as rules in query programs. However, the user has to perform the appropriate menu selection. In the context of temporal databases, in addition to the normal ICs arising in any database application, certain ICs are implicitly needed to insure consistency [14]. The unique *key* constraint for temporal relations is defined with respect to valid intervals or valid events such that uniqueness is only required with respect to a sequence of ticks. In the spirit of duplicate removal, sets of concurrent tuples with the same non-temporal attributes are combined into one tuple with the appropriate valid interval. Finally, in keeping with the closed world assumption (see [13]) approach to implicitly represent negative information in base relations, each tuple t such that $t.\text{To} < t.\text{From}$ is disallowed. The formal description of these ICs and our proposal for their implementation are detailed in [11].

4.2 Finiteness of Query Answers

Function symbols are needed for queries about the passage of time. For example, the following rule might be used by a company to express the idea that if an available employee is not assigned today, he/she will be available for assignment tomorrow.

```
available(E, D+1) :- available(E, D), not on-assignment(E, D).
```

However, allowing function symbols raises some difficult questions about the finiteness of query answers. Finiteness is known to be undecidable in general for datalog with function symbols. Ramakrishnan, *et al.* [12] and Kifer, *et al.* [8] have developed a methodology which consists of (i) approximating the logic program with function symbols, with a function-free program together with infinite base relations satisfying *finiteness constraints* (FCs) and (ii) testing a stronger notion called *superfiniteness* on the resulting program. They have developed a complete axiom system and a decision procedure for superfiniteness. Unfortunately, the time complexity of their algorithm is exponential in the size of the program and the FCs. We have developed a methodology based on transforming the program together with given FCs for (EDB) predicates into a non-deterministic finite automaton (nfa) when the FCs are unary [6]. We say that an nfa is *permissive* if every string over the alphabet of the nfa is a prefix of some string that is accepted by the nfa. In [10] we develop an algorithm based on pebbling to decide this property in polynomial time. Among other things, we establish the following results in [10]. (i) For a subclass of linear programs, together with unary FCs, superfiniteness reduces to permissiveness of the nfa associated with the program and, therefore, it can be tested in polynomial time. (ii) For the class of single linear recursive rule programs, superfiniteness reduces to the non-emptiness of the nfa associated with the program and, again, this can be tested in polynomial time.

4.3 The Implementation of TKL

We are currently implementing TKL as an interface to the deductive database system LDL. (See [5] for the syntax and the features of LDL.) LDL is used as the underlying inference engine for TKL. It is also used as a 'rapid prototyping' language for implementing aspects of TKL. For example, TKL database scheme definitions are stored as data in LDL. This allows type-consistency checking on TKL constants and variables in queries to be implemented easily using rules. TKL schemes are stored in LDL relations of the following form.

---

[6] A FC on a predicate a (which may be infinite,) is of the form $a_{i_1}, \ldots, a_{i_k} \rightarrow a_{i_l}$ and says that with any given tuple of values for the arguments $a_{i_1}, \ldots, a_{i_k}$, a associates a finite number of values for its argument a_{i_l}. An FC is *unary* if the number of arguments on its LHS is less than or equal to 1.

```
scheme(Pred_Name, Arg_Position, Attr_Name, Attr_Type).
```

The value of the attribute *Pred_Name* is the predicate symbol corresponding to a TKL form; *Arg_Position* is the relative position of an argument in the predicate corresponding to *Pred_Name*; *Attr_Name* and *Attr_Type* are the attribute name and attribute type associated with that argument position.

Information about forms used in statements is stored in the *literal* relation in LDL. There is a tuple in this relation for each attribute field in the corresponding form.

```
literal(Sid, Pred_Name, Pred_Position, Arg, Value, Type).
```

The value of *Sid* is a unique statement identifier for each rule, query, and IC defined by the user; *Pred_Name* is the predicate symbol corresponding to a TKL form; *Pred_Position* is the position of the predicate in the statement, relative to the other subgoals; *Arg* is an argument position, and *Value* and *Type* are its value and type. The type of the field value is determined by lexical analysis of the tokens in the corresponding fields. The allowed types are *integer, real, string, boolean, DATE*, and user-defined temporal data types.

Two rules are used for type checking. The first rule type checks constants by verifying if the lexical type of each constant corresponds to the type declared for that argument in the scheme declaration. Underscores are used to indicate unique 'don't care' variables.

```
constant_type_error(Sid, Position, Arg, Value, Type, Right_Type)
    :- literal(Sid, P_Name, Position, Arg, Value, Type),
       not equal(Type, 'variable'),
       scheme(P_Name, Arg, _, Right_Type),
       not equal(Type, Right_Type).
```

Variables are type checked for consistency in their usage. We define consistent usage as follows. Let A_i and B_j be arguments of literals used in the same statement such that the same variable X appears in both arguments. Then the usage of X is type consistent if the type of A_i is the same as the type of B_j. The following rule performs this check. The atom literal(_, _, _, _, _, 'variable') is true whenever the corresponding TKL field contains a variable.

```
variable_type_error(Sid, Position, Arg, Value)
    :- literal(Sid, Pred, Position, Arg, Value, 'variable'),
       scheme(Pred, Arg, _, Type),
       literal(Sid, Other_Pred, _, Other_Arg, Value, 'variable'),
       scheme(Other_Pred, Other_Arg, _, Other_Type),
       not equal(Type, Other_Type).
```

A type error is reported to the user whenever either of the relations **constant_type_error** or **variable_type_error** is non-empty.

5 Conclusion

A uniform treatment of temporal information is a natural extension to database technology that can aid in the design and the use of databases maintaining the history of objects they model. We take the temporal extension one step further to deductive temporal databases. Our deductive temporal database query language, TKL, offers some important innovations: its graphic user interface is designed to make the meaning of queries as transparent as possible; user-defined temporal data types help adapt the representation of temporal data to fit the user's needs; finally, we provide a simple semantics for temporal imprecision using *broad* and *narrow* interpretation policies. A spin-off of our treatment of flexible granularity is that null values can be stored in temporal terms and used effectively in queries that reason about time.

Our future research follows two paths. The first is to extend the capabilities of TKL. An interesting problem we are pursuing is to allow user-defined temporal interpretation policies in addition to the predefined *narrow* and *broad* policies. For example, it may be known that the probability that a temporal tuple holds in the imprecise temporal intervals which the `From` and the `To`, and `At` attribute values can represent, follows a normal distribution. In such cases where the probability distribution is known, it should be possible to associate a probability with a tuple that is in the temporal join of two temporal relations.

The second path is to extend our work on the finiteness problem due to the introduction of function symbols. The detection of queries with finite answers is undecidable in general. We can now determine whether subclasses of linear programs have finite answers when the finiteness constraints are given for the EDB predicates, by testing if they satisfy a stronger condition, superfiniteness. We are currently working on extending this approach to other classes of programs. We are also working on relaxing the restriction to testing for superfiniteness by searching for interesting classes of programs for which finiteness can be determined, when the finiteness constraints are known.

References

[1] Abadi, M., Z. Manna. "Temporal logic programming," *Proc. Symposium on Logic Programming*, 1987, pp. 4-16.

[2] Apt, K., H. Blair, A. Walker. "Towards a theory of declarative knowledge," in Foundations of Deductive Databases and Logic Programming, Morgan Kaufmann, Los Altos, Ca., 1988, pp. 89-142.

[3] Biskup, J. "Null values in database relations," in *Advances in Data Base Theory*, Vol. 1, H.Gallaire, J.Minker, J.M. Nicolas, eds., Plenum Press, New York, 1981.

[4] Chellas, B. F. *Modal logic: an introduction*, Cambridge Univ. Press, 1980.

[5] Chimenti, D. *et al.* "The LDL system prototype," *IEEE Trans. on Knowledge and Data Eng.*, 2(1), 1989, pp. 76-90.

[6] Chomicki, J., T. Imieliński. *Finite representation of infinite query answers*, Tech. Report TR-CS-90-10, Dept. of Comp. and Information Sciences, Kansas State Univ., 1990.

[7] Gunadhi, H., A. Segev. "Query processing for algorithms for temporal intersection joins," in *Proc. of the 7th International Conf. on Data Eng.*, Kobe, Japan, 1991, pp. 336-344.

[8] Kifer, M., R. Ramakrishnan and A. Silberschatz. "An axiomatic approach to deciding finiteness of queries in deductive databases," Tech. Report, Department of Comp. Sci., SUNY, Stony Brook, NY, 1991. (Preliminary version appeared in *ACM PODS*, 1988.)

[9] Lakshmanan, V.S. "Query evaluation with null values: how complex is completeness?," *Proc. 6th Foundations of Software Technology and Computer Science*, Springer-Verlag 1989, pp. 204-222.

[10] Lakshmanan, V.S., D. Nonen. "Superfiniteness of query answers in deductive databases: an automata-theoretic approach," To appear in *Proc. 9th Foundations of Software Technology and Computer Science*, 1992.

[11] Nonen, D., V.S. Lakshmanan. "TKL: A Deductive Temporal Database Management System," Tech. Report, Concordia University, Montréal, (in preparation).

[12] Ramakrishnan, R., F. Bancilhon, and A. Silberschatz. "Safety of recursive Horn clauses with infinite relations," *ACM Principles of Databases Systems*, 1987, pp. 328-339.

[13] Reiter, R. "On closed world databases," in Gallaire and Minker, 1978, pp. 55-76.

[14] Sarda, N. "Extensions to SQL for historical databases," *IEEE Transactions on Knowledge and Data Engineering*, 2(2), June 1990, pp. 220-230.

[15] Snodgrass, R. "The temporal query language TQuel," *ACM Transactions on Database Systems*, 12(2), June 1987, pp. 247-298.

[16] Soo, M.D. "Bibliography of temporal databases," *Sigmod Record*, 20(1), March, 1991, pp. 14-23.

[17] Ullman, J.D. *Principles of Database and Knowledge-Base Systems*, Vol. I & II, Computer Science Press, 1989.

[18] Zloof, M. "Query-by-example: a database language," *IBM Systems J.* 16(4):324-343.

Intuitionistic Interpretation of Deductive Databases with Incomplete Information

Fangqing Dong* and Laks V.S. Lakshmanan †

Computer Science Department

Concordia University

Montreal, Quebec, Canada H3G 1M8

Abstract

We consider the semantics of deductive databases with incomplete information in the form of null values. We motivate query answering against a deductive database with nulls as the problem of extracting the maximal information from a (deductive) database in response to queries, and formalize this in the form of *conditional answers*. We give an intuitionistic model theoretic semantics and a fixpoint semantics to deductive databases with nulls, and examine the relationship between existing recursive query processing techniques and the proof procedure for deductive databases with nulls. We then examine hypothetical reasoning using (extended) embedded implications and develop an algorithm for transforming extended embedded implications into deductive databases with nulls. This result shows that the important functionality of hypothetical reasoning can be implemented within the framework of deductive databases with null values.

1 Introduction

Most of the works on deductive databases have only considered a complete information model for the set of facts available for the EDB (or base) relations. For many applications, available information is typically incomplete. One form of incomplete information that has been researched extensively in the context of relational databases is the well-known *null values* (see [1] for a survey). Of the many different types of null values, the kind most researched are the so-called "exists but unknown" type of null values. Both logical (*e.g.*, Gallaire et al [7], Reiter [13], Vardi [15]) and algebraic (*e.g.*, Abiteboul et al [1]) approaches have been investigated in the literature. The question of query processing in deductive databases in the presence of incomplete information (*e.g.*, in the form of nulls) has received relatively little attention. Abiteboul et al [1], Demolombe and Cerro [5], Liu [8], and Dong and Lakshmanan [6] are the representative works.

Abiteboul et al explored the question of extracting *possible* facts to answer queries against incomplete information databases. They interpreted null values

---

*This author's research was supported by a grant from (FCAR) Quebec

†This author's work was supported in part by grants from NSERC (Canada) and FCAR (Quebec)

176

as variables bound by the constraints on nulls, and formalized *possible* answers to the queries as facts satisfiable in *some* models of the underlying theory of the database. Liu [8] considers incomplete information in the form of "S-constants" which are similar to marked nulls with additional information in the form of a set of possible values that the null may take. Dong and Lakshmanan studied query answering against deductive databases containing null values in terms of extracting the maximal amount of information from the databases. Following Vardi [15], they treated null values as mapping functions to constants, and defined the answers extracted in that form to be *conditional* answers to the queries. These answers to the queries are facts true over *all* models satisfying certain conditions supposed on nulls. Furthermore, they indicated the information extracted in that manner may be applicable to hypothetical query answering (see Naqvi and Rossi [12]) and to answering queries in the context of design databases where specifications are often incomplete and one may want to know what would be the eventual outcomes if various design alternatives were chosen. Indeed, the idea behind possible and conditional answers can be regarded as extracting the facts which are derivable under assumptions on how null values can be replaced by constants available in the domain. Those assumptions can be supposed if they do not contradict existing knowledge on nulls. This is certain a kind of hypothetical reasoning.

Theoretical research on hypothetical reasoning has received some attention in the database community. Many researchers explored the possibility of extending the power of databases and logic programming by integrating the ability of hypothetical reasoning into existing approaches. One promising approach for incorporating hypothetical reasoning is the use of embedded implications [2, 3, 4, 10, 11]. In particular, Bonner [2] has developed an elegant approach to hypothetical reasoning based on an intuitionistic interpretation of embedded implications. Embedded implications are rules of the form $(A \leftarrow (B \leftarrow C))$, which represents the knowledge that A is derivable, provided B would be if (the assumption) C were added into the database. The theoretical foundation of embedded implications has been investigated in the literature [2, 3, 4, 10, 11].

In this paper, we continue research on query answering against deductive databases in the presence of nulls along the line of hypothetical reasoning, in two ways. Firstly, we model deductive databases with null values in terms of extended embedded implications, and formalize query answering against databases with null values as hypothetical query answering against the databases expressed in the form of extended embedded implications. Since Bonner's declarative language for hypothetical reasoning cannot handle integrity constraints among predicates, we need to extend embedded implications to allow Horn rules as the heads of extended embedded implications so that information on nulls can be correctly delivered from rule bodies to heads, and constraints on nulls can be verified whenever it is necessary. An example is given to show the motivation and intuition behind the ideas discussed in this paper. We develop an intuitionistic model theoretic semantics using a "canonical" Kripke model to interpret null values as mapping functions which obey the constraints on nulls. We not only allow nulls which can be mapped to some (existing or completely new) constant, but also deal with those nulls which may correspond to a set of constants under the constraints on nulls. We also develop a fixpoint semantics for database logic programs with nulls, which is defined by an iterative operator T_P similar to that used in logic programming argumented with a consistency checking module. Following from this result, it is easy to see that query answering against databases with nulls can be implemented based on existing query processing strategies (also see [6]).

Secondly, we develop an algorithm to transform extended embedded implications into databases with null values. This result implicitly suggests that extracting hypothetical answers against extended embedded implications is essentially similar to the question of query processing against databases with null values. Since many commercial and experimental query languages have been developed for deductive databases, this result provides a new perspective for implementing hypothetical reasoning. It shows the possibilities of integrating the ability of hypothetical reasoning into existing approaches to deductive databases and of implementing hypothetical query processing within the same framework of deductive databases.

2 Motivation

Null values have been recognized to be a convenient way of representing incomplete information of the "exists but unknown" kind in databases. Consider a file system design situation[1] where it is desired to make use of available file organization strategies and their strengths in terms of efficiently supporting various types of queries. Suppose that information known to the database administrator (DBA) is represented in the form of the relations *good_for(Strategy, Query-type)* and *implemented(File, Strategy)*, where *Strategy* refers to file organization strategies and the other attributes and relations have the obvious meaning. Suppose the available knowledge is represented as the following facts together with the constraint $C = \{\perp_1 \neq \perp_2\}$. Here, $b = B^+\text{-}tree$, $h = hashing$, $m = multilist$, $s = simple$, $r = range$, $bl = boolean$, and f_1, f_2, f_3 denote files.

r_1 : $good\_for(b, s)$. $\qquad$ r_6 : $implemented(f_1, h)$.

r_2 : $good\_for(b, r)$. $\qquad$ r_7 : $implemented(f_2, \perp_1)$.

r_3 : $good\_for(m, bl)$. $\qquad$ r_8 : $implemented(f_3, \perp_2)$.

r_4 : $good\_for(h, s)$. $\qquad$ C : $\{\perp_1 \neq \perp_2\}$

r_5 : $good\_for(\perp_2, r)$.

Here, r_5 corresponds to the DBA's knowledge that there is a strategy $\perp_2$ which is good for range queries, and this strategy could be one of the known ones, or could be something he did not encounter before (perhaps a recent invention). Also, r_7 and r_8 correspond to the facts that the access strategies for files f_2, f_3 have not been decided on yet, although there is a constraint to implement them with different strategies. Let $supports(F, Q)$ mean that file F supports queries of type Q efficiently. This can be defined as the following rule r_9 : $supports(F, Q) \leftarrow implemented(F, S), good\_for(S, Q)$. Now, consider the query $Q :\leftarrow supports(F, r)$, which asks for the files supporting range queries. Mechanically resolving the given query against rule r_9, and resolving the second subgoal in the resulting goal against r_2 gives us the new goal $\leftarrow implemented(F, b)$. Under the usual least Herbrand model semantics, an attempt to unify this subgoal with r_7 fails, essentially because b and $\perp_1$ are

---

[1]The example that follows is an adaptation of the one in [6]. The main difference is that here query answering is motivated in terms of extended embedded implications, rather than conditional answers.

treated as distinct entities. However, what we really need is to be able to match the null $\perp_1$ with a (normal) constant like b as long as the constraints on the null values are not violated. Thus, we need to be able to conclude something like the following:

$$r_{10} : (implemented(f_2, b) \leftarrow \perp_1 = b) \leftarrow (implemented(f_2, \perp_1) \leftarrow \perp_1 = b),$$

to assert that $implemented(f_2, b)$ is derivable under the condition $\perp_1 = b$ if $implemented(f_2, \perp_1)$ would be whenever the null constant $\perp_1$ and the normal constant b were interpreted to be the same constant, provided the interpretation for the null $\perp_1$ to be the constant b does not violate the constraints $\mathcal{C}$. In this case, since the constraint is not violated, we would like to be able to conclude "$supports(f_2, r)$ provided the condition $\perp_1 = b$ holds", *i.e.*, $supports(f_2, r)$ holds in every model satisfying the constraints $\mathcal{C} \cup \{\perp_1 = b\}$ (as long as the constraints are consistent). Answers extracted in this form from a deductive database are called conditional answers to the query Q. The idea behind conditional answers is to extract tuples which would be answers if certain conditions held. The notion of conditional answer is formalized in the next sections and we will eventually derive this conditional answer formally (Example 4.1). For lack of space, we only sketch the proofs of our results in this paper.

3 Datalog$^\perp$ Programs

In this section, we formalize the intuition developed in the previous section. We assume the reader is familiar with the general notions of deductive databases and logic programming [9, 14]. Datalog, the language of function-free Horn clauses, is the vehicle query language for deductive databases [14]. A datalog query program consists of (*i*) a finite set of unit clauses representing facts for the base (EDB) predicates, (*ii*) a finite set of Horn clause rules defining the derived (IDB) predicates, and (*iii*) a goal clause, representing the query. We next extend datalog programs to *datalog$^\perp$ programs*.

Consider a first order language L, with a vocabulary consisting of finitely many constant symbols, denoted by D, finitely many predicate symbols p_i, q_j, and infinitely many variables X_i, Y_j, Z_k. We assume the vocabulary includes the arithmetic relations $=, \neq, <, \leq$, and the set relations $=, \prec, \preceq$ (set inclusion), $\in, \notin$ (membership). Set relations are introduced to represent a new form of nulls, called set nulls, which capture those cases where more than one constant may simultaneously satisfy given relations. For example, given an *EDB* fact *father($\perp$, john)*, we know from common sense some one (and only one) is *john*'s father. If we have a fact *neighbor($\perp$, john)* and we do not know exactly how many neighbors *john* has, then it is natural to interpret this null constant corresponding to multiple elements as long as this interpretation is reasonable. In our language L, we assume that the universe D consists of a set of *constants* d_i and a set of *set constants* s_l. The constants d_i are either *normal constants* c_j, or *nulls* $\perp_k$, and the set constants s_l are either *(normal) set constants* s_m, or *set nulls* ω_n. We make use of the membership predicate $d_i \in s_l$ to assert that the constant d_i is a member of the set constant s_l. A predicate such as $p(\omega_1, \omega_2)$ represents that for every member $d_1 \in \omega_1$ and every member $d_2 \in \omega_2$ $p(d_1, d_2)$ is true. We denote by $\bar{d}$ a tuple of constants $(d_1, \cdots, d_k)$, and by $\bar{X}$ a tuple of variables $(X_1, \cdots, X_k)$. Given tuples of variables $\bar{X} = (X_1, \cdots, X_k)$

and $\bar{Y} = (Y_1, \cdots, Y_k)$, $\bar{X} = \bar{Y}$ is the abbreviation for $X_1 = Y_1 \wedge \cdots \wedge X_k = Y_k$, and $\bar{X} \in \bar{Y}$ is the abbreviation for $X_1 \in Y_1 \wedge \cdots \wedge X_k \in Y_k$, where we abuse that the variables X_i and Y_i are of the appropriate type so that the predicate atoms above are well defined.

We need equality and membership predicates to satisfy the following *rewriting axioms* for every k-ary predicate p:

$$(p(\bar{Y}) \leftarrow \bar{X} = \bar{Y}) \leftarrow (p(\bar{X}) \leftarrow \bar{X} = \bar{Y}), \quad and$$
$$(p(\bar{Y}) \leftarrow \bar{Y}' \in \bar{X}') \leftarrow (p(\bar{X}) \leftarrow \bar{Y}' \in \bar{X}'),$$

where $\bar{X}'$ is a tuple of variables contained in $\bar{X}$ which are supposed to be instantiated by set nulls, and $\bar{Y}'$ are the tuple of variables occurring at the same positions as $\bar{X}'$ in the predicate p. These rewriting axioms assert the knowledge that $p(\bar{Y})$ is derivable under the conditions $\bar{X} = \bar{Y}$ (or $\bar{Y}' \in \bar{X}'$) if $p(\bar{X})$ would be whenever the conditions $\bar{X} = \bar{Y}$ (or $\bar{Y}' \in \bar{X}'$) were added into the database, provided those conditions are consistent with existing constraints on nulls. Notice that we can not omit the conditions associated with $p(\bar{Y})$ since conditional answers following from a deductive database with nulls are distinguished from (normal) logic consequences (see the example in Section 4.1). These axioms provide us a theoretical mechanism to treat equality constraints and membership constraints using rewriting axioms so that nulls can be replaced by any other constants as long as those replacements respect the constraints on nulls. The exact meaning of these axioms will be discussed in the section 4.2.

We are now going to introduce datalog$^\perp$ programs which are intended to model deductive databases with null values. A *datalog$^\perp$ program P* is a first order theory of the language L consisting of a datalog program Π, the standard axioms on arithmetic predicates and set predicates, rewriting axioms on database predicates, and a set $\mathcal{C}$ of constraints. The set $\mathcal{C}$ of constraints contains (i) *Unique Name Axioms (UNA)*: $c_i \neq c_j$ for every pair of distinct normal constants c_i and c_j of D, and $s_i \neq d_j$, $s_i \notin d_j$, $s_i \notin s_j$, $d_i \notin d_j$ for every set constant s_i (s_j) and constant d_i (d_j); (ii) *Constraints* on nulls: a set of constraints of the forms: $d_i R d_j$, where R is one of $=, \neq, <, \leq, \prec, \preceq, \in, \notin$. The *UNA*s force the true identity of each normal constant to be fully specified, and make constants and set constants distinguished from each other. The constraints on nulls allow the representation of partial knowledge on the nulls. Besides, we require the constraints $\mathcal{C}$ to be consistent. A set $\mathcal{C}$ of constraints is *consistent* if $\mathcal{C}$ together with all the axioms on arithmetic predicates and set predicates is satisfiable, otherwise, $\mathcal{C}$ is said to be *inconsistent*.

A query Q in L is a goal clause of the form $\leftarrow p(\bar{X})$, where p is any database predicate and $\bar{X}$ is a k-tuple of free variables. We generalize the notion of answers to that of conditional answers. Let P be a datalog$^\perp$ program, and $Q \equiv \leftarrow p(\bar{X})$ be a query. The *conditional answers* to Q against P are defined to be the following set

$$\|Q\|_P = \{(\bar{d}, E) \mid P \models_i p(\bar{d}) \leftarrow E, \ \bar{d} \in D^k\},$$

where $\models_i$ represents intuitionistic implication[2] and E is a set of consistent equality and membership constraints. To capture correct meaning of conditional answers, we can interpret them in terms of hypothetical reasoning (see

---

[2]Notice that E is a set of equality and membership constraints. For simplicity, we abuse notion and use E to represent both a set of conditions and their conjunction.

[2, 3]) as follows: $P \models_i p(\bar{d}) \leftarrow E$ *iff* $P \cup E \models_i p(\bar{d})$, provided $P \cup E$ is satisfiable. In general, this answer set may include redundant answers. To exclude them, we need the notion of minimality. We say that a conditional answer $(\bar{d}, E)$ to a query Q is *minimal* provided for any conditional answer $(\bar{d}, E')$ of Q, if $P \models_i E' \rightarrow E$, then $P \models_i E \rightarrow E'$. Normal answers can be seen to be a special case of conditional answers where the condition set is empty. Clearly, a set of minimal conditional answers are always non-redundant.

4 Intuitionistic Interpretation of Datalog$^\perp$ Programs

Several researchers have explored the fundamental issues on extending the functionalities of logic programming by integrating ability of hypothetical reasoning. It has been revealed that embedded implications argumented with intuitionistic semantics capture knowledge related to hypothetical reasoning. The intuitionistic fixpoint semantics for rules involving embedded implications was first established by McCarty [10]. Bonner proposed a canonical Kripke model semantics for embedded implications which can be constructed proof-theoretically and developed an extension to logic programming to incorporate hypothetical reasoning [2, 3, 4]. In this section, we develop an intuitionistic semantics for datalog programs with nulls. We also develop a fixpoint characterization of this semantics. Our results show the close relationships between "extended" embedded implications (see Section 4.1) useful for hypothetical reasoning and deductive databases with nulls. Specifically, we show that the semantics of deductive databases with nulls can be established in a hypothetical reasoning framework.

We develop a notion of a "canonical" Kripke model and use it as a formal tool to characterize conditional answers as those facts associated with a set of consistent equality and membership constraints, and to interpret null values as mapping functions which match them to constants as long as those mappings do not violate constraints on nulls. We use fixpoint semantics to establish the computational relationship between existing query processing techniques and the proof procedure for deductive databases with nulls. Our fixpoint semantics is defined by an operator T_P over Herbrand base, which is very similar to that widely used in logic programming. With every ground atom, we associate a set of conditions to state that atom is derivable whenever the associated conditions are added into the database. Our fixpoint semantics implicitly suggests that the query processing against deductive databases with nulls can be achieved using existing query answering strategies in the domain of logic programming and databases. Indeed, Dong and Lakshmanan [6] proposed both top-down and bottom-up approaches to query answering. Those strategies show a justification for implementing query answering based on existing approaches. The semantics developed in this paper, in turn, provides an alternative semantical foundation underlying those strategies.

4.1 Embedded Implications

Embedded implications are expressions of the form $A \leftarrow r_1, \cdots, r_n$, where A is an atom and r_i's are Horn rules. Clearly, Horn rules and EDB facts are special cases of embedded implications. An embedded implication such as $(A \leftarrow (B \leftarrow C))$ expresses the knowledge that A is derivable from a database provided B would be whenever C were added into the database.

We have indicated that approaches to incomplete information databases make use of strategies to replace nulls by constants and these strategies are related with hypothetical reasoning. A careful examination would show that query answering against databases with nulls is not a simple variant of hypothetical query answering against embedded implications, since existing approaches to hypothetical reasoning do not capture possible integrity constraints on predicates in the embedded implications. In realistic problems, integrity constraints on predicates may naturally arise and they could effectively restrict the number of possible hypothetical answers. Without allowing integrity constraints, the space of possible answers would be very large, and might contain many undesired conclusions. Consider the following deductive database with nulls:

$$r_1 : p(X,Y) \leftarrow q(X), q(Y); \quad r_2 : q(\perp); \quad r_3 : r(a); \quad r_4 : r(b).$$

We can make use of embedded implications to capture the meaning of nulls by interpreting nulls as mapping functions. The rule $r_5 : q(Y) \leftarrow (q(X) \leftarrow X = Y)$ is one possible way to express nulls as mappings. It asserts that $q(X)$ is derivable if $q(Y)$ would be whenever the corresponding condition $X = Y$ were added into the database. Following this rule, it is easy to see we can get $q(a)$ and $q(b)$ by replacing $\perp$ by a and b, respectively. Following the rule r_1, then we get $p(a,b)$. However, $p(a,b)$ is derivable only if we add *both* $\perp = a$ and $\perp = b$ into the database. Since the same null can not be mapped to distinct constants, the hypothetical answer is obviously incorrect. The key point is that embedded implications can not force the answers for queries against incomplete information databases to respect constraints on nulls. So we need to extend embedded implications in such a way that the information on nulls can be delivered from the rule bodies to the heads, and constraints on nulls can be confirmed whenever it is necessary. The following section will discuss *extended embedded implications* and give an intuitionistic interpretation to extended embedded implications.

4.2 Intuitionistic Semantics

Extended embedded implications are extended form of embedded implications where Horn rules can occur in both the rule heads and the rule bodies. An *extended embedded implication* is defined as follows: an atom A is an extended embedded implication, a Horn rule r is an extended embedded implication, and an expression of the form $r \leftarrow r_1, \cdots, r_n$ is an extended embedded implication if r and r_i's are Horn rules. Clearly, Horn rules, EDB facts and embedded implications are special cases of extended embedded implications. To capture the correct meaning of extended embedded implications *w.r.t.* hypothetical reasoning, it turns out that they should be interpreted under intuitionistic semantics.

Given a set R of extended embedded implications, let D be a set of constants, and H be the Herbrand base *w.r.t.* D. An intuitionistic structure is a collection of subsets of the Herbrand base H, called substates. More precisely, an intuitionistic structure is a Kripke structure $(M, \preceq, \pi)$, where M is a subset of 2^H, $\preceq$ is the partial order corresponding to the usual set inclusion, and π is a truth assignment function $\pi(A) = \{s \mid s \in M, A \in s\}$ for every ground atom A. For our convenience, we denote by M an intuitionistic structure without explicitly mentioning the partial order $\preceq$ and the truth-assignment function π.

Let M be an intuitionistic structure. Then the (intuitionistic) satisfaction of a formula ψ at s by M, denoted by $s, M \models_i \psi$, is recursively defined as follows:

$$
\begin{array}{ll}
s, M \models_i A & \text{iff } A \in s, \text{ for any ground atom } A; \\
s, M \models_i \psi_1 \wedge \psi_2 & \text{iff } s, M \models_i \psi_1, \text{ and } s, M \models_i \psi_2; \\
s, M \models_i \psi_1 \vee \psi_2 & \text{iff } s, M \models_i \psi_1, \text{ or } s, M \models_i \psi_2; \\
s, M \models_i \neg \psi & \text{iff } r, M \not\models_i \psi, \text{ for every } r \succeq s \text{ in } M; \\
s, M \models_i \psi_1 \leftarrow \psi_2 & \text{iff } r, M \models_i \psi_1, \text{ if } r, M \models_i \psi_2, \text{ for every } r \succeq s \text{ in } M,
\end{array}
$$

where $\models_i$ expresses intuitionistic satisfaction. M satisfies a formula ψ iff $s, M \models_i \psi$ for every substate s of M. M is a Kripke model of R if M satisfies all the extended embedded implications of R. A datalog$^\perp$ program formalized in the previous section is a set of extended embedded implications, since all datalog rules, *EDB* facts, and constraints are special cases of extended embedded implications, and rewriting axioms are of the form of extended embedded implications, used to generate conditional answers from nulls.

4.3 Canonical (Kripke) Model

As is common in logic programming and deductive databases (with negation), we base the model theoretic semantics of deductive databases with nulls on the notion of a canonical (Kripke) model. Our semantics provides a foundation for the idea of conditional answers. In particular, we would like to characterize nulls as mapping functions and conditional answers as facts valid *w.r.t.* a set of consistent equality and membership constraints.

Let P be a datalog$^\perp$ program with constraints $\mathcal{C}$, D be the universe of P, and H be the Herbrand base *w.r.t.* D. Let M be a classical model of P excluding the rewriting axioms (see section 3). Define the extension of P *w.r.t.* M to be the following set: $E_M(P) = \{p(\bar{d}) \mid p(\bar{d}) \in H, \text{ and } \models_M p(\bar{d})\}$, *i.e.*, an extension *w.r.t.* a model M is the set of all the ground atoms which are interpreted to be true *w.r.t.* the model M. We define an intuitionistic structure $\mathcal{M}$ of P to be the collection of all the extensions of P, *i.e.*,

$$\mathcal{M} = \{E_M(P) \mid \text{for any classical model } M \text{ of } P \text{ excluding rewriting rules}\}.$$

In our definition of extensions and that of intuitionistic structures, we consider all predicates including the built-in predicates $=, <, \leq$ and the set predicates $=, \in, \prec, \preceq$. The domain of every substate of this intuitionistic structure is the Herbrand universe H of P, where every constant including nulls are treated as distinct constants. In order to correctly capture the meaning of constants, we interpret the equality predicates semantically, rather than syntactically, *i.e.*, a constant d_i is interpreted to be the same constant as d_j at a substate s of $\mathcal{M}$

only if there is an equality predicate $d_i = d_j$ in s. In the same way, a set null ω_i is mapped to a set of constants at a substate s if we have a set constant s_l s.t. the equality predicate $\omega_i = s_l$ is true at the substate. It is easy to see $\mathcal{M}$ is an intuitionistic model of P, as each substate of $\mathcal{M}$ satisfies every datalog rule of P. The functionality of every rewriting axiom is to replace a tuple of constants by semantically equivalent other ones. Thus, it can be verified that every substate of $\mathcal{M}$ satisfies all rewriting axioms. Also, we can construct a classical model of P (excluding rewriting axioms) from each substate of a Kripke model of P. This guarantees the Kripke model $\mathcal{M}$ to be the greatest one. We have the following theorem to characterize the properties of $\mathcal{M}$.

Theorem 4.1 *Let P be a datalog$^\perp$ program with constraints C, and $\mathcal{M}$ be the Kripke structure of P defined above. Then (i) $\mathcal{M}$ is the greatest Kripke model of P w.r.t. the partial order $\preceq$; (ii) for any query $Q \equiv \leftarrow p(\bar{X})$, $(\bar{d}, E)$ is a conditional answer to the query Q against P, iff $\mathcal{M} \models_i p(\bar{d}) \leftarrow E$, provided E is a set of consistent equality and membership constraints.* □

We define this greatest Kripke model to be the *canonical Kripke model* of P. It is easy to see that this canonical Kripke model semantics correctly captures the meaning of nulls and conditional answers, since nulls are characterized exactly to be mapping functions bound by the constraints on nulls, and conditional answers are interpreted as those ground atoms valid *w.r.t.* a set of consistent equality and membership constraints. While the canonical Kripke model of a program P may be very large (and is thus impractical to physically materialize), it offers a very simple and intuitive conceptual picture of the semantics of P.

4.4 Fixed-point Semantics

The main work of this section is to develop a constrained operator T_P for generating conditional answers. The intuition behind this fixpoint semantics is to show a computationally strong connection between the existing query processing techniques and the proof procedure for incomplete information databases. Instead of constructing canonical Kripke model, we can make use of this constrained operator T_P to generate only conditional answers directly.

The operator T_P is defined over the Herbrand base, argumented with a set of conditions associated with every ground atom. A ground atom A with the associated conditions E asserts the derivability of A hypothetically depends on E. Whenever a ground atom A is derived using a rule $A \leftarrow B_1, \cdots, B_k$, we can verify if the conditions associated with all the subgoals B_i's are consistent. A can be a conditional answer only if all the conditions are consistent.

Now, we are going to introduce the notion of constrained Herbrand base. Let P be a datalog$^\perp$ program with constraints C. Let D be the universe of P, and H be the Herbrand base *w.r.t.* D. Let $\mathcal{E}$ be the power set of all the equality constraints of the form $\perp = d$, and all the membership constraints of the form $d \in \omega$, where $\perp$ is any null constant of D, ω is any set null of D, and d is a constant of D. Then the constrained Herbrand base H_E is defined to be the Cartesian product of $H \times \mathcal{E}$. We refer to a pair $(A, E) \in H \times \mathcal{E}$ as a constrained ground atom, and denote it as $(A|E)$ for convenience.

The operator T_P is defined to be the mapping from 2^{H_E} to 2^{H_E}. Let M_E be an element of 2^{H_E}, and P^* be the Herbrand instantiation of P *w.r.t.* H. Then, for any ground atom A associated with a set E of conditions, $(A|E) \in T_P(M_E)$ *iff*

- there is some Horn rule $A \leftarrow B_1 \cdots B_k$ in P^*, and there exists a constrained ground atom $(B_j|E_j) \in M_E$, for $j = 1, \cdots, k$ *s.t.* $E = E_1 \cup \cdots \cup E_k$, provided $C \cup E$ is consistent; or

- there is some extended embedded implication[3] $(A \leftarrow E') \leftarrow (B \leftarrow E')$, and some $(B|E'') \in M_E$ *s.t.* $E = E' \cup E''$, provided $C \cup E$ is consistent.

We define a sequence of constrained interpretations of P as follows:

$M_0 = \{(\phi|\phi)\};$ *where* ϕ *denotes empty set*;

$M_{j+1} = T_P(M_j);$

$M_\omega = \bigcup_j M_j,$ *where* ω *is the limit ordinal*.

We have the following theorem establishing the relationship between canonical Kripke model semantics and fixpoint semantics. This theorem shows that a ground atom A associated with a set E of conditions can be a conditional answer against the datalog$^\perp$ program, only if E is consistent and A is derivable when E is added to the theory associated with the program.

Theorem 4.2 *Let P be a datalog$^\perp$ program with constraints C, and $\mathcal{M}$ be the canonical Kripke model of P. Then (i) for some n, $M_n = lfp(T_P)$; (ii) for every constrained ground atom, $(A|E) \in M_n$ iff $\mathcal{M} \models_i A \leftarrow E$, where A is a ground atom, and E is a set of consistent equality and membership constraints.* □

Theorem 4.2 generalizes the classical result due to Van Emden and Kowalski, to the class of datalog programs with nulls. Notice that this fixpoint semantics makes use of an operator T_P which is similar to that defined in logic programming, argumented with a consistency checking module. Several efficient consistency checking algorithms have been extensively studied in the domain of constraint logic programming, and for the sake of space, we omit the details for consistency checking. It can also be implemented based on techniques as discussed in[6].

Example 4.1 Let us revisit the example in Section 2 and consider the query $Q \equiv \leftarrow supports(f_2, r)$. First, we introduce an embedded implication associated with every predicate *good_for*, *implemented* and *supports*. Thus, we get three

---

[3]Recall that the rewriting axioms are of the form of extended embedded implications.

more extended embedded implications r_{10}, r_{11} and r_{12}.

$$r_1 : \quad good\_for(b,s).$$
$$r_2 : \quad good\_for(b,r).$$
$$r_3 : \quad good\_for(m,bl).$$
$$r_4 : \quad good\_for(h,s).$$
$$r_5 : \quad good\_for(\perp_2, r).$$
$$r_6 : \quad implemented(f_1, h).$$
$$r_7 : \quad implemented(f_2, \perp_1).$$
$$r_8 : \quad implemented(f_3, \perp_2).$$
$$r_9 : \quad supports(F,Q) \leftarrow implemented(F,S), \; good\_for(S,Q).$$
$$r_{10} : \quad (good\_for(Y_1,Y_2) \leftarrow X_1 = Y_1, X_2 = Y_2) \leftarrow$$
$$(good\_for(X_1,X_2) \leftarrow X_1 = Y_1, X_2 = Y_2).$$
$$r_{11} : \quad (implemented(Y_1,Y_2) \leftarrow X_1 = Y_1, X_2 = Y_2) \leftarrow$$
$$(implemented(X_1,X_2) \leftarrow X_1 = Y_1, X_2 = Y_2).$$
$$r_{12} : \quad (supports(Y_1,Y_2) \leftarrow X_1 = Y_1, X_2 = Y_2) \leftarrow$$
$$(supports(X_1,X_2) \leftarrow X_1 = Y_1, X_2 = Y_2).$$
$$\mathcal{C} : \quad \{\perp_1 \neq \perp_2\}.$$

Notice that the resulting program P consists of extended embedded implications $r_1, \cdots, r_{12}$, and the constraint $\mathcal{C}$ including the axioms UNA's. To the query Q, we apply the constrained operator T_P to generate conditional answers:

1. $M_0 = \{(\phi|\phi)\}$;
2. $M_1 = \{(r_1|\phi), \cdots, (r_8|\phi)\}$ obtained from $r_1, \cdots, r_8$;
3. $(good\_for(\perp_1, r)|\{\perp_1 = b\}) \in M_2$ obtained from r_{10} and $(r_2|\phi)$;
4. $(supports(f_2, r)|\{\perp_1 = b\}) \in M_3$ obtained from r_9, $(r_7|\phi)$ and 3.

So we get a conditional answer $(\epsilon, \{\perp_1 = b\})$ to the query, where ϵ denotes a tuple of zero length, corresponding to the answer "yes". We next consider a recursive example.   □

Example 4.2 Consider the query $Q \equiv \leftarrow ancestor(paul, Y)$, from the following program:

$$r_1 : \quad ancestor(X,Y) \leftarrow parent(X,Z), ancestor(Z,Y).$$
$$r_2 : \quad ancestor(X,Y) \leftarrow parent(X,Y).$$
$$r_3 : \quad parent(\perp_1, jim).$$
$$r_4 : \quad parent(paul, \perp_1).$$
$$r_5 : \quad parent(\perp_2, george).$$
$$r_6 : \quad parent(john, joe).$$
$$r_7 : \quad (parent(Y_1,Y_2) \leftarrow X_1 = Y_1, X_2 = Y_2) \leftarrow$$
$$(parent(X_1,X_2) \leftarrow X_1 = Y_1, X_2 = Y_2).$$
$$r_8 : \quad (ancestor(Y_1,Y_2) \leftarrow X_1 = Y_1, X_2 = Y_2) \leftarrow$$
$$(ancestor(X_1,X_2) \leftarrow X_1 = Y_1, X_2 = Y_2).$$
$$\mathcal{C} : \quad \{\perp_1 \neq \perp_2, \perp_1 \neq jim, \perp_1 \neq paul, \perp_2 \neq george\}.$$

Let P be the resulting program consisting of rules r_1 to r_8, as well as the constraints $\mathcal{C}$. Then there are three conditional answers to the query Q:

$\|Q\|_P = \{((joe), \{\perp_1 = john\}), ((jim), \phi), ((\perp_1), \phi)\}$. Here, we only show the procedure for getting the first answer to the query Q.

1. $M_0 = \{(\phi|\phi)\}$;
2. $M_1 = \{(r_3|\phi), \cdots, (r_6|\phi)\}$ obtained from $r_3, \cdots, r_6$;
3. $(parent(\perp_1, joe)|\{\perp_1 = john\}) \in M_2$ obtained from r_7 and $(r_6|\phi)$;
4. $(ancestor(\perp_1, joe)|\{\perp_1 = john\}) \in M_3$ obtained from r_2 and 3;
5. $(ancestor(paul, joe)|\{\perp_1 = john\}) \in M_4$ obtained from r_1, $(r_4|\phi)$ and 4.

So, we get the conditional answer $((joe), \{\perp_1 = john\})$ to the query Q. In a similar way, we can get the other conditional answers to Q.   □

5   Transforming Extended Embedded Implications

In spite of numerous efforts to explore theoretical properties and proof procedures for embedded implications, it is still not very clear how hypothetical query answering can be implemented without complicating the existing framework of deductive databases. The main purpose of this section is to develop an approach to transforming extended embedded implications into datalog programs so that hypothetical reasoning can be implemented in the framework of deductive databases. In this paper, we only consider the extended embedded implications without local universal quantifiers occurring in the bodies and without integrity constraints[4]. Bonner [2, 3] has developed a proof system for embedded implications. It is not hard to see that this proof system is also sound and complete for the extended embedded implications discussed in this paper.

Let R be a set of extended embedded implications. A hypothetical query Q, like any normal query, is just a goal clause of the form $Q \equiv \leftarrow p(\bar{X})$, where p is database predicate and $\bar{X}$ is k-tuple of free variables. The hypothetical answers for the query Q are all tuples of constants satisfying

$$\|Q\|_R = \{\bar{d} \mid R \models_i p(\bar{d}), \ \bar{d} \in D^{|\bar{X}|}\}.$$

Example 5.1 Consider hypothetical query answering to the query $Q \equiv \leftarrow within1(X)$ against the following set R of embedded implications:

$r_1 : grad(X) \leftarrow take(X, his101), take(X, eng201)$.
$r_2 : within1(X) \leftarrow \exists Y(grad(X) \leftarrow take(X, Y))$.
$r_3 : take(john, his101)$. $r_4 : take(joe, eng201)$. $r_5 : take(paul, phy301)$.

This example is due to Bonner [2, 3]. Here the rule r_1 expresses X can graduate if X has taken both the courses *his101* and *eng201*. The rule r_2 is an embedded implication which expresses that X is within one course of graduation. Suppose that the universe of R is $\{john, joe, paul, his101, eng201, phy301\}$. The hypothetical answers to the query Q are the following tuples: $\{(john), (joe)\}$. For example, if we add *take(john, eng201)* into the database, then *grad(john)*

---

[4] We will discuss transformation on the whole class of extended embedded implications involving integrity constraints in a full paper which will appear later.

follows from the first Horn rule. Thus, $grad(john) \leftarrow take(john, eng201)$ follows from R. So, $within1(john)$ is hypothetically derivable from R due to the rule r_2. □

The essential difference between reasoning with extended embedded implications and that present in deductive databases is the ability of *deriving new Horn rules*. So, to transform extended embedded implications into datalog programs, we need somehow to replace the embedded Horn rules by other predicates and make sure these predicates can be derivable only when the embedded Horn rules are. Based on this idea, in this section we develop an algorithm to transform extended embedded implications into deductive databases with nulls. Given a set of extended embedded implications, the resulting database is equivalent to the extended embedded implications in the sense that the transformed database procedures the same answers to queries. The algorithm associates an extra argument with every predicate to express the set of ground atoms from which the predicate would be derivable if those atoms were added into the database. Associated with each extended embedded implication such as $(A \leftarrow (B \leftarrow C))$, we introduce a new predicate D to replace the embedded Horn rule $B \leftarrow C$, define a new rule with the head D, with B and C as subgoals in the rule body, and add C as new *EDB* facts with nulls which are obtained by replacing each variable occurring in C by a set null. We use this strategy to transform a set R of embedded implications into a datalog$^\perp$ program $ddb(R)$. To the end, we extend the language L to contain a special symbol ϕ to represent empty set, and use the notation $[\cdots]$ to express a set of terms. Besides, we introduce two primitive predicates *union* and *diff*. $union(S_1, S_2, S)$ asserts S to be the union of S_1 and S_2. $diff(S_1, S_2, S)$ gives S to be the difference of $S_1 - S_2$. Let R be a set of extended embedded implications. Then the following algorithm transforms the extended embedded implications R into a datalog$^\perp$ program $ddb(R)$.

Input: a set R of extended embedded implications;

Output: a datalog$^\perp$ program $ddb(R)$ transformed from R with constraints C.

FOR every extended embedded implication r of R **DO** {

1. If r is an *EDB* fact $p(\bar{c})$, then transform $p(\bar{c})$ to the form $p(\bar{c}, \phi)$;
   /* This says $p(\bar{c})$ is unconditionally true; */

2. If $r \equiv p(\bar{X}) \leftarrow q_1(\bar{Y}_1) \cdots, q_k(\bar{Y}_k)$ is a Horn rule, then introduce a new argument associated with every predicate and modify the rule r into the following form:

$$p(\bar{X}, S) \leftarrow q_1(\bar{Y}_1, S_1) \cdots, q_k(\bar{Y}_k, S_k), union^*(S_1, \cdots, S_k, S),$$

where $union^*(S_1, \cdots, S_k, S)$ is the abbreviation for $union(S_1, S_2, S_2'), \cdots,$ $union(S_{k-1}', S_k, S)$; /* This rule asserts that $p(\bar{X})$ is true under assumptions S if every $q_j(\bar{Y}_j)$ is true under the associated assumptions S_j $j = 1, \cdots, k$, and S is the union of all the assumptions; */

3. If r is an extended embedded implication $(p(\bar{X}) \leftarrow A_1(\bar{X}_1), \cdots A_l(\bar{X}_l)) \leftarrow r_1(\bar{Y}_1) \cdots, r_k(\bar{Y}_k)$, then associate an extra argument with the head $p(\bar{X})$

and introduce a new predicate $p_i(\bar{Y}_i, S_i)$ to replace every r_i, where $\bar{Y}_i$'s are the tuples of the variables occurring in the ith embedded Horn rule r_i. Modify the rule r into the following form:

$$p(\bar{X}, S) \leftarrow A_1(\bar{X}_1, S_1), \cdots A_l(\bar{X}_l, S_l),$$
$$p_1(\bar{Y}_1, S_{l+1}) \cdots, p_k(\bar{Y}_k, S_{l+k}), \; union^*(S_1, \cdots, S_{l+k}, S).$$

Write the rules for the predicates p_i as follows:

FOR $i = 1, \cdots, k$ **DO** {

(a) if r_i is an atom $q_i(\bar{Y}_i)$, then simply let p_i be q_i in the previous rule;
/* Thus, no new rule for $p_i \equiv q_i$ is necessary; */

(b) if r_i is a Horn rule of the form $b_i(\bar{Y}_i') \leftarrow c_1(\bar{W}_{i1}), \cdots, c_n(\bar{W}_{in})$, then

   i. Introduce the following rule to define the predicate p_i:
   $$p_i(\bar{Y}_i, S_i) \leftarrow b_i(\bar{Y}_i', S_i'), c_1'(\bar{W}_{i1}, [c1(\bar{W}_{i1})]), \cdots,$$
   $$c_n'(\bar{W}_{in}, [cn(\bar{W}_{in})]), \; diff(S_i', [c1(\bar{W}_{i1}), \cdots, cn(\bar{W}_{in})], S_i),$$
   where $c_j'(\bar{W}_{ij}, S_{ij})$ is a new predicate associated with $c_j(\bar{W}_{ij})$;
   /* Here, a term $cj(\bar{W}_{ij})$ represents the assumption corresponding to the atom $c_j(\bar{W}_{ij})$. The above rule simply asserts that the assumptions (S_i) under which the rule r_i is true, are the assumptions (S_i') under which its head $b_i(\bar{Y}_i')$ is true, less any assumptions $[c1(\bar{W}_{i1}), \cdots, cn(\bar{W}_{in})]$ under which r_i's body is true; */

   ii. Generate the following rules for the new predicates $c_j'(\bar{W}_{ij}, S_{ij})$:
   $$c_j'(\bar{W}_{ij}, [cj(\bar{W}_{ij})]) \leftarrow c_j(\bar{W}_{ij});$$
   $$c_j(\omega_{j1}, \cdots, \omega_{jm});$$
   Here cj is a newly introduced function symbol associated with the predicate c_j, and $(\omega_{j1}, \cdots, \omega_{jm})$ is a tuple of set nulls corresponds to the tuple of variables $\bar{W}_{ij}$. /* Every $cj(\bar{W}_{ij})$ represents an assumption corresponding to the atom $c_j(\bar{W}_{ij})$, and every set null ω stands for the set of constants which can instantiate the associated variable. */

   }

}
At last, add all the transformed rules and all newly introduced Horn rules into $ddb(R)$, and add all the following constraints into $\mathcal{C}$:

$\omega_i \neq d$, $\omega_i \not\in d$, for every newly introduced set null ω_i and every constant d,
$\quad \omega_i \not\in \omega_j$, for every pair of set nulls ω_i and ω_j.

The transformed datalog$^\perp$ program $ddb(R)$ is said to be the datalog$^\perp$ program associated with R. Notice that the size of the resulting program $ddb(R)$ is comparable to the size of R, since every newly introduced predicate p_i is associated with an embedded Horn rule, and each predicate c' is associated with a subgoal

c occurring in the embedded Horn rules.

Example 5.2 We revisit the example we discussed at the beginning of the section. R are the following (extended) embedded implications:

$$r_1 : grad(X) \leftarrow take(X, his101), take(X, eng201).$$
$$r_2 : within1(X) \leftarrow \exists Y(grad(X) \leftarrow take(X, Y)).$$
$$r_3 : take(john, his101). \quad r_4 : take(joe, eng201). \quad r_5 : take(paul, phy301).$$

The embedded implications R can be transformed into the following datalog$^\perp$ program $ddb(R)$ with nulls:

$r_1' : grad(X, S) \leftarrow take(X, his101, S_1), take(X, eng201, S_2), union(S_1, S_2, S).$	2.
$r_2' : within1(X, S) \leftarrow p_1(X, S).$	3.
$r_3' : p_1(X, S) \leftarrow grad(X, S'), take'(X, Y, [t1(X, Y)]), diff(S', [t1(X, Y)], S).$	3.b.i.
$r_4' : take'(X, Y, [t1(X, Y)]) \leftarrow take(X, Y).$	3.b.ii.
$r_5' : take(\omega_1, \omega_2).$	3.b.ii.
$r_6' : take(john, his101, \phi).$	1.
$\quad hspace * -2.5 em r_7' : take(joe, eng201, \phi).$	1.
$r_8' : take(paul, phy301, \phi).$	1.
$\mathcal{C} : \omega_i \neq d, \omega_i \notin d, d \in \{john, joe, paul, his101, eng201, phy301\}, i = 1, 2,$	
$\quad\quad \omega_1 \neq \omega_2, \omega_2 \neq \omega_1.$	

where $t1$ is a newly introduced function symbol associated with the predicate *take*. Suppose that the universe of R is $\{john, joe, paul, his101, eng201, phy301\}$. Consider the hypothetical query $Q \equiv \leftarrow within1(X)$. Associated with the hypothetical query, we have a datalog query $Q' \equiv \leftarrow within1(X, \phi)$, where ϕ expresses empty set. From transformed datalog$^\perp$ program $ddb(R)$, then we can get the following conditional answers:

$$((john, \phi), \{john \in \omega_1, eng201 \in \omega_2\}), ((joe, \phi), \{joe \in \omega_1, his101 \in \omega_2\}))\}.$$

For the sake of space, we omit details for getting conditional answers to the query Q'. □

The main result of this section is that the resulting datalog$^\perp$ program $ddb(R)$ is query equivalent to the original extended embedded implications. In other words, the hypothetical answers to the queries against R can be obtained by deductively querying the associated datalog$^\perp$ program $ddb(R)$. We have the following theorem to state the equivalence formally.

Theorem 5.1 *Let R be a set of extended embedded implications, and $Q \equiv \leftarrow p(\bar{X})$ be a hypothetical query against R. Let $ddb(R)$ be the datalog$^\perp$ program associated with R, and $Q' \equiv p(\bar{X}, \phi)$ be a datalog query against $ddb(R)$. Then $\bar{d} \in \|Q\|_R$ iff $((\bar{d}, \phi), E) \in \|Q'\|_{ddb(R)}$, where ϕ stands for empty set, and E is a set of consistent equality and membership constraints.*

Proof (Sketch): It is sufficient to prove that (i) $R \cup \{A_1, \cdots, A_k\} \vdash_i p(\bar{d}) \Leftrightarrow ddb(R) \models_i (p(\bar{d}, S) \leftarrow E)$ for some $S \subseteq [A_1, \cdots, A_k]$, where E is a set of consistent membership constraints, and (ii) $R \vdash_i B \leftarrow C_1, \cdots, C_n$ (that is, $R \cup \{C_1, \cdots, C_n\} \vdash_i B) \Leftrightarrow$ in $ddb(R)$ we have a rule of the form $p(\bar{X}, S) \leftarrow B'(S'), C_1', \cdots, C_n', \text{diff}(S', [c1, \cdots, cn], S)$ (3.b.i) s.t. $(p(\bar{X}, \phi) \leftarrow E), (B'(S') \leftarrow$

$E'), (C_1' \leftarrow E_1), \cdots, (C_n' \leftarrow E_n)$ are derivable from $ddb(R)$, provided $S = \phi$ and $S' \subseteq [c1, \cdots, cn]$. Here all E's are sets of consistent membership constraints, $E = E' \cup E_1 \cup \cdots \cup E_n$, and $\vdash_i$ stands for the proof system defined in Bonner [2, 3]. The proof is based on induction on the deductive steps of the proof system [2] and on the number of iterations of the operator T_P. □

Notice that in the transformed program every predicate is associated with one more argument to represent the set of atoms on which the truth of p hypothetically depends. Therefore, querying Q against R is equivalent to querying Q' against $ddb(R)$.

Achieving efficient hypothetical query answering is the motivation of this research. In view of the rapid progress of query processing techniques in the domain of relational databases and deductive databases, this approach shows the promising possibility of implementing hypothetical query answering within the framework of deductive databases. [6] has proposed an approach to query answering against deductive databases with nulls based on existing top-down and bottom-up query processing techniques. So hypothetical query answering against extended embedded implications can be achieved by transforming extended embedded implications into deductive databases with nulls. To implement efficient hypothetical query answering, we now still need the following restrictions on extended embedded implications, and we believe these restrictions are realistic requirements. Firstly, we need integrity constraints to limit answer sets. Without any limitation on hypothetical answers, the number of hypothetical answers would be prohibitively large. Secondly, if we limit the number of possible assumptions allowed in hypothetical query answering, query answering can be done in polynomial time in the database size.

6 Conclusion

We proposed an intuitionistic semantics for deductive databases in presence of incomplete information. We motivated the problem of querying deductive databases containing null values as extracting conditional answers against the database, where null values are treated as mapping functions to match themselves to constants, provided the mappings respect the existing knowledge on nulls. We developed both an intuitionistic declarative semantics and a fixpoint semantics for deductive databases with nulls. Our results are not only characterized the formal semantics of conditional answers, but also established a computationally close relationship between existing query processing techniques and the proof procedure for the deductive databases containing nulls. Furthermore, we developed an algorithm to transform extended embedded implications (with some restrictions) into query-equivalent deductive databases with nulls. This result shows the possibilities of implementing hypothetical reasoning within the same framework of deductive databases, and achieving hypothetical query answering based on existing techniques of query processing.

In future research, we would like to implement hypothetical query answering based on the query processing strategies developed for deductive databases with null values, and further to characterize the form of extended embedded implications which can be more efficiently computed within the framework of deductive databases.

References

[1] Abiteboul, S., Kanellakis, P. and Grahne, G., "On the representation and querying of sets of possible worlds", *Theoretical Computer Science*, 78 (1991), 159-187.

[2] Bonner, A.J., "A logic for hypothetical reasoning", *AAAI'88*, 480-484

[3] Bonner, A.J., McCarty, L.T. and Vadaparty, K., "Expressing database queries with intuitionistic logic", *Proc. North American on Logic Programming Conference* (1989), 831-850.

[4] Bonner, A.J., "Hypothetical Datalog: complexity and expressibility", *Theoretical Computer Science*, 76 (1990), 3-51.

[5] Demolombe, R. and Cerro, L.F.D., "An algebraic evaluation method for deduction in incomplete data bases", *The Journal of Logic Programming*, No. 5 (1988), 183-205.

[6] Dong, F. and Lakshmanan, V.S., "Deductive databases with incomplete information", *Tech. Report, Dept. of Computer Science, Concordia University* (March 1992). (A modified version to appear in *1992 Joint International Conference and Symposium on Logic Programming, 1992*).

[7] Gallaire, H., Minker, J. and Nicolas, J.-M., "Logic and databases: a deductive approach", *Computing Surveys*, 16(2), (June 1984), 151-185.

[8] Liu, Y., "Null values in definite programs", *Proc. North American on Logic Programming Conference*, (1990), 273-288.

[9] Lloyd, J.W., **Foundations of Logic Programming**, Springer-Verlag, New York (1987).

[10] McCarty, L.T., "Clausal intuitionistic logic. i. fixed-point procedures", *Journal of Logic Programming*, 5 (1988), 1-31.

[11] McCarty, L.T., "Clausal intuitionistic logic. ii. tableau proof procedures", *Journal of Logic Programming*, 5 (1988), 93-132.

[12] Naqvi, S.A. and Rossi, F., "Reasoning in inconsistent databases", *Proc. North American on Logic Programming Conference*, (1990), 255-272.

[13] Reiter, R., "A sound and sometimes complete query evaluation algorithm for relational databases with null values", *JACM*, 33(2), (April 1986), 349-370.

[14] Ullman, J.D., **Principles of Database and Knowledge-Base Systems**, Vol. I&II, Comp. Sci. Press, MD (1989).

[15] Vardi, M.Y., "Querying logical databases", *Journal of Computer and System Sciences*, 33 (1986), 142-160.

Author Index

Published in 1990–91

AI and Cognitive Science '89, Dublin City University, Eire, 14–15 September 1989
A. F. Smeaton and G. McDermott (Eds.)

Specification and Verification of Concurrent Systems, University of Stirling, Scotland, 6–8 July 1988
C. Rattray (Ed.)

Semantics for Concurrency, Proceedings of the International BCS-FACS Workshop, Sponsored by Logic for IT (S.E.R.C.), University of Leicester, UK, 23–25 July 1990
M. Z. Kwiatkowska, M. W. Shields and R. M. Thomas (Eds.)

Functional Programming, Glasgow 1989
Proceedings of the 1989 Glasgow Workshop, Fraserburgh, Scotland, 21–23 August 1989
K. Davis and J. Hughes (Eds.)

Persistent Object Systems, Proceedings of the Third International Workshop, Newcastle, Australia, 10–13 January 1989
J. Rosenberg and D. Koch (Eds.)

Z User Workshop, Oxford 1989, Proceedings of the Fourth Annual Z User Meeting, Oxford, 15 December 1989
J. E. Nicholls (Ed.)

Formal Methods for Trustworthy Computer Systems (FM89), Halifax, Canada, 23–27 July 1989
Dan Craigen (Editor) and Karen Summerskill (Assistant Editor)

Security and Persistence, Proceedings of the International Workshop on Computer Architecture to Support Security and Persistence of Information, Bremen, West Germany, 8–11 May 1990
John Rosenberg and J. Leslie Keedy (Eds.)

Women into Computing: Selected Papers 1988–1990
Gillian Lovegrove and Barbara Segal (Eds.)

3rd Refinement Workshop (organised by BCS-FACS, and sponsored by IBM UK Laboratories, Hursley Park and the Programming Research Group, University of Oxford), Hursley Park, 9–11 January 1990
Carroll Morgan and J. C. P. Woodcock (Eds.)

Designing Correct Circuits, Workshop jointly organised by the Universities of Oxford and Glasgow, Oxford, 26–28 September 1990
Geraint Jones and Mary Sheeran (Eds.)

Functional Programming, Glasgow 1990
Proceedings of the 1990 Glasgow Workshop on Functional Programming, Ullapool, Scotland, 13–15 August 1990
Simon L. Peyton Jones, Graham Hutton and Carsten Kehler Holst (Eds.)

4th Refinement Workshop, Proceedings of the 4th Refinement Workshop, organised by BCS-FACS, Cambridge, 9–11 January 1991
Joseph M. Morris and Roger C. Shaw (Eds.)

AI and Cognitive Science '90, University of Ulster at Jordanstown, 20–21 September 1990
Michael F. McTear and Norman Creaney (Eds.)

Software Re-use, Utrecht 1989, Proceedings of the Software Re-use Workshop, Utrecht, The Netherlands, 23–24 November 1989
Liesbeth Dusink and Patrick Hall (Eds.)

Z User Workshop, 1990, Proceedings of the Fifth Annual Z User Meeting, Oxford, 17–18 December 1990
J.E. Nicholls (Ed.)

IV Higher Order Workshop, Banff 1990
Proceedings of the IV Higher Order Workshop, Banff, Alberta, Canada, 10–14 September 1990
Graham Birtwistle (Ed.)

Printing: Weihert-Druck GmbH, Darmstadt
Binding: Theo Gansert Buchbinderei GmbH, Weinheim